RISING FROM THE ASHES?

LABOR IN THE AGE OF "GLOBAL" CAPITALISM

RISING FROM THE ASHES?

LABOR IN THE AGE OF "GLOBAL" CAPITALISM

Edited by Ellen Meiksins Wood,
Peter Meiksins,
and Michael Yates

Monthly Review Press
New York

Library of Congress Cataloging-in-Publication Data

Rising from the ashes? : labor in the age of global capitalism /
    edited by Ellen Meiksins Wood, Peter Meiksins, and Michael Yates.
        p.   cm.
    Includes bibliographical references and index.
    ISBN 0-85345-939-8 (pbk.) — ISBN 0-85345-949-5 (cloth)
    1. Labor movement. 2. Capitalism. 3. International trade.
I. Wood, Ellen Meiksins. II. Meiksins, Peter, 1953-
III. Yates, Michael, 1946-
HD4901.R57 1998
331.88—dc21   98-48886
                                                                           CIP
                                                                          r 98

Monthly Review Press
122 West 27th Street
New York NY 10001

Manufactured in Canada
10 9 8 7 6 5 4 3 2

CONTENTS

3. A WORLD TO WIN?

1
LABOR AND CLASS
IN A CHANGING WORLD

Labor, Class, and State in Global Capitalism

Ellen Meiksins Wood

The U.S. labor movement has never really had a political organization of its own, whether a strong socialist, social democratic, or British-style labor party, and the Democratic Party has even less to offer the labor movement now than it had in the past. But the American case today seems less exceptional than it once did, as the most well-established working-class parties—communist, socialist, social democratic, and labor—have effectively cut themselves off from their class roots, especially in Europe.

European communist and socialist parties, for instance, have generally retreated from the politics and language of class struggle, while the election of New Labour in Britain brought to power a leadership bent on cutting the party's historic ties with the trade union movement, leaving Britain, at least for the moment, with something close to the U.S. model of a one-party state, or as Gore Vidal has put it, one party with two right wings.

It is possible that even this ambiguous victory for the left, or the subsequent election of social democratic governments in France and Germany, will open up new political prospects. But for the moment, many people seem to take it for granted that the disappearance of working-class politics is only natural, that the political terrain on which both revolutionary and electoral working-class parties traditionally operated simply no longer exists. That terrain has been more or less obliterated, mainly by "globalization," or so we are told.

But we need to look more closely at that assumption. We must explore more critically the political consequences of globalization and what they mean for the labor movement and class struggle.

What Is Globalization?

The current global crisis has, of course, tarnished the whole idea of globalization to such an extent that formerly enthusiastic advocates are questioning its most basic principles. Neoliberal financial wizards are not only contemplating measures, like capital controls, which just yesterday would have seemed to them horrific violations of natural law, but are even raising nervous questions

3

about "free market" capitalism in general. While a great deal of rethinking is bound to follow from the crisis, however, the idea of globalization is certainly not dead, and it represents a serious concern to labor movements everywhere.

What, then, does globalization mean? The basic outlines of the conventional conception, or what some have called the "globalization thesis," are familiar enough: in the early 1970s, or thereabouts, the world entered a new epoch of "globalization," marked by an increasing internationalization of capital—not just a global market but internationalized production and even an internationalized capitalist class; the growing power of international agencies of capital like the IMF, the World Bank, the WTO; rapid movements of finance capital, accelerated by new information technologies; the movement of capital from economies with high labor costs to low-wage economies, which serves as a justification for lowering wages and attacking social welfare in advanced capitalist countries; and a shift of sovereignty away from the nation-state.[1]

The conventional conception of globalization is not, of course, universally accepted.[2] No one doubts that capitalism has become a more *universal* system than ever before, nor does anyone doubt that we are living in a "global" economy with increasingly international markets and economic transactions of all kinds that span the whole planet. But some writers on the left have expressed doubts about how much production has really been internationalized, about how mobile industrial capital really is, about the very existence of "multinational" corporations. Such critics have pointed out that the vast majority of production still goes on in nationally-based companies in single locales. They have argued that there is no such thing as a "multinational" corporation, that there are only nationally-based corporations with a transnational reach.

Critics of conventional ideas of globalization have also pointed out that, while capital flights to low-wage economies may be a serious problem, foreign direct investment has been overwhelmingly concentrated in advanced capitalist countries, with capital moving from one such country to another. There are, of course, differences among the big capitalist economies, with some more exposed than others to international competitive pressures. The U.S., for example, is sheltered from some forms of competition because a relatively small proportion of its economy is devoted to manufacturing and the proportion of the U.S. labor force employed in manufacturing is even smaller. As other contributors to this volume point out, for instance, more than 70 percent of all employment in the United States is in the service sector, much of it in industries that cannot simply be shifted to other economies with cheap and unorganized labor forces.

But whatever the proportion of the manufacturing industry in the U.S. economy (or in other advanced capitalist countries), it is still—and is likely to remain—a disproportionately large share of the production in the world as a whole. In this sector, competition has certainly intensified, but that competition typically takes place among the advanced capitalist countries themselves. The United States, in particular, has been profoundly affected by competition from Japan and Germany. At the same time, the preferred solution has not been simply to export industry to Third World countries. Manufacturing industries are much less mobile than conventions about globalization suggest—not least because large-scale and long-term capital investments are hard to abandon. Competitive strategies in this situation are no more likely to take the form of moving capital elsewhere than of reducing labor costs at home. In fact, one of the most notable features of the current global economy is not the industrialization and enrichment of the poorest Third World countries but, on the contrary, a growing impoverishment of economies left on the margins of globalization and an increasing polarization between rich and poor.

At the very least, then, it is difficult to formulate any simple proposition about the competition between low-wage and higher-wage economies or about the dangers of capital flights in response to working-class organization and struggle. More generally, there is no simple correlation between the politics or ideology of "globalization" and the actual exposure of advanced capitalist economies to international competition, at least to competition from low-wage economies. "Globalization" is certainly an effective threat, and hence a powerful *political* strategy. But we must not uncritically identify threat with reality.

Beyond these empirical challenges to the conventional notion of globalization, there are also larger questions, two of which need to be canvassed here. First, we should ask how new this phenomenon is. According to the globalization thesis, we have been living in a new epoch since the early 1970s. Yet nothing could be more obvious than the uncanny resemblance between the "bourgeois" world so vividly portrayed by *The Communist Manifesto* in 1848 and the "epoch of globalization" in which we are living today:

> Exploitation of the world market [has] given a cosmopolitan character to production and consumption in every country. . . . All old-established national industries have been destroyed or are daily being destroyed. They are dislodged by new industries...that no longer work up indigenous raw material but raw material drawn from the remotest zones, industries whose products are consumed not only at home but in every quarter of the globe. In place of old wants, satisfied by the production of the country, we find new wants, requiring for their satisfaction the products of distant lands. . . . In place of the old local and national seclusion and self-sufficiency, we have intercourse in every direction, universal interdependence of nations. . . .

And all the crises of the twentieth century, up to and including the recent one in Asia, are anticipated here:

> A society that has conjured up such gigantic means of production and exchange is like the sorcerer who is no longer able to control the powers of the nether world whom he has called up by his spells. . . . It is enough to mention the commercial crises that by their periodical return put the existence of the entire bourgeois society on trial. . . . In these crises, there breaks out an epidemic that, in all earlier epochs, would have seemed an absurdity—the epidemic of over-production. . . .

In the face of Marx's prescience, how can we possibly sustain the notion that "globalization" marks a new epoch that began in the early 1970s? A much more plausible explanation for the connection between Marx's world and our own is that globalization is not a new epoch but a long-term process, not a new kind of capitalism but the logic of capitalism as it has been from the start.

This view, of course, does not ignore the massive changes that have taken place in the past century and a half. On the contrary, capitalist "laws of motion"—as Marx knew better than anyone else—are precisely laws of *constant* change. But how we interpret those changes very much depends on the vantage point from which we observe them. For instance, seen as an epoch, from the perspective of conventional globalization theories, globalization tends to look like a whole new age, in which the final triumph of capitalism has closed off all alternatives. Seen from Marx's perspective, as a long-term process, globalization looks like a deeply contradictory process, where every advance in the expansion of capitalism has, from the beginning, brought with it new instabilities and new possibilities of struggle.

This brings us to the second large question about globalization, which concerns the role of competition in the globalization thesis. On the face of it, competition seems to lie at the very heart of the thesis: on the right, every effort by capital to worsen the conditions of workers, every attack on the "welfare state," is justified in the name of competitiveness and the stringent new requirements of competition in a globalized economy; on the left, much the same assumptions have led to defeatism and the conviction that all we can do is work out our own, more humane, strategies of competitiveness.

Yet there is a curious contradiction in the globalization thesis, and oddly enough, that contradiction is most visible in some of its left variants. The thesis is based on the premise—and this is why it has such wide-ranging *political* implications—that the effect of globalization is an increasingly united and all-powerful international capital, against which anticapitalist forces are pretty much powerless. But when we examine that assumption, we see some inconsistencies. It looks as if, in the globalization thesis, the transnationalization of capital means not the *intensification* of competition but, on the contrary, the *decline* of competition among major capitalist powers. It means the *interpenetration* of national capitals, their increasing collaboration, apparently *instead* of competition.[3]

Now, of course, even the most extreme globalization theorist would never claim that globalization is creating a single, unified international capital. Obviously, globalization still has a long way to go, and for the foreseeable future, all participants in the market will have to fight to stay on top. But the very strong implication of the globalization thesis, or at least some versions of it, is that there is an inverse relation between globalization and competition: the more globally integrated capitalism becomes, the more unified the capitalist class will be. This seems to imply that globalization is not the *growth* of competition but its suppression.

According to such arguments, it is true that a highly mobile capital roams freely across national borders in search of cheap labor and, at the same time, drives down wages in its country of origin. But that happens, apparently, not because of the old imperatives of competition among capitalists that have *always* driven them to increase profitability and market share by driving down the costs of labor. It happens just because capital is now free to throw its weight around in a simple exercise of raw power. The globalization thesis, then, which constantly invokes the need for competitiveness, is also predicated on an internationalization of capital that drives out competition, unites capital into a single international class, and disables all opposition.

But looked at from a different vantage point, globalization means exactly the reverse. First, we must never forget that capitalism always and necessarily means competition. Competition is at the very heart of the system. This obviously does not mean that capital will not do everything possible to *circumvent* competition. On the contrary, it is a law of competition that capital will try to *evade* competition. Capitalist competition means trying always to maintain and increase market share, and one classic way of doing so is to collude with competitors, to create monopolies, as Adam Smith already knew very well, or to drive out rivals by the sheer force of size and economies of scale. And, of course, one of the consequences of competition is that losers can be swallowed up by winners—though winners on one day may be losers the next.

So increasing concentration and centralization of capital is not the *antithesis* of competition but one of its expressions. The units of competition may have become larger: not only huge domestic companies but transnational companies (and that, again, usually means not *non*-national companies but *national* companies with a transnational reach). But this certainly has not diminished competition. On the contrary, competition between advanced capitalist economies has intensified as new aggressive players have entered the field.

For instance, take the classic case of a hegemonic, monopolistic capitalism—the United States in the early postwar period. The U.S. economy was temporarily hegemonic and almost unchallenged, mainly because of the war. But the recovery of the defeated powers soon put new and more dynamic competitors into play (and here, the period of U.S. hegemony may even have become a competitive liability). The result was, no doubt, more capitalist "monopolies"—not only American, but also Japanese and German—but that certainly did not mean less competition. On the contrary, larger units have made competition more fierce and destructive. On the one hand, this kind of competition means the collapse of small companies, and on the other, we now see new kinds of macro-competition, if you will, with whole national economies engaged in cutthroat rivalries and new forms of state intervention to help them.

So capitalist collaboration has never been incompatible with competition. In fact, the interaction of the two is another one of those characteristic contradictions of capitalism. Even the most advanced transnational collaboration lives side by side with fierce competition. Just look at the European Union today. The Union is meant precisely to strengthen European economies in their competition with the U.S. and Japan. But it is also the terrain of competition *among* European states. In fact, one of the expected, even desired, outcomes of the European Monetary Union and the common currency is intensified competition within European economies and even between them, as the various national economies are deprived of their domestic protections (e.g., monetary policy and manipulation of exchange rates) against the full force of the competitive market.

What conclusions, then, should we draw from this intensified competition among advanced capitalist countries? One obvious conclusion is that globalization may mean less, not more, capitalist unity. So at least that part of the globalization thesis which assumes an increasingly unified international capital is contradicted by capitalist competition.

But does the intensification of competition mean that globalization theorists are right in invoking the requirements of competitiveness? More than one piece in this volume will expose the flaws in left-wing competitive strategies and explain why they are bad for workers, so I will confine my argument to a single point: the main conclusion the labor movement and the left should draw from globalization, or the universalization of capitalism, is that capitalism is now, more than ever, riddled with internal contradictions and that this is a reason for stepping up, not abandoning, anticapitalist struggles.

The universalization of capitalism means that more capitalist economies are entering into global competition, major capitalist economies are depending on export to almost suicidal degrees, and crises of overcapacity are increasingly severe. At the same time, to make themselves competitive, those capitalist economies restrict the buying power of the very consumers they are competing to reach. Maximum profitability for capital today depends less and less on absolute growth or outward expansion and more on redistribution and a widening gap between rich and poor, both within and between nation-states.

You can't get much more contradictory than that. The point, then, is that capitalism's strengths are also its vulnerabilities, and that globalization may be widening, not constricting, the space for oppositional politics.

The State and Class Struggle

But this claim about the new political possibilities would be empty if the globalization thesis were right in its basic assumptions about the state and the transfer of sovereignty from the state to global capital. We are repeatedly told that globalization has made the nation-state irrelevant. For some, this means that nothing can be done at all, that there is no real space for socialist politics, because its traditional target is gone. For others, it means that struggle has to move immediately to the international plane. In either case, a working-class politics in any recognizable sense seems to be ruled out.

That, then, is the assumption I now want to challenge. I want to argue that globalization has made class politics—a politics directed at the state and at class power concentrated in the state—more, rather than less, possible and important.

Marxists used to emphasize the ways in which the growth of capitalism encourages the development of class consciousness and class organization. The socialization of production and the homogenization of work, and the national, supranational, and even global interdependence of its constituent parts, were all supposed to create the conditions for working class consciousness and organization on a mass scale, and even for international solidarity. But developments in the twentieth century have increasingly and, some would say, fatally undermined that conviction.

The failure of the working class to fulfill the expectations of traditional Marxism is typically cited by leftist intellectuals as the main reason for abandoning socialism, or at least for looking for alternative agencies. In recent decades, Western Marxism, then post-Marxism and postmodernism, have, one after the other, assigned historical agency (if they believe in history or agency at all) to intellectuals, to students, to "new social movements"—to anyone but the working class. Today, the labor movement has all but disappeared from the most fashionable types of leftist theory and politics. And globalization seems to have struck the final blow.

Most people who talk about globalization, for instance, are likely to say that in the age of global capitalism, the working class, if it exists at all, is more fragmented than ever before. And if they are on the left, they are likely to say that there is no alternative, that the best we can do is liberate a little more space in the interstices of capitalism by means of many particular and separate struggles—the kind of struggles that sometimes go under the name of identity politics.

Now, there are many reasons for this tendency to reject class politics in favor of political fragmentation and the politics of identity. But surely one major reason is the assumption that the more *global* capitalism becomes, the more global the *struggle* against it will have to be. After all, the argument goes, isn't it true that globalization has shifted power away from the nation-state to transnational institutions and forces? And doesn't this obviously mean that any struggle against capitalism will have to operate on that transnational level?

So since most people, reasonably enough, have trouble believing in that degree of internationalism and in the very possibility of organizing on that level, they naturally conclude that the game is up. They conclude that capitalism is here for good, that there is no longer any point in trying to construct a mass political movement, an inclusive and wide-ranging political force of the kind that old working-class parties aspired to be. Class as a political force, in other words, has disappeared, together with socialism, as a political objective. If we can't organize on a global level, all we can do is go to the other extreme. All we can do, apparently, is turn inward, toward our own very local and particular oppressions.

At the other extreme there is a kind of abstract internationalism without material foundations. It is one thing to recognize the importance of international solidarity and cooperation among national labor movements. That kind of internationalism is not only essential to socialist values but strategically indispensable to the success of many domestic class struggles. But some on the left invoke an "international civil society" as the new arena of struggle, or "global citizenship" as the basis of a new solidarity—and that sounds less like an anti-capitalist strategy than like a kind of whistling in the dark. When people say that the international arena is the *only* one for socialists, that global capital can *only* be met with a truly global response, they seem to be saying, no less surely than the advocates of a fragmented politics, that the struggle against capitalism is effectively over.

My own conclusion is a different one, because I start from different premises. Let me say first of all that I have always had reservations about the direct relationship between the growth of capitalism and the unity of the working class. About seventeen years ago, in an article called "The Separation of the Economic and the Political in Capitalism," I talked about the centrifugal force of capitalism, the ways in which, contrary to conventional Marxist wisdom, the very structure of production and exploitation in a fully developed capitalism tends to *fragment* class struggle and to *domesticate* it, to turn class struggle inward, to make it very local and particularistic.[4] Capitalism certainly has homogenizing effects, and the integration of the capitalist economy certainly provides a material foundation for working-class solidarity beyond the walls of the individual enterprise and even across national frontiers. But the more immediate effect of capitalism is to enclose class conflict within individual units of production, to *de*centralize and localize class struggle.

This is not, it must be emphasized, a failure of working-class consciousness. It is a response to a material reality, to the way the social world is really organized by capitalism. It is worth adding here that, even as class conflicts are localized in this way, the working class is paradoxically divided further by competition among enterprises, in which workers are made to see themselves as allied with their exploiters against their competitors, both capitalists and other workers. This is a tendency that the ideology of globalization is doing its best to promote.

The turning inward of class struggle also means, I suggested, that in capitalism political issues are, in a sense, privatized. The conflicts over authority and domination, which in precapitalist societies are directly aimed at the jurisdictional or political powers of lords and states, in capitalism have shifted to the individual capitalist enterprise. Although capital certainly depends on the power of the state to sustain the system of property and to maintain social order, it is not in the state but in the process of production, and in its hierarchical organization, that capital exerts its power over workers most directly.

I also thought this had something to do with the fact that modern revolutions have tended to take place where capitalism was *less,* rather than more, developed. Where the state itself is a primary exploiter—for example, exploiting peasants by means of taxation—economic and political struggles are hard to separate, and in cases like that, the state can readily become a focus of mass struggles. It is, after all, a much more visible and centralized class enemy than capital by itself could ever be. When people confront capital directly, it is generally only in the form of individual, separate capitals or individual employers. So even proletarian revolutions have tended to occur where working-class conflicts with capital have merged with other, precapitalist struggles, notably peasant struggles against landlords and exploitative states.

But while I was arguing that capitalism has a tendency to fragment and to privatize struggle, it also seemed to me that there were some new countervailing tendencies: the increasing international integration of the capitalist market was shifting the problems of capitalist accumulation from the individual enterprise to the macroeconomic sphere, and capital was being forced to rely more and more on the state to create the right conditions for accumulation. So I suggested that the state's growing complicity in capital's antisocial purposes might mean that the state would increasingly become a prime target of resistance in advanced capitalist countries and might begin to counteract some of the centrifugal effects of capitalism, such as its tendency to fragment and domesticate class struggle.

Now, I had never heard of globalization back then, and I didn't know that people would soon be taking it for granted that the international integration of the capitalist market would weaken the nation-state and shift the focus of capitalist power away from the state. Lately, when globalization is on everyone's lips, I have found myself arguing against the popular assumption that globalization is making the nation-state increasingly irrelevant. I have been arguing that, whatever functions the state may be losing, it is gaining new ones as the main conduit between capital and the global market. Now I want to suggest that this development may be starting to have the consequences for class struggle that, back in 1981, I thought might be a prospect for the future.

We can debate how much globalization has actually taken place, what has and what has not been truly internationalized. But one thing is clear: in the global market, capital *needs* the state. Capital needs the state to maintain the conditions of accumulation and competitiveness in various ways, including direct subsidies and rescue operations at taxpayers' expense (Mexico, the Asian Tigers). It needs the state to preserve labor discipline and social order in the face of austerity and "flexibility," and to enhance of the mobility of capital while blocking the mobility of labor.

Behind every transnational corporation is a national base that depends on its local state to sustain its viability and on other states to give it access to other markets and other labor forces. "Executives," writes *New York Times* journalist Thomas L. Friedman, "say things like 'We are not an American company. We are IBM U.S., IBM Canada, IBM Australia, IBM China.' Oh yeah? Well, the next time you get in trouble in China, then call Li Peng for help. And the next time Congress closes another military base in Asia . . . call Microsoft's navy to secure the sea-lanes of Asia."[5]

In a way, the whole point of "globalization" is that competition is not just—or even mainly—between individual firms but between whole national economies. And as a consequence, the nation-state has acquired new functions as an instrument of competition. If anything, the nation-state is the *main agent* of globalization. U.S. capital, in its quest for competitiveness, demands a state that will keep social costs to a minimum, while keeping in check the social conflict and disorder generated by the absence of social provision. In the European Union, which is supposed to be the model of *trans*national organization, each European state is the principal agent forcing on its citizens the austerities and hardships necessarily for compliance with the stringent requirements of monetary union, and each state is the main instrument for containing the conflicts engendered by these policies—the main agent for maintaining order and labor discipline. Even if the strongly national impulses of the European states allow integration to continue, once these states give up their traditional instruments, such as deficit spending and currency devaluations, for absorbing economic shocks, the state will be needed even more to quell social unrest (or, as many critics expect, individual states will simply violate the Union's rules). Monetary union may then shatter on the rocks of social upheaval. But even if the union survives, it is more than likely that these nation-states will, in the foreseeable future, continue to play a central role in maintaining the right environment for capital accumulation and competitiveness.

The state in various countries plays other roles too. In particular, again, it keeps labor immobilized while capital moves across national boundaries, or in less developed capitalisms, it may act as a transmission belt for other, more powerful, capitalist states. It is, of course, possible that the state will change its form and that the traditional nation-state will gradually give way, on the one hand, to more narrowly local states and, on the other, to larger, regional political authorities. But whatever its form, the state will continue to be crucial, and it is likely that for a long time to come the old nation-state will continue to play its dominant role.

So what has been the effect of the state's new functions? What have been the consequences for class struggle? Has it proved to be true, as I suggested it might, that the new functions of the state in a "globalized," "flexible" capitalism are making it a target of class struggle and a new focus of working-class unity? It is still too early to judge, but at the very least we can take note of a spate of mass protests and street demonstrations in France, Germany, Canada, South Korea, Poland, Argentina, Mexico, and elsewhere, some of which are discussed in this volume. Without making too much of them or their likely effects, it is worth considering their common denominator.

No doubt most people would accept that it has something to do with globalization. Even if we have our doubts about certain aspects of "globalization," let us consider just those aspects we can all agree on: the restructuring of capitalism taking place in every advanced capitalist country and, as a major part of this restructuring, the efforts to eliminate various kinds of social provision in the interests of competitiveness. This is exactly the kind of complicity between the state and capital I was talking about: not just the retreat of the state from its ameliorative functions but also its increasingly active role in restructuring the economy in the interests of capital and to the detriment of everyone else. The actions of the state have driven people into the streets, to oppose state policies in countries as diverse as Canada and South Korea.

In this volume, Sam Gindin suggests that globalization has actually created new opportunities for struggle. With "national and international economic restructuring comes a higher degree of integration of components and services, specialization, lean inventories," he writes, and this makes corporations more vulnerable to certain kinds of local, regional, and national struggles. What I am saying here is that precisely this kind of integration has made the state in many ways more important to capital than ever. In this way and others, the symbiosis between capital and the state is *closer* than ever, and that is making each individual state a potential focus of conflict and class struggle to a greater degree than ever before in advanced capitalist economies.

So now is hardly the time for the left to abandon this political terrain in favor of fragmented politics or a completely abstract internationalism. If the state is the principal agent of globalization, by the same token, the state, especially in advanced capitalist countries, still has the most powerful weapons for *blocking* globalization. If the state is the channel through which capital moves in the globalized economy, then it is equally the means by which an anticapitalist force could sever capital's life line. Old forms of "Keynesian" intervention may be even less effective now than they were before, but this means that political action can no longer simply take the form of *intervening* in the capitalist economy. It is now more a question of *detaching* material life from the logic of capitalism.

In the short term, this means that political action cannot be directed just at offering capital incentives to do socially productive things, or at compensating for the ravages of capital by means of "safety nets." Politics must be increasingly about using state power to *control* the movements of capital and to bring the allocation of capital and the disposition of economic surpluses increasingly within the reach of democratic accountability, in accordance with a social logic different from the logic of capitalist competition and profitability.[6]

Conclusion

One of the main problems in organizing anticapitalist struggles has always been that capital presents no single, visible target. And the formal separation of economic and political spheres that is characteristic of capitalism—in which exploitation takes place by means of an apparently free exchange between juridical "equals," in a contract between capital and labor, and in which the relationship between them is mediated by an impersonal "market"—has created what looks, on the surface, like a "neutral" state that does not visibly intervene in the daily confrontations between capital and labor. But as capital depends on the state to clear its path through the global economy, whether bu means of neoliberal policies or by some other means, the power of capital becomes more concentrated in the state, and the state's collusion with capital becomes increasingly transparent.

This is one major reason why we need to be so careful about how we use the term "globalization." We have to guard against treating the trends that go under that name as if they were natural, inevitable processes, instead of historically specific *capitalist* processes, the capitalist exploitation of human beings and natural resources, aided and abetted by a direct collaboration between the state and capital. In fact, the concept of globalization today plays such a prominent role in capitalist ideology precisely because powerful ideological weapons are now needed to disguise and mystify this increasingly direct and obvious collusion.

If the state can now more than ever serve as a target in an anticapitalist struggle, it can also, as the focus of local and national class struggles, be a unifying force within the working class, against its internal fragmentation, and also between the labor movement and its allies in the community. At the same time, as the destructive logic of capitalismbecomes more universal, domestic struggles against that common logic can be the strongest basis of a new internationalism. This internationalism would be founded not on some unrealistic and abstract notion of an international civil society or global citizenship, nor on the illusion that we can make things better by increasing the left's representation in transnational organizations of capital like the IMF, but rather on mutual support among various local and national movements in their struggles against their own domestic capitalists and states.

This does not mean that there is no place for common, transnational struggles, or that the labor movement should neglect transnational organizations, such as the European Union, in which it can make a difference. But cooperative struggles of this kind ultimately depend on a strong and well-organized domestic labor movement. So if there is a motto that sums up this kind of internationalism, it might be this: "Workers of all countries unite—but unity begins at home."

Even if, as now seems possible, the current global crisis puts the brakes on neoliberal globalization, it will not end the universalization of capitalism and the growing contradictions that come with it, and capital will continue to need the help of the state in navigating the turbulent global economy. The political organization of the working class is now more important and potentially effective than ever.

Notes

1. Readers will no doubt be familiar with conventional versions of the globalization thesis just from reading the daily newspaper. There are also several leftist variants of the thesis. For a moderate and relatively judicious version, see Richard B. DuBoff and Edward S. Herman, "A Critique of Tabb on Globalization," *Monthly Review* 49 (November 1997): 27-35. A rather more exaggerated version can be found in A. Sivanandan, "Capitalism, Globalization, and Epochal Shifts: An Exchange," *Monthly Review* 48 (February 1997): 19-21. For a particularly extreme version, see Roger Burbach, "The Epoch of Globalization," *URPE Newsletter* 29 (Fall 1997): 3-5.

2. See, for example, Greg Albo, "The World Economy, Market Imperatives, and Alternatives," *Monthly Review* 48 (December 1996): 6-22; Doug Henwood, "Post What?" *Monthly Review* 48 (September 1996): 1-11; Harry Magdoff, *Globalization: To What End?* (New York: Monthly Review Press, 1992); L. Panitch, "Globalisation and the State," in R. Miliband and L. Panitch, eds., *Socialist*

Register 1994: Between Globalism and Nationalism (London: Merlin, 1994), 60-93; William K. Tabb, "Globalism Is *an* Issue, The Power of Capital Is *the* Issue," *Monthly Review* 49 (June 1997): 20-30.

3. For the most explicit and extreme statement of this position, see Burbach, "The Epoch of Globalization."

4. That article, published in 1981 in *New Left Review,* has more recently appeared in my book, *Democracy Against Capitalism: Renewing Historical Materialism* (Cambridge: Cambridge University Press, 1995), 19-48.

5. *New York Times,* 10 April 1998.

6. On these themes, see Albo, "The World Economy."

Talking About Work

Doug Henwood

Mainstream discourse about work is heavy with nonsense, but, sadly, so is a lot of leftish talk. The two versions are tightly bound together. The orthodox spin tales of productivity miracles and smart machines, and too many people take them seriously. George Gilder's cheerful tales of fully automated lifestyles (like his book *Microcosm)* metamorphose into Jeremy Rifkin's *End of Work* or Stanley Aronowitz and William DiFazio's *Jobless Future.*[1] Fortunately for their argument, none of these writers seems to care much about rigorous evidence, but, unfortunately, they've acquired some influence.

It's quite reminiscent of the buzz around globalization. Ancient features of capitalism, job-displacing technical innovation, and the lust to cross national borders are posited as recent transformations. This leads to a dramatic misspecification of the enemy: instead of capital and its lust for profit, innovation and cosmopolitanism are demonized. Demonizing these things, instead of talking about their radical transformation, is one of the worst consequences of the rejection of Marx.

Bright Future

The optimistic line is known to anyone who picks up a copy of *Wired,* or even just watches TV.[2] Technology is changing everything. All the old fixities—big industry, big government, big things—have become endlessly fluid. Hierarchy is gone in the new team-oriented world; innovation is ceaseless, bubbling up from the bottom. Self-reliance and interconnectivity together make the future, and a libertarian spirit pervades it all. Education and skill are the keys to the new world, not ownership or connection.

This mode comes in several flavors. The right wing one, exemplified by George Gilder and the "digerati" of *Wired,* is deeply laissez-faire. But there's a liberal one as well, embodied by Robert Reich and even Bill Clinton. A few years ago, when he was secretary of labor, Reich said: "The most rapidly growing job categories are knowledge-intensive; I've called them 'symbolic analysts.' Why are they growing so quickly? Why are they paying so well? Because technology is generating all sorts of new possibilities. . . . The problem is that many people don't have the right skills."[3] (The "problem" Reich is talking about is

17

presumably poverty and social decay.) Clinton believes and says very similar things. Reich, it seems, didn't pay much attention to the projections of an agency he once supervised, the Bureau of Labor Statistics (BLS), nor, apparently, does Clinton. Listed below are the BLS's projections of the fastest-growing occupations between 1996 and 2006; they bear no relation to Reich's fantasies, or to those filling the pages of *Wired*.

Cashiers	Childcare workers	Computer engineers
Systems analysts	Clerical supervisors and managers	Food-preparation workers
General managers and top executives		Hand packers and packagers
Registered nurses	Databasead ministrators, computer support specialists, and all other computer scientists	Guards
Salespersons, retail		General office clerks
Truck drivers, light and heavy		Waiters and waitresses
Home health aides	Marketing and sales-worker supervisors	Social workers
Teacher's aides and educational assistants		Adjustment clerks
Nursing aides, orderlies, and attendants	Maintenance repairers, general utility	Cooks, short order and fast food
Receptionists and information clerks	Food counter, fountain, and related workers	Personal and home-care aides
Teachers, secondary school	Teachers, special education	Food service and lodging managers
		Medical assistants

These thirty job categories alone account for almost one-third of total employment today, and for 46 percent of the next decade's projected growth. Of the top thirty, those that look like symbolic analysts account for 9 percent of employment now, and 16 percent of projected growth. Most look quite mundane. It's hard to see from this how "the problem is that many people don't have the right skills." It is, however, easy to see the polarizing tendencies in today's labor market. Of the top thirty occupations, about 40 percent of the job growth will be among those in the lowest quarter of the earnings distribution. Another 28 precent will be in the top-paying quarter, with only 31 percent in the middle half.

About a third (34 percent) of new openings will require a bachelor's degree or more (meaning, of course, that two-thirds won't), well under the 39 percent that will require no more than "short on-the-job training."[4]

Unpacking "Skills"

Just what do people mean by skills anyway? If the U.S. ruling class were seriously worried about illiteracy and innumeracy, its members would spend more money on education. While it may be that we'd all be better off if workers were better trained, there's no sign that actual employers are demanding such a workforce now.

One problem with analyzing skill is that it's a difficult concept to define and measure. Economists typically use a mix of education and experience to describe the skill of workers, but these are only inexact proxies. At the big-picture level, the rising "education premium"—the earnings advantage enjoyed by those with advanced degrees—is often cited as proof of the rising demand for skilled workers. But comparisons of U.S. regions show that the higher the unemployment rate, the greater the education premium.

Since average unemployment rates have drifted upwards since the golden age—they averaged 4.6 percent in the 1950s and 1960s, and they have averaged 6.8 percent since 1980—it may be that the rising education premium is just a sign of a slack labor market. More direct attempts to measure employers' wants offer no support for the skills thesis. To measure the changes in skills requirements in the United States, David Howell and Edward Wolff linked changes in employment in 64 industrial and 264 occupational categories from 1960-1985 to their descriptions in the BLS's *Dictionary of Occupational Titles*. They found that low-skilled service-industry work grew more quickly than high-skilled—and that, perversely, the more rapidly growing service industries "required higher skills but paid lower wages than the low-growth service industries." The picture was brighter in manufacturing, but it's a shrinking field. For nonsupervisory workers as a whole, the most rapid growth "was in the highest skill segment but in the lowest wage segment." If the "problem" that Reich was talking about was social polarization, then there's not much evidence that skills or their lack have much to do with it. Most of the increase in inequality over the past twenty-five years has come *within* demographic groups—people grouped by occupation, age, sex, and schooling—and not between them. A better place to look for explanations of polarization would be the erosion of the working class's bargaining power because of union busting, deregulation, and capital mobility.[5]

Why do employers and their mouthpieces keep talking about skills then? It may be that they mean something other than mental or manual dexterity.

Of course, formal training does impart certain skills; there are no self-taught neurosurgeons. But work training at less elite levels has proved disappointing; for example, people with (nonprofessional) vocational training in high school find it easier to get jobs, but there's no evidence that they do any better once they're working. And while having a high school diploma is necessary to snag certain kinds of jobs, grade average correlates neither with the probability of getting a job nor with one's pay upon landing a position. Studies of the relations among wages, schooling, and scores on standardized tests—admittedly imperfect measures of skills— show that, while people with more education make higher scores on the tests, this advantage pales next to the higher wages earned by the credentialed; nothing in the scores can explain why college grads earn 60 percent more than those with only a high school diploma.[6] Writing in the *California Management Review,* Peter Cappelli asked, "Is the 'skills gap' really about attitudes?" He carefully answered his own question "yes." In the 1970s, Cappelli reminds us, there was lots of worry about bad worker attitudes: the "blue collar blues"—an alienation that expressed itself in strikes, sabotage, and general truculence. By the mid-1980s, though, the complaints were all about "skills": workers just didn't have what it took to cut it in the modern world. Education summits were convened to address the skills problem, though, of course, little new funding for primary and secondary schooling was on offer. Clinton has offered some measly tax breaks for education, of disproportional benefit to rich folks,, but no serious schooling initiative. Employer surveys reveal that bosses care less about their employees' candlepower than they do about "character," by which they mean self-discipline, enthusiasm, and responsibility. Bosses want underlings who are steadfast, dependable, consistent, punctual, and tactful, and who identify with their work and show sympathy for others; those who are labeled creative and independent received low marks. (A survey of high-school teachers showed almost identical results about students.) Workers are rarely dismissed for incompetence, but rather for absenteeism and other irresponsible behavior. An extensive 1991 review of research showed "conscientiousness" the best of five personality predictors for job success, and "openness to experience," the psychologists' odd name for smarts, the least impressive.

Employers want the can-do, self-starters of classified-ad boilerplate, not adepts at C++ or vector autoregressions.[7] Another trait that's valued highly, according to the psychomanagerial literature, is a knack for "prosocial" behavior—doing more for others, which, in this case, means more for the boss. Such devotion is especially welcome in these days of employee "empowerment" programs and leaderless teams; workers are expected to be the architects of their own better exploitation.[8]

The challenge to educators is to produce that kind of worker. According to Cappelli, it's not enough to teach students "responsibility, self-discipline, and adherence to rules"; they must produce graduates with good attitudes, which, as we've learned, means cheerful, self-sacrificing, and prosocial. Though he is too respectable to say so, Cappelli makes it clear that talk of teaching "values" in the classroom is, in part, about the most important value of all, shareholder value. Employers, Cappelli and his sources say, should use fear of "losing face" as a motivational tool and, through "role modeling," use "conformity pressures [to] produce a positive result." It's not enough that employers control your time; they should control your mind and heart as well.

No More Work?

But complaints of the sort I've just lodged may strike some readers as carping: isn't employment scarce these days, and growing scarcer? Well, yes, in the sense that full employment is impossible under capitalism, but it's highly unlikely that we've entered a new era of 25 percent unemployment rates. The argument that technology has finally advanced enough to render human workers obsolete is old, very old, but its most popular recent embodiments are Jeremy Rifkin's *The End of Work* and Aronowitz and DiFazio's *The Jobless Future*. Rifkin's book was for a popular audience published by a trade house;[9] Aronowitz and DiFazio are academics, and their book was published by a university press, but neither book is based on sound evidence.

Aronowitz and DiFazio's whole book flows essentially from the assertions of its first paragraph:

> We live in hard times. The economic stagnation and decline that changed many lives after the stock market crash of 1987 and blossomed into a full-blown recession in 1990 lingers despite frequent self-satisfied statements by politicians and economists that the recovery has finally arrived (1992, 1993, 1994). Nevertheless, there are frequent puzzled statements by the same savants to the effect that although we are once again on the road to economic growth, it is a jobless recovery. Then, in the months in which the Department of Labor records job growth, we are dismayed to discover that most of the jobs are part-time, near the minimum wage.

Virtually every assertion in this paragraph except the first sentence is wrong. Growth in the two years after the 1987 crash averaged a respectable 3.4 percent. The recession that followed was briefer and milder than the post-Second World War average. The recovery from that slump was admittedly weak and tentative at first, but it did happen, and it ceased being "jobless" in early 1992. Over 1.4 million new jobs were created in 1992, and the total between the recession's trough and the spring of 1998 was almost 17 million new jobs.[10] While many of them are lousy, most are not part-time and few are near the minimum wage.

Our authors' claim about part-time jobs deserves closer scrutiny, since it has taken on a life of its own. The BLS divides part-time work into two categories: for economic reasons and for noneconomic reasons. (The BLS's old terms for these categories were clearer: involuntary and voluntary.) People who are working part-time for economic reasons would like full-time work, but can find only the part-time variety; those who are working part-time for noneconomic reasons want only part-time employment. Between the February 1992 trough in employment (which came eleven months after the official end of the 1990-1991 recession) and April 1998, part-time employment grew by 609,000 jobs. But all of that growth, and then some, has been of the noneconomic or voluntary kind; involuntary and economic part-timing fell by 2.6 million jobs. Over the past forty years, the share of employed workers working part-time for economic reasons rises in recessions and falls in expansions, but without any upward drift over the long term; in other words, no trend exists. Overwork is at least as characteristic of the U.S. labor market now as is underwork.

Nearly twice as many people hold down multiple jobs as are involuntarily limited to part-time work (7.9 million vs. 4.1 million), and well over half the multiply employed hold at least one full-time job. As the webzine *Suck* (http://www.suck.com) reported on January 21, 1997, "Since 1969, full-time employees in the United States have increased by a full workday the hours they put in each week, and in the past two decades, the number of people working over fifty hours a week has increased by a third." Or, as a recent BLS study has shown, the total number of annual hours put in by the average employed male increased by one hundred hours between 1976 and 1993, or two-and-a-half full workweeks. More eye-poppingly, the number clocked by the average working woman increased by 223 hours, or nearly six full workweeks.[11] (And for women, that doesn't include the unpaid labor at home that men are still so expert at shirking.) What does a book called *The Jobless Future* have to say to them?

Temporary jobs, another favorite of the Aronowitz-DiFazio and Rifkin schools, are growing, but they account for just 10 percent of the total growth in jobs since 1992, and just over 2 percent of total employment.

All in all, according to a BLS survey, workers classified as "contingent"—temp and contract workers with explicitly limited job tenure—accounted for 4.4 percent of total employment in 1997, a fall from 4.9 percent in 1995.[12] Job-tenure statistics also counsel skepticism about epochal transformations. BLS surveys show that, in 1996, the average (median) worker had been at his or her job for 3.8 years, only a little less than 3.5 years in 1983. A look at workers classified by age and sex shows less stability. Tenure for men in every age group fell, with tenure for those fifty-five to sixty-four years old falling the most, from 15.3 to 10.5 years, and the tenure for those thirty-five to forty-four falling from 7.3 to 6.1 years. But since workers are, on average, getting older, and tenure rises with age, the average for all men fell only slightly, from 4.1 to 4.0 years. Tenure for women rose on average from 3.1 to 3.5 years, and in half the age groups.[13] This looks like a picture of increasing volatility for older men, part of a slow convergence of the work lives of the genders, but not a sea change.

Bad Science

One reason that mass job death may not be appearing on schedule is that the productivity miracle is a bit delayed. The BLS offers two measures of productivity, one strictly of labor productivity—real (inflation-adjusted) output per hour worked—and one of "multifactor" productivity, which includes capital inputs along with labor. Now the concept of productivity of capital is very problematic, conceptually and practically. An hour of labor is an hour of labor, but just what is a unit of capital? What is a unit of drill press or a unit of computer? You can express all those material things in dollar terms, but at what value—purchase price or its cost today? How do you handle computers, whose real price continues to drop like a stone? But for all those problems, let's see if the official numbers match the assertions of the gloomsters.

Annual Growth in Labor Productivity by Decade, U.S.

	nonfarm business	manufacturing
1950-60	2.5%	2.2%
1960-70	2.5	2.6
1970-80	1.9	2.9
1980-90	1.1	2.7
1990-98	1.1	3.6

This chart offers no evidence for a technological miracle. Manufacturing productivity has picked up a bit, but these figures may be inflated by the manufacturers' strategy of contracting out for services ranging from mopping to accounting.[14] Besides, the Aronowitz-DiFazio-Rifkin crowd claims that the real job-killing techno-action is in the service industries, where computers are allegedly making human workers obsolete—but they're not.

Nor does the capital productivity series offer any evidence of a fundamental change; quite the contrary, output per unit of real capital has been flat to down for more than forty years, and even in manufacturing! Maybe the sea change is ahead of us, not upon us. But there is just no evidence, aside from some gee-whiz anecdotes Aronowitz and DiFazio picked up in the business press, that things have fundamentally changed. Our authors have rather loose standards of evidence. "Most recently," they write, "Alvin Toffler and Jacques Attali have offered futurologies that confirm prognostications of the workerless factory and office." Very nice indeed; today's futurologists are called in to confirm the wrong predictions of yesterday's soothsayers!

Abroad

So far, I've focused mainly on U.S. experience. In this case, such provincialism is defensible; the United States, despite its many problems, is the most technically advanced of all the major economies (with the possible exception of Japan), and the United States has one of the least-regulated labor markets in the first world. So if the Aronowitz-DiFazio-Rifkin diagnosis were correct, it would be most visible in the United States. But it's not. We see plenty of wage polarization, a disappearance of middle-income jobs, the loss of fringe benefits, longer hours, speedup, and rising stress, but no generalized disappearance of work. Quite the contrary, in fact. But non-U.S. experience offers no backup for Aronowitz and DiFazio either. Asian statistics on capital productivity show no great leaps forward in the East. A recent survey of employers in New Zealand, which has experienced one of the world's most extreme bouts of deregulation during the past decade, shows a decline in reliance on "casual" labor (temp, part-time, contract, etc.), to the surprise of the surveyors. An OECD study shows an increase in the share of temporary arrangements in total employment since the early 1980s in Australia, France, the Netherlands, and Spain; little change in Denmark, Finland, Germany, Ireland, Italy, Japan, Sweden, and the U.K.; and drops in Belgium, Greece, and Portugal - in other words, a very mixed picture. In the cases of France and Spain, the growth in temp work can be traced to legal changes more than anything else.[15] Another end-of-worker, Roger Burbach, has turned to the International Labour Office (ILO) for support. In a paper read at the *Rethinking Marxism* conference (held at the University of Massachusetts in December 1996), Burbach cited the ILO's estimate of a 30 percent global unemployment rate as proof that I was "dead wrong" in my "criticism of Jeremy Rifkin's book *The End of Work*" in my article in the September 1996 issue of *Monthly Review*. I assume that that estimate came from the ILO's 1996-1997 World Employment Report; the wire service stories on it, circulated all over the Internet, featured the 30 percent figure. But if Burbach read the original, he might have noticed that the ILO spent a whole chapter refuting Rifkin and his ilk. In that chapter, the ILO reviewed all the empirical evidence and concluded that there was no support for end-of-work theories.

There's been no long-term structural change in the relationship between economic growth and employment growth. In areas of high unemployment, such as Western and Eastern Europe, the main causes are slow growth and economic collapse, respectively, not technological transformation. Faster growth may not be politically possible or ecologically desirable, but those are different matters entirely. In Latin America and Asia, paid employment is growing, as peasants are daily transformed into industrial workers, for good or ill. Let's look a bit at what economists call the employment intensity of growth: how much employment a given amount of gross domestic product (GDP) growth is associated with. Every major rich industrialized country, including the United States, has seen slower job growth since 1990 than over the previous two or three decades. And in every one of those countries, the employment slowdown has come with a GDP slowdown. Contradicting the bedrock thesis of jobless-future proponents, there's no evidence that some technological revolution means that a given amount of GDP growth today generates less employment growth than in the past; if anything, the gap between GDP and job growth is narrower now than in earlier decades. In the 1960s, for example, Japanese GDP growth averaged 10.5 percent a year, and employment growth, 1.5 percent, a difference of 9 percentage points. The Western European economies that were enjoying fabulous, if not quite Japanese, rates of growth between the early 1950s and the early 1970s also saw employment growth trail GDP growth by 2 to 4 percentage points. As growth fell to 1 to 2 percent for Japan and Western Europe in the early 1990s, employment fell proportionally with it. Nothing magical has happened to sever growth in real GDP and growth in employment.[16] Further, says the ILO, "[W]hile there has been some increase in self-employment, part-time work and other non-standard forms of employment, this has not meant the disappearance of regular jobs. Data on job tenure do not show any generalized decline in either the period employed individuals have been with their current employer or projected future tenure. At the same time there is also no evidence that the rate of job change has increased in labour markets. . . ."

The Meaning of It All

Of course, none of this is meant to argue that the world of work is wondrously pleasant or secure. It rarely is. But for all the centuries of its history, capitalism has drawn an ever-larger share of the population into paid labor while never supplying as many jobs as people would like.

In other words, unemployment is a constant feature of economic life in capitalist societies, rising in bad times and falling in good. Times of mass unemployment, as in the 1930s, are rare in the rich industrialized countries, but so are times of low unemployment, as in the 1960s. There's no evidence that this fundamental fact of capitalist life has changed. The increasing harshness characterizing economic life can be traced to some very old-fashioned causes—tight money, tight budgets, increased capital mobility, and union-busting—rather than to epochal technological transformations. The recent U.S. downsizing mania, which now may be waning, was much more the result of pressures from Wall Street for fatter profits and higher stock prices than of snazzier microprocessors or Malaysian competition.[17] As all the welfare-state buffers that once softened the market's disciplines are dismantled, we're being returned to the savage rule of pure nineteenth century capitalism. In many ways, the recent past and imaginable future resemble the Victorian world more than they do the futurist fantasies of science fictioneers. In fact, few things could make the world's bosses happier than blaming abstractions like "technology" and "globalization" rather than themselves or the charming system known as capitalism; blaming impersonal forces is one giant step toward naturalizing a problem that's really social in origin. Worse, by encouraging a belief in the inevitability of downsizing, the end-of-work crowd may be deepening the sense of resignation that lubricates the austerity agenda, rather than encouraging a challenge to it. The fact that people believe deeply in technological hyperspace and jobs vanishing en masse (and along with these beliefs, the allegedly rampant, recent globalization of everything) has greatly weakened the bargaining power of workers, both organized and unorganized.

Obviously, merely being acquainted with the truth won't change the political balance of forces. Even if the economy is nowhere near as seamlessly globalized as the cheerleaders and worrywarts say, individual employers are still quite adept at using the threat of a move to Mexico to cow their workers into submission. But straightening out these facts is essential to any working-class political renaissance. Capitalism is fundamentally still the same beast that Ricardo and Marx described: a rudely expansive, ceaselessly innovative system (whose innovations are only of the sort that increase profits, it must be noted), based on a fundamental hostility between the classes and a brutally destructive appropriation of nature. The detailed realizations of those fundamental principles vary over time and space, but the fundamentals are still with us. The beast seems harder to fight than ever, but at least we should study its physiology.

Notes

1. George Gilder, *Microcosm: The Quantum Revolution in Economics and Technology* (New York: Touchstone Books, 1990); Jeremy Rifkin, *The End of Work:The Decline of the Global Labor Force and the Dawn of the Post-Market Era* (New York: Putnam, 1995); Stanley Aronowitz and William DiFazio, *The Jobless Future: Sci-Tech and the Dogma of Work* (Minneapolis: University of Minnesota Press, 1995).

2. The magazine's classic manifesto is Peter Schwartz and Peter Leyden, "The Long Boom: A History of the Future, 1980-2020," *Wired,* July 1997. The text, minus the vertiginous graphics, is available on the magazine's web site at *http://www.wired.com/wired/5.07/longboom.html.*

3. From an interview with Reich, conducted by David Bennahum, published in the webzine *Meme* no. 2.02, at *http://memex.org/meme2-02.html.*

4. Author's calculations based on George T. Silvestri, "Occupational Employment Projections to 2006," *Monthly Labor Review* 120 (November 1997): 58-83, especially tables 4 and 6. This article and other employment projections are available from the BLS web site at *http://stats.bls.gov/emphome.htm.*

5. David R. Howell and Edward N. Wolff, "Trends in the Growth and Distribution of Skills in the U.S. Workplace, 1960-1985," *Industrial and Labor Relations Review* 44 (April 1991): 486-502.

6. Samuel Bowles and Herbert Gintis, "Why do the Educated Earn More? Productive Skills, Labor Discipline, and the Returns to Schooling," unpublished paper, University of Massachusetts Department of Economics, 28 November 1995.

7. Peter Cappelli, "Is the 'Skills Gap' Really About Attitudes," *California Management Review* 37 (Summer 1995): 108-124.

8. Thomas S. Bateman and Dennis W. Organ, "Job Satisfaction and the Good Soldier: The Relationship Between Affect and Employee 'Citizenship'," *Academy of Management Journal* 26 (1983): 587-95; Arthur P. Brief, "Prosocial Organizational Behaviors," *Academy of Management Review* 11 (1986): 710-25; Peter Cappelli, "College Students and the Workplace: Assessing Performance to Improve the Fit," *Change,* November/December 1992: 55-61; Richard C. Edwards, "Personal Traits and 'Success' in Schooling and Work," *Educational and Psychological Measurement* 37 (1977): 125-38.

9. For a critique of Rifkin, see Doug Henwood, "Post What?" *Monthly Review* 48, no. 4 (September 1997).

10. Author's calculations based on U.S. Bureau of Labor Statistics data, available at *http://www.bls.gov/sahome.html.*

11. U.S. Bureau of Labor Statistics, "Workers Are on the Job More Hours Over the Course of the Year," *Issues in Labor Statistics* 97, no. 3 (February 1997).

12. U.S. Bureau of Labor Statistics, "Contingent and Alternative Employment Arrangements, February 1997," News Release USDL 97-422, 2 December 1997, available at *http://stats.bls.gov/news.release/conemp.toc.htm.*

13. U.S. Bureau of Labor Statistics, "Employee Tenure in the Mid-1990s," News Release USDL 97-25, 30 January 1997, available at *http://stats.bls.gov/news.release/tenure.toc.htm.*

14. Author's calculations from Bureau of Labor Statistics productivity data, available at *http://www.bls.gov/sahome.html.*

15. On part-time and temporary work, see the 1995 and 1996 editions of the OECD's *Employment Outlook* (Paris: Organisation for Economic Cooperation and Development).

16. Author's calculations from U.S. Bureau of Labor Statistics figures, at *http://www.bls.gov/sahome.html.*

17. See Doug Henwood, *Wall Street: How It Works and For Whom,* updated paperback edition (New York and London: Verso, 1998).

"Same As It Ever Was"? The Structure of the Working Class

Peter Meiksins

There is a story you will hear told over and over again in sympathetic commentary on the contemporary American labor movement:

The American labor movement has declared its intent to organize, once again, the American working class. After decades of stagnation and decline, and faced with the virtual extinction of private sector unionism, organized labor has finally realized that it needs to return to the aggressive organizing tactics that were the key to its success in the past. But, while the tactics may be old, those being organized are not. In fact, one of the reasons for the decline of American unionism has been the unions' inability and unwillingness to grasp that there is a new work force in the United States. This has developed as the demographic composition of the workforce has changed, and as the evolution of capitalism has altered the overall occupational structure and the conditions of work in both old and new occupations. This new work force needs to be organized, to be sure. But it will not be, unless the labor movement abandons the narrow unionism of the past, with its focus on white, male industrial workers, and replaces it with a more flexible, diverse unionism responsive to the diverse employees and workplaces of the post-industrial age.

This story contains two crucial assumptions about the structure of the working class and about the way in which that structure is likely to affect the future of the labor movement. It assumes, first of all, that the working class has developed a structure that is fundamentally different from what it was in the past, obliging the labor movement to adopt fundamentally new tactics. The second assumption is that the principal problem posed by the structure of the working class is one of organizing, i.e., getting new kinds of workers to join unions. These assumptions are logically connected. Should we accept these assumptions underlying the conventional story being told about the contemporary working class?

While it is obvious that the contemporary working class is diverse and structurally complex, it is not clear that this is something entirely new. Diversity and complexity may have taken new forms, but this is not the same thing as saying that what preceded it was simple or homogeneous. In fact, the "old" working class was diverse, too, and the traditional labor movement's experience with organizing a diverse working class can teach us something about the prospects for working-class organization in the present. The problem with the story being told about contemporary workers is that it obscures the lessons that can be learned from past experiences with diversity and complexity by defining diversity and complexity as something entirely new.

Working Class Diversity

Let us begin with some facts about the structure of the contemporary working class and the ways in which it represents a departure from the past. For the sake of simplicity, I will focus on two major sets of changes: (1) demographic changes in the composition of the working class, particularly gender and race; and (2) changes in occupational structure and the organization of work brought about by trends in contemporary capitalism.

There is, to begin with, the remarkable growth of female employment in the decades since World War II. In 1995, 64.1 percent of American women participated in the labor force up, from about 33 percent in 1950. The vast increase of women in the labor force has been more than a matter of numbers; the female labor force has also become considerably more diverse, as groups of women who, in the past, tended not to seek paid employment (middle-income, married women, women with small children at home) were both pushed and pulled into the wage economy.

The influx of women into the paid labor force has produced a more diverse, but highly segmented working class. Women workers remain heavily concentrated in a narrow range of largely female occupations (secretary, nurse, teacher, etc.). Even those occupations which appear to have achieved a degree of gender integration (such as commercial baking or real-estate sales) remain segregated, with women concentrated in less lucrative, less desirable portions of the "trade."[1] Despite some improvement, women workers continue to earn only 70 percent of what male workers earn.

Racial and ethnic diversity has also taken on new importance in the contemporary workforce. African Americans have always formed a significant part of the American labor force, but their numbers have increased slightly in recent decades to slightly more than 11 percent of the total population of the country, and slightly less than 11 percent of the workforce. But the fact that African Americans are far less concentrated in agricultural employment than they were in the past makes them increasingly important to the future of union organizing. Meanwhile, the number of Hispanics in the population and the labor force has grown sharply; Hispanics are now more than 9 percent of the civilian labor force. To this can be added growing numbers of Asian Americans, so that, by some estimates, nonwhites are now almost 25 percent of the labor force.

Like women, nonwhites are highly segregated into certain occupations and economic sectors. While there are few (if any) occupations which are predominately African-American or Hispanic, workers from these groups are disproportionately concentrated in a number of occupations, many of which are low-paying and low-status (e.g., private household workers; security guards; nurses' aides; correctional officers; freight, stock, and material handlers, and taxi drivers). There is also a pattern of sectorial segregation, with minority workers being unusually numerous in government employment, for example. Indeed, sectorial segregation intersects with economic stratification; most of the gains in high-wage employment of African Americans have occurred in the public sector, while racial inequality remains sharper in the private sector.[2] Overall, as with women's employment, the increasing numbers of nonwhite workers have also created a highly segmented labor force.

The second major reason for the diversity and complexity in the American working class has been the evolution of American capitalism. The rise of global capitalism, increasing capital mobility, the shift towards "flexible" production, technological change, and a series of other developments have transformed occupational structure and stimulated the development of a variety of "new" employment relationships.

The most significant change in occupational structure has been the shift away from manufacturing toward service work, as a result of a variety of changes in capitalism, including the replacement of direct labor by technology; the shift of production and assembly work overseas; the rise of new "service-intensive" industries, such as the production of software; and the growing administrative complexity of capitalist firms. Manufacturing work in the United States employed 35.9 percent of the labor force in 1950, but this figure was projected to decline to as little as 20 percent by the year 2000. The manufacturing sector actually experienced absolute declines in employment over the past few decades. At the same time, "services" now employ over 70 percent of the overall labor force, up from only 52 percent in 1950. Women and minorities are disproportionately employed in the service sector, so this shift in employment intersects with the demographic changes outlined above.[3]

Not only is the service sector large, but it is extraordinarily diverse. Included under this general heading is a wide range of occupations, from low-pay janitors and health-care workers to middle-income teachers and nurses, and on to affluent engineers, lawyers, and other professionals. Some of these workers (e.g., engineers) are in positions of authority over manual and/or lower-level service workers, and others work in sectors (retail sales, health care, education) far removed from the traditional industrial working class. Paid employment has taken on a variety of new meanings as a result of the proliferation of different kinds of service work.

The evolution of contemporary capitalism has also produced a final source of complexity within the contemporary working class: the proliferation of forms of employment relationships. Technological changes have made possible new kinds of employment arrangements, ranging from "just-in-time" production to telecommuting and working at home. Economic pressures have led to experiments with decentralized production, the internal reorganization of companies (downsizing, flattened hierarchies, etc.), and the attempt to develop a more "flexible" labor force. Globalization has also affected the structure of the workplace, for example, by stimulating the dissemination of managerial techniques from abroad. The effects on the structure of the work-force are too numerous to mention here. Let us simply indicate the scope of the changes by mentioning two or three.

First, one can point to the growth of temporary and part-time employment (so-called "contingent" work), a phenomenon heavily skewed towards, but by no means confined to, the service sector. As other contributors to this volume note, the growth of contingent work has probably been exaggerated. Estimates as high as 25 percent of the workforce have given way to more conservative estimates in the 6 to 7 percent range. Nevertheless, temporary employment and involuntary part-time employment are growing faster than the workforce as a whole, and there is abundant evidence of growing employment insecurity even among permanent employees. The expansion of contingent employment threatens to create a "class" of workers whose relationship to employers is quite different from that experienced by traditional employees in all sectors of the economy.

Many of the changes described above have also helped to fuel the much-publicized expansion of smaller workplaces. The subcontracting of work and the rise of small, flexible enterprises serving niche markets, among other developments, have spawned numerous small companies whose employees' work conditions are quite different from those of employees of large organizations (including reduced employment security and bureaucracy).

One can also note the emergence of a wide range of "interactive service work," in which workers (salesworkers, flight attendants, etc.) interact directly with clients. As Dorothy Sue Cobble notes, the relationship between these workers and their employers is complicated by the introduction of a third party, the customer. The customer may appear as the central determinant of wages and/or as the principal source of stress and conflict at work.[4] These workers thus experience a different set of social relationships at work than do conventional workers in manufacturing or even in many service jobs.

Finally, there are the many innovations associated with the globalization of production. Most notable among these are Japanese management practices, which have been imported directly by Japanese producers and emulated by many American employers. These practices, while hardly as benign as they have often been presented,[5] do tend to create a different relationship between employer and employee. By deliberately selecting cooperative employees, businesses can effectively divide the workforce into pro-union and anti-union segments. The use of quality circles and other forms of quasi-participation creates at least the illusion of voice, something traditional employees rarely possess. And the division of the workforce into a permanent core and a temporary periphery tends to divide the labor force socially as well.

The Lesson(s) of Working Class Diversity

These (and other) facts indicate that it is entirely appropriate and necessary to see the contemporary working class as diverse and structurally complex. Any serious effort to organize such a class must adopt a wide range of strategies and approaches appropriate to the differences of circumstance and demography described above. Relying on a single mode of organizing or on traditional union messages is unlikely to reach many segments of the new work force.

Morever, there is considerable truth in the argument that contemporary forms of working-class diversity and complexity present real obstacles to union organization. While there has been some statistical progress in organizing women and nonwhite workers, much of this can be attributed to their over-representation in the highly organized public sector. American unions have not improved their poor record in organizing nonwhites and women in the private sector or in heavily female occupations, such as clerical work, in the service sector. Similarly, the obstacles to unionization presented by the proliferation of service work are significant. Many service workers are employed in small businesses or organizations, which have been historically difficult to organize. Add to this the fact that the service sector includes many highly educated, high-status employees (including engineers, accountants, and computer professionals) whose professional ideologies and occupational cultures may discourage them from joining traditional unions (or from joining unions at all), and it is obvious that organizing the service sector is both crucial to the survival of organized labor and likely to require new strategies to overcome these (and other) obstacles.

Finally, workplace cultures and management practices vary considerably, and not just in the service sector. Unionization is less likely to take traditional forms (or to take any form at all) in workplaces where there is close, personal contact between employees and employers, or where occupational or workplace cultures create a strong emphasis on (and real prospects for) individual upward mobility or individual career building (as, for example, in the case of engineers).[6] One could add that an important feature of new management strategies has been the development of effective anti-union practices. Indeed, some have argued that one of the major reasons for the introduction of Japanese management techniques has been the desire to short-circuit unions and block the independent organization of the workforce.[7]

These and other obstacles to contemporary unionization must be acknowledged. However, we must also ask how much of this is entirely new. And we must consider whether the old labor movement was completely without responses to these kinds of problems and whether the solutions proposed by the new movement are always superior.

First, it is too often forgotten that the old labor movement had much in common with the new. It was, to begin with, ethnically divided and diverse, including workers from a wide variety of ethnic backgrounds, and sometimes organized on the basis of ethnicity. While minority workers were largely excluded from traditional labor organizations, the movement has had to wrestle with the problems of accommodating workers from different cultural backgrounds who often mistrusted or hated one another.

Perhaps more important, the labor movement has always organized employees in a wide variety of employment contexts into a wide variety of unions. While American unions have traditionally been concentrated in the manufacturing sector, this sector includes many different kinds of workers, ranging from skilled workers organized by occupation into unions that emphasized craft exclusivity, to mass production workers organized into industrial unions that accepted a wide range of occupational groups. Nor has the labor movement been entirely without experience with many of the new kinds of service worker. As indicated earlier, it has had considerable success with certain kinds of service workers, most notably government employees and teachers. It has even had experience with organizing professional workers and with the distinctive kinds of concerns (often elitist and exclusive) their unions emphasized. There is, in other words, a degree of caricature involved in portraying the old union movement as a monolith composed of a homogeneous group of workers. Even the Taft-Hartley Act, which channelled and homogenized labor organizations to a degree,[8] was unable completely to eliminate the diversity that has long characterized American unions.

The fact that unions have long confronted a diverse workforce, and have had some success in the past in organizing it, is reason for optimism. And there is evidence that the labor movement can succeed in organizing new constituencies. Labor movements in other countries (Sweden, Great Britain, and even Canada) have been able to organize large numbers of service and professional workers. The American labor movement can also point to evidence that it is already succeeding with certain groups of service and professional workers: in 1996, 20.4 percent of "professional speciality" employees (including teachers) were unionized, as were 39.5% of protective service workers, and 37.7 percent of the government sector as a whole. Similarly, it can point to the above-average rates of unionization among minorities and to the fact that rates of female unionization have risen somewhat in recent decades (until the past decade or so, men were roughly twice as unionized as women, but this ratio has now dropped considerably).[9] Female workers are also becoming more like male workers, in that they are more likely to work full-time, to work all their life, and to be the primary earner in their household. All these characteristics help to explain the growth of female unionism and of female interest in organizing. It could be added that promising models for organizing new constituencies already exist. As is pointed out elsewhere in this volume, the Justice for Janitors campaign has been identified as a potential model for organizing low-pay service workers (especially minority workers). Others have suggested that occupational unionism, which emphasizes the union's role in providing portable benefits, setting industry-wide employment standards, and serving as a "hiring hall" for members, might be attractive to the growing numbers of temporary workers and others in unstable forms of employment.[10]

As we consider the problems of organizing the contemporary labor force, we also must avoid caricaturing both the old and the new labor movements. The old labor movement was not a monolith and, at times, it developed strategies very much like contemporary "best practice" strategies. At the same time, not all that is new is good, as several examples of contemporary union strategy demonstrate.

Critics of traditional unions argue that there is a need to develop new organizing strategies appropriate to the realities of the contemporary workplace. For example, they point to the need to adopt long-term organizing campaigns (rather than blitz campaigns led by outside organizers) to succeed with recalcitrant groups such as clerical workers. Similarly, they argue that organizing must go beyond the workplace into the community if it is to address the concerns of ethnic and racial minorities and of women.[11] All of this is true. But are these strategies new? As Elly Leary and Jean Alonso point out, these practices sound very much like the organizing strategies adopted by the pre-Second World War CIO in its attempts to organize new, anti-union industries with ethnically diverse workforces.[12]

Thus, the old labor movement may have more to teach us than we acknowledge. Moreover, its lessons may also help us avoid some of the problems of the new. For example, the much-praised campaign to organize Harvard's clerical workers did succeed, but it adopted a strategy of rejecting adversarial relations with management. Critics of this campaign correctly note that this strategy needs to be considered in the light of a long history of disastrous attempts to foster cooperation between labor and management.[13]

Or consider the argument that a new approach to organizing is dictated by the racial composition of the working class. Robin Kelley has recently argued that a new community-based strategy is needed for the new urban working class: "Increasingly, the battle lines are drawn in these cities between a multiracial working class that is primarily African-American, Latino and Asian-American and a multiracial management class that is primarily white." Fair enough; but what of the lessons of the past? Does not a strategy focused on a racially divided city run the risk of reproducing old patterns of racial segregation within the labor movement? How will the African-American, Latino, and Asian-American workers of Los Angeles connect with the many white workers employed in suburban New Jersey or Ohio, or in rural Kentucky or Tennessee? It is also worth noting the tendency to adopt a very traditional definition of the working class that tends to exclude from the labor movement middle-class workers (semiprofessionals and various kinds of educated labor) unless, as in the case of teachers, they are already organized. The American labor movement has long been impaled on such a narrow definition; the greater strength of European labor has much to do with its ability to avoid it. In short, the new urban unionism risks repeating the errors of the very old unionism it rejects.

This leads us to what is probably the most important lesson to be learned from the history of the old labor movement. The experience of the past also suggests that simply organizing a structurally complex working class is only the beginning of the solution. For once the various groups and occupations are organized, the labor movement is faced with making them into a unified class, something which they are not automatically.

Organizing the Working Class

Capitalism has never, not in the past, and not now, generated a homogeneous working class. On the contrary, it has consistently created a varied, highly stratified working class, and capitalists have had an inherent interest in making sure that it is as divided as it possibly can be. Capitalism spawns a wide variety of workers who share the characteristic of being wage-laborers, and it brings them together within a complex, collective labor process. But that labor process, although it requires cooperation among various kinds of labor, is organized hierarchically so as to obscure and distort cooperation. One has only to think of the relationship between an engineer and a machinist or a machine operator, who collectively design and produce the product (and who could not function without one another), but whose relationships are often antagonistic and shaped by status concerns, to see that this is true.[14] Add to this the fact that deliberate employer policy and the working of capitalist labor markets create significant differences of reward among various categories of worker. Add, as well, the fact that capitalists have a long history of dividing the working class by encouraging competition among individual workers and by pitting groups of workers against one another, often by using demographic differences such as race, ethnicity, and gender. All of these parts of the working class can be organized into something called unions. But that does not, in itself, produce a united labor movement or working class.

The history of the old labor movement indicates this quite clearly. Even in its heyday, in periods when unions were powerful and growing, the American labor movement was divided in all sorts of ways, many of which were directly related to the internal complexity of the working class. Thus, quite apart from the political and ideological conflicts that have always plagued organized labor, one can point to the conflicts between craft and industrial unions that, in turn, reflect the different occupational experiences of craft and industrial workers. Similarly, racial and ethnic conflicts have a long history within the labor movement. And unions of professionals have generally been reluctant to identify themselves with their blue-collar counterparts or even to affiliate with national labor organizations; in some cases, as in the case of post-Second World War engineering unions, unions of professionals have actually disbanded over the issue of relations with lower-status employees.[15]

Overcoming these kinds of divisions, forging harmonious relations among workers from different racial and ethnic backgrounds, overcoming differences of status within the waged labor force, and unifying workers with different occupational experiences requires a real "class" project, something American labor, like most organized labor movements, has approached reluctantly at best. Such a project would mean mounting a real challenge to the hegemony of capitalism, to its claim to be able to organize production in a rational, effective way. To overcome the divisions within the working class, organized labor would have to create an alternative model for the organization of production, one that would make apparent and real the possibility of cooperation and the transcendance of hierarchy in production. It would also have to build institutions through which this cooperation could be realized in practice. This was what Antonio Gramsci seemed to imagine in his early writings on the labor movement in Turin. He envisaged the factory council as more than a body for workers' self-defence: as a way of effecting a transition to real cooperation within the labor process and mounting a challenge to the capitalist organization of production.[16] The Lucas Aerospace Plan, in which engineers and production workers collectively proposed alternatives to plant closure, could be viewed as a contemporary, embryonic version of the same idea.[17] At the same time, a real "class" project for labor would require a political challenge to capitalism as a whole, a challenge which would unite various kinds of wage labor on the basis of their shared interest in eliminating a mode of production that exploits all of them (even if the symptoms of their exploitation vary).

In the absence of this class project, organized labor has tended to fall victim to the very diversity it had been relatively successful in organizing. American labor has largely shied away from direct challenges to the capitalist organization and control of production and to capitalism as a system, concentrating instead on the short-term defence of workers' positions and improving the workers' lot within capitalism. But this leaves in place the social arrangements that divide workers and pit groups of them against one another, both in the labor market and in the labor process; the aforementioned conflicts within the labor movement thus become inevitable.

The contemporary labor movement runs the risk of repeating this pattern, both by retreating further from the use of class as an organizing principle and by relying on a variety of vague formulations that create the illusion of unity rather than its reality. AFL-CIO leaders, including John Sweeney, have acknowledged the need for labor unity and have at least nodded in the direction of trying to create it in two significant ways. On the one hand, there is the widespread use of rhetoric, disturbingly similar to that of the Clinton-led Democratic party, emphasizing the plight of "working families." This phrase implies that the various constituencies represented by organized labor share a common characteristic. At the same time, it explicitly rejects the idea of class, suggesting instead that it is work (as opposed to idleness?) that brings these groups together.

On the other hand, there is a strong emphasis in contemporary labor-movement rhetoric on the homogenizing character of the present economic situation. For example, in *America Needs a Raise,* John Sweeney attempts to document the ways in which working people from all walks of life (including women, men, Blacks, whites, and professionals) have suffered from the effects of downsizing, capital mobility, and growing social inequality, suggesting that while we may not all have been in the same boat before, we are finding ourselves in the same boat now.[18]

Neither of these rhetorical strategies is a viable basis for overcoming the internal divisions of the working class. The phrase "working families" represents a significant retreat from even the traditional labor movement's view of the capitalist system. Traditional images (workers and bosses, haves and have-nots, and occasionally class) at least conveyed the sense that the capitalist system was divided by relations of conflict between those who ran things and those who did not. The newer formulation eliminates this conflict by a kind of rhetorical sleight-of-hand, replacing it with a moralizing appeal to the virtues of work (presumably, "working families" excludes both the idle rich and the idle poor) and to the "deserving" character of those who engage in it. Indeed, Sweeney makes this explicit in his recent book, in which he declares that America needs a raise (and accepts that someone else must provide it) and in which he accepts the idea of modifying, but not directly challenging, the employer's right to control the enterprise.

The second rhetorical strategy is effectively delusional. History demonstrates clearly that the ebb and flow of capitalism never has and never will yield a homogenized working class that is not divided socially, economically and ideologically. The present period is no different: if the labor movement succeeds in organizing new constituencies, it will undoubtedly consist of a bewildering array of different kinds of unions—occupational unions, mass unions, professional unions, etc.—with very different concerns reflecting their different memberships.

Moreover, while the present conjuncture may be affecting a wide variety of workers in similar ways, it must be remembered that different groups of workers respond to similar experiences in different ways. Salaried doctors may react to the increasing bureaucratization of practice and deteriorating economic conditions by forming unions; but these unions are likely to be built around the idea of recovering past privilege and achieving autonomy in a way that would place doctors in positions of authority over other groups of (unionized) health care workers.[19]

Conclusion

Thus, the moral of the story is different from the one with which we began. There are, in fact, two morals. First, it is obvious that unions need to organize the unorganized, bringing their efforts directly to a diverse, heterogeneous working class. This diversity is not new, but it has taken on new forms, and older aspects of working-class diversity have taken on increasing importance. A successful organizing campaign is likely to yield a labor movement composed of a variety of different kinds of unions that include constituencies traditionally under-represented (or not represented at all).

The second moral follows from this point. The labor movement, even if it is successful in organizing the unorganized, also will need to unify the organized behind a single class project. Because the working class is diverse, and because it has always been diverse in various ways, any labor movement must confront the fact that the working class is not, by itself, united. On the contrary, history demonstrates that even the allegedly homogeneous labor movement of the past (which was not so homogeneous, as we have seen) was hampered by disunity and conflict among different kinds of workers and different kinds of unions. Present patterns of diversity are likely to yield a labor movement at least as complex and disunited.

While one can question tactics and the depth of commitment (as some of the contributors to this volume have done), it seems clear that the labor movement has understood the first moral of the story—it seems more serious than it has in the past about organizing traditionally excluded groups of workers, incorporating new kinds of workers, and confronting new employment relations that call for different organizing strategies. But what about the second moral? Here, the labor movement, at least thus far, offers little but rhetorical flourishes ("working families") that gloss over or even discount the reality of working-class disunity. Rather than treating the contemporary working class as fundamentally new in its diversity, it would be wise to recall that the working class has always been diverse, and consequently disunited, and that there has never been a solution to this problem other than concerted action on the part of the labor movement.

Notes

1. Barbara Reskin and Patricia Roos, *Job Queues, Gender Queues* (Philadelphia: Temple University Press, 1990).
2. John Zipp, "Government Employment and Black-White Earnings Inequality," *Social Problems* 41, no. 3 (1994): 363-82.
3. Teresa A. Sullivan, "Women and Minority Workers in the New Economy," *Work and Occupations* 16, no. 4 (1989).
4. Dorothy Sue Cobble, *Women and Unions: Forging a Partnership* (Ithaca: ILR Press, 1993), 14.
5. See Laurie Graham, *On the Line at Subaru-Isuzu* (Ithaca: ILR Press, 1995) for a good description of the harsh side of Japanese management in the United States.
6. For a discussion of this and other obstacles to unionization in the case of engineering, see Peter Meiksins and Chris Smith, "Why American Engineers Aren't Unionized," *Theory and Society* 22 (1993): 57-97.
7. For example, Guillermo Grenier, *Inhuman Relations* (Philadelphia: Temple University Press, 1988).
8. See Dorothy Sue Cobble, "Organizing the Postindustrial Work Force: Lessons From the History of Waitress Unionism," *Industrial and Labor Relations Review* 44, no. 3 (1991): 419-36, for an analysis of the ways in which Taft-Hartley eliminated some of the variety in union organization.
9. Ruth Milkman, "Organizing the Sexual Division of Labor: Historical Perspectives on 'Women's Work' and the American Labor Movement," *Socialist Review* 10 (1981): 95-151.
10. See Cobble, "Organizing," and Chris Tilly, *Half a Job* (Philadelphia: Temple University Press, 1996), ch. 8.
11. See Robin D. G. Kelley, "The New Urban Working Class," *New Labor Forum* 1, no. 1 (1997): 8 for an example of this kind of argument.
12. Elly Leary and Jean Alonso, "The Women Who Organized Harvard: A Feminist Model of Labor Organization?" *Monthly Review* 49, no. 7 (1997):1-7.
13. Ibid.
14. See Peter Meiksins and Chris Smith, *Engineering Labour: Technical Workers in Comparative Perspective* (London: Verso Books, 1996), especially chapters 1 and 9, for an extended statement of this argument.

15. See Meiksins and Smith, "Why," for a discussion of this episode.

16. Some of Gramsci's early writings on Turin factory councils are collected in Antonio Gramsci, *Selections from the Political Writings, 1910-1920* (New York: International Publishers, 1977).

17. See Mike Rustin, *For a Pluralist Socialism* (London: Verso Books, 1995), for a view of the Lucas episode as a prefiguring of a challenge to the capitalist organization of production.

18. John Sweeney, *America Needs a Raise* (New York: Houghton Mifflin & Co, 1996), especially chapter 2.

19. For a recent example of the formation of a doctor's union, see "Challenging Corporate Power," *In These Times,* 28 April-11 May 1997: 2. This article tends to play down the differences between such unions and those of more subordinate workers. For a more sustained, somewhat hostile analysis of professional unions, see Bob Carter, *Capitalism, Class Conflict and the New Middle Class* (London: Routledge, 1985).

On Gender and Class in U.S. Labor History

Johanna Brenner

The relationship between gender and class, central to understanding the history of the labor movement, raises important issues for Marxist analysis in general. Grappling with the complexities of this relationship forces us to confront a wide range of theoretical and practical questions. What is the connection between "material conditions" and "identity"? What role do culture, discourses, sexuality, and emotions play in shaping people's responses to their material conditions? How are the varieties of consciousness of class related to other identities and affiliations? These questions challenge us theoretically and politically, as we seek to develop a working-class politics that incorporates struggles against all forms of oppression.

Feminist labor historians have asked the question: why is it that throughout the history of the labor movement, working class men have often pursued strategies that systematically disadvantaged women workers: excluding women from their unions and, when they did organize with women, accepting, even demanding, gendered occupations and wage differentials where men's jobs paid more. Feminist answers to this question originally focused on how working class men's gendered material "interests" or psycho-sexual "needs" overrode their interests as workers. These analyses illuminated working-class men's privilege, but they also tended to attribute a fixed set of motivations to men as a group. Material interests and emotional needs may be powerful wellsprings of human action. However, it is also important to contextualize them historically. How people understand their interests and experience their needs varies tremendously and is shaped by the possibilities and constraints of a given historical moment.

More recent feminist approaches have moved away from an attribution of gendered interests/needs to more historically specific accounts of, in Ava Baron's words, "the construction of gender identity and its role in shaping workers' lives."[1] Here, explanations focus on how cultural meanings of sexual difference, expressed in discourses of gender, affected action. Efforts to secure a stable gender identity underlay men's job choices, the ways they defined and

41

did their work and the strategies they chose to fight their employers, decisively shaping the sexual division of waged labor and the structure of work and unions.

But still, recognizing that many different meanings of sexual difference circulate at the same time, we must explain why some discourses of gender and not others took the stage, why certain gendered identities were mobilized in workplace and communal struggles, how particular definitions of gender came to be institutionalized in workplaces, families and communities.

This question points toward an analysis of relations of power between employers and workers and between men and women within working class households, communities and workplaces. It brings us back to looking at interests that arise as working-class men and women attempt to survive within the competitive structures of a capitalist economy. And it brings us back to the socio-emotional needs that individuals develop in the context of organizing daily life on and off the job. Rather than counterposing explanations which draw on interests, needs, and discourses, I want to suggest some ways to understand how they are linked.

Survival Projects

I would start with the concept of *survival projects*, the ways people group together in order to live in capitalist society. These projects take different forms, from the most narrow and individualistic modes of striving to mass collective action. Individuals may be very conscious of making strategic choices, or they may adopt them more or less unconsciously. In either case, people must enter into various kinds of affiliation to secure the basic necessities of life. These patterns of affiliation are fundamental to how individuals define the boundaries of their solidarities, how they position themselves in relation to others, how they organize a worldview, and how they develop their various definitions of self, including their gendered identities.

I want to use the notion of survival projects because it is a way of talking about material life that recognizes the importance of individuals' motives and action, while placing these in specific social and historical contexts. We can conceptualize resistance and accommodation as outcomes of a process that is simultaneously cultural, individual, psychological, collective, and social. Individuals are situated in workplaces and communities, within which they develop understandings, feelings, and intentions. Through groups, individuals try to establish some control over their situation in the labor market as well as vis a vis particular employers. And because most working-class people (in contrast to more affluent professionals and managers) cannot reproduce themselves entirely through the market, groups are also constituted by exchanges (of money and unpaid labor) outside the capitalist economy.

There is no such thing as an identity abstracted from social practice. Like other identities, gender is negotiated and renegotiated in the practices of everyday life. Strategies that working-class people adopt for economic survival within the rules of the capitalist game shape these everyday practices in fundamental ways. These survival strategies will necessarily include forms of mutual support, not only in the workplace but outside of waged work—relations of sharing and solidarity across households, in neighborhoods, in kinship and friendship networks, in communities, and so on. Key resources include sharing cash income, bartering services such as childcare, and sharing living space.

Although historically women have predominated in creating social networks outside the workplace, I am not at all suggesting that we should locate *gender* in community while *class* belongs at work. Rather, I am suggesting that households, survival networks (of kin, fictive kin and friends), neighborhoods, and workplaces are interrelated. Until well into the twentieth century, communal ties created a base of support for worker protest and trade union organization, as well as women's community organizing (the cooperative movement, rent strikes, and so forth). But communal ties can also be sources of ethnic and racial hostility as communities, formed through particularistic and local sharing networks, compete with each other for scarce resources (jobs, better neighborhoods, and the like).

In contemporary capitalism, personal survival networks may not be as centered within spatial communities as they once were (although this might be debated). Yet they remain crucial resources, determining the level of individual and family well-being. And, operating in a normal everyday way, they reproduce distributions of relative privilege among groups within the working class. The role that friends and kin play, for example, in facilitating access to employment is well-documented and an important source of racial and ethnic segregation in the occupational structure.

Many feminists have rightly argued that identities are multiple (one is never simply a worker) and that different identities are not lived separately. One is not a worker here, a woman there, and a person of color elsewhere. Feminist labor historians have also emphasized that women, like men, develop identities as workers. Further, while feelings mobilized by workplace-based identity, the intense commitment to a particular self-definition, have a gendered character, these feelings and commitments do not arise only from meanings of gender.

This is important to emphasize from the start. When we talk about gendered workers, we risk associating with gender the emotional components of identity in which gender "modifies" workers, as if *workers'* identities reflect rational calculations of material interest, while *gender* arises from sexuality, culture, and emotion. But workers' identities, in their many variations, also have unconscious and emotional components. They mobilize feelings as much as gender does. And, on the other side, gender identities, while drawing on cultural meanings and mobilizing sexuality, are constructed within material relations, relations defined by the survival strategies through which people accomplish their basic life tasks.

Cultural meanings of gender, like cultural meanings of class, are produced by men and women within group life, on and off the job. However, because the production of meaning is itself a group process, it is also intensely political. The choices that groups of people make about such matters as how to organize their survival, how to represent themselves, how to resist and where to accommodate, and who within the group has rights to what valued goods, is a product of negotiation and struggle. The outcome, therefore, reflects the different kinds and levels of resources that men and women bring into the process (as, for example, skilled craft workers, unskilled workers, legal or undocumented immigrants, married women, or single mothers).

How men and women affiliate—at work and outside it—both reflects gender identities and creates them. Group affiliations respond to a complex set of constraints and opportunities. These constraints and opportunities cannot be reduced to the operations of the capitalist economy, but neither can they be divorced from them. In what follows, I give some examples of how we might make the connection.

Sectorial Strategies and Market Competition

Workers in capitalism are pulled apart as much as (perhaps even more than) they are pushed toward collective action. The operations of the capitalist market constrain the strategies of both employers and workers and tend to reproduce particularistic group identities and exclusionary strategies. If workplace relations tend to enhance workers' recognition of their common condition, competition in the labor market tends to encourage individualistic strategies for survival. That workers have been able to overcome individualistic tendencies through unionization should not blind us to the very real difficulties and barriers that have to be faced and overcome.

An analysis of gender and strategic choices ought to take these difficulties sufficiently into account, acknowledging that the competitive structure of the labor market threatens to undermine solidarity and divide groups of workers from each other. Although trade unions are common strategies for countering employers, trade unions have often organized on a relatively narrow basis, hardly constituted as organizations of the working class as a whole. Organizing to secure immediate, short-run economic advantages often runs counter to organizing based on longer-run possibilities for challenging employers on a more class-wide basis. From this point of view, working men's individualistic or narrowly-based group strategies for survival may have been the source for certain kinds of masculine identities as much as a consequence of them.

The fact that male workers have adopted exclusionary and elitist attitudes toward other men and not just toward women further supports this idea. Control over a craft, for instance, required control over apprenticeship and employment. Skilled workers narrowed the potential labor pool by using many different criteria for entry into their trade: not only gender, but kinship (training only sons or close relatives), geography (city printers refusal to unionize country printers who undercut them), ethnicity, race, and so forth. Faced with employers' efforts to avoid established apprenticeship systems and to use lower-paid skilled male workers (immigrants, rural workers, etc.) to undercut their rates, craft unions followed the same exclusionary tactics, striking against the employment of non-union workers rather than attempting to unionize them. Masculinity of a certain sort (e.g., white or native-born) was produced and mobilized to delimit the areas of labor belonging to unionized men and to justify their exclusionary strategies.

In following sectorial strategies, male craft workers were not unique. Competition among workers over jobs and as members of different occupations and industries can and often does overwhelm and obscure the common interests that they have as a class. The skilled disregard the unskilled, the organized disregard the unorganized, the stronger unions disregard the weaker ones—and this happens among workers who share ethnic identity or gender as well as those who do not. Sectorial organization, narrow strategies in which some sets of workers secure their immediate economic interests even to the detriment of others, can characterize industrial as well as craft unions. (Conversely, skilled craft workers are as capable as industrial workers of developing very broad-based conceptions of solidarity—for example, the Knights of Labor in 1884-1887.) The point is that when we look at labor history we don't necessarily see "working-class identities" arising out of trade union organization. We may see a range of understandings, organizations, and practices within trade unions, reflecting very different conceptions of what it means to be a worker and even very different views of whether all workers belong to a "working class."

When working women have organized on the basis of craft exclusion rather than industrial organization, they have, like nineteenth-century male craft workers, adopted patronizing attitudes toward other workers and profound emotional commitments to maintaining occupational boundaries and divisions of labor in the workplace.[2] Registered nurses have been no more willing to take "less credentialed" hospital workers into their unions than male craftsmen were willing to assimilate the "lesser skilled" women workers into theirs. Unionized women teachers have often made separate contract deals with school administrations and failed to support the demands and organizing of clerical workers and teachers' aides.

If craftsmen clung to masculine craft identities rather than adopt new strategies as their industries changed and women entered their workplaces, so have women workers developed feminine craft identities embedded in particular strategies for organizing against their employers. Conflicts among women workers can look very much like those between women and men. Waitresses successfully organized along gender-segregated craft lines in the 1920s and 1930s, developing fierce commitments to an identity as female workers, doing work that was different from that of men but equally skilled. In the 1960s, they clung to these identities, and to the forms of organization that had served them so well as against a younger generation of waitresses, working under very different conditions in an expanding and reorganizing food service industry.

By the early 1970s, at the height of the feminist movement, younger waitresses turned to the courts to demand access to jobs (elite food service, bartending) that had previously been closed to women. They also sought to change union strategy, abandoning craft unionism for a more industrial mode. According to historian Dorothy Sue Cobble, older waitress leaders experienced this challenge as an assault on their identities as skilled craft workers as well as their leadership positions, reacting with anger and mobilizing to squelch the opposition. The highly factionalized political situation starkly counterposed strategies which otherwise might have been melded together and, preserving some of the older strategies, strengthened waitress organizing even in the new conditions.[3]

Gender Divisions of Labor and Strategic Choices

More privileged workers can choose to protect themselves on the labor market by organizing to establish or defend a racialized or gendered occupational structure. But whether workers can successfully carry out this kind of strategy depends upon whether employers are willing to accommodate the particular distribution of relative privilege and upon whether marginalized groups are in a position to challenge these strategies. To understand whether and when women successfully resist, we need to consider both how they might have construed their interests and the resources for contestation available to them at different times and places. We must look beyond the workplace and labor market to survival networks organized around a gendered division of labor, networks which have and continue to be primary strategies for working people to secure their conditions of life.

Women's responsibilities for care giving have provided resources and posed limitations. They have structured women's interests as well as their identities. On the one hand, women have used these responsibilities to successfully make claims on men and on their communities. In the past (and even today, to a certain extent), women's sharing networks enabled mothers to participate in wage work. And out of these networks women developed solidarity for political action—as community members and as trade union activists.[4]

On the other hand, care-giving responsibilities are also constraints. They hamper women's collective self-organization, especially in organizations and struggles which extend beyond the community level. Historically, the more localized and communal working-class organization is, the easier it has been for women to participate in action and organization, to take on leadership roles, to develop their own demands and ways of representing themselves, and to contest with men. The more centralized, bureaucratic, and trans-local working-class organizations are, the easier it is for men to monopolize decision making and marginalize women. Limitations on women's participation were cultural (definitions of leadership, and notions of masculine authority and the role of women in the public sphere) but also material. In the first instance, care-giving responsibilities restricted women's leadership beyond the local level. Until quite recently most women union leaders and organizers were single, childless, or had grown children. But even when individual women fought their way into leadership at the regional or national level, they were isolated, lacking a collective political base.[5]

Care-giving responsibilities shaped working-class women's interests, creating potentials for both solidarity and conflict. Single women, daughters of working-class families, single mothers, and married women have adopted different survival strategies, which in turn shape their own as well as their family members' participation in work and workers' protest. Married women dependent on a male breadwinner and young single women workers living in male-headed households had very different real interests from those women workers who were sole or primary wage-earners for themselves or their families. In many instances, married women supported the efforts of predominantly young and single female workers to unionize and receive higher wages. And at times female solidarity has been built across significant divides—for instance, between married women home workers and single women factory workers.[6] On the other hand, in struggles where men have promoted their own interests at the expense of single female workers, cross-cutting alliances have sometimes undermined female solidarity, as married women have thrown their support behind the men of the community.[7]

Conflicts surfaced between married and single women workers in the electrical industry in the years immediately following the Second World War over who had more "right" to hold onto their wartime jobs. This division occurred in the context of pervasive fears about post-war unemployment, unions dominated by men numerically and politically, and a hegemonic male breadwinner ideology unchallenged by any feminist organization either inside or outside the trade unions.[8]

Women's strategic choices are, like men's, shaped by a complex set of constraints and resources, needs and opportunities. These, again, reflect not only their position in the labor market (e.g., their levels of skill, the demand for their labor) but also how they are positioned within the communities on which they depend for their survival and how their communities are positioned in relation to others. Some of the key factors here are the degree of political support for women's claims to wage work, the degree to which women can actually rely on male breadwinners for support, and, in relation to the former, their community's norms of motherhood and womanhood. The different strategic choices of white and black women workers in one case study illuminates this point.

After the Second World War, the predominantly male unionized bartenders mobilized to drive women who had entered bartending during the war from the trade. Most of the white women unionists, who had in fact fought men for the right to serve liquor (previously a male preserve), did not mobilize to hold onto bartending work. But three hundred black women bartenders in Chicago launched a strong protest. Their all-black union local leadership conceded to the women, continuing to dispatch women bartenders from the hiring hall. In 1961, however, when a city ordinance banning women from bartending was finally enforced, four hundred women lost their jobs. The male-dominated local (as well as the international) refused to help, so the barmaids turned to the community for support and picketed city hall. Black community newspapers ran stories sympathetic to the women; however, the ordinance was allowed to stand.[9]

Black women and white women workers pursued different strategies, because discrimination in the food service industry limited black women's access to higher paid employment as waitresses at the same time that industry growth was expanding white waitresses' opportunities. Black women, although faced with opposition from black men, also had more space to assert their own "breadwinner" claims, because their right to living wage work was more supported in the black community. Where white waitresses found their main support for their identities as craft workers inside the union and the trade-union movement, black women belonged to a racially oppressed community which generated its own oppositional organizations, including black newspapers. Perhaps because the women bartenders' struggle focused more on the white-dominated city council than their own black union local, it was easier for the women to win community support. Although many white waitresses were also single mothers, they did not have the same sorts of community institutions to turn to and so were under more pressure to come to terms with the men in their union.

Thus, the different sources of group support for women at work and outside of it shaped the ways in which they developed gendered work identities and structured the risks they faced and the resources they had available to contest with men about what was and was not gender-appropriate work for women. White women had stronger ties to the union, fewer resources outside it than black women, and, perhaps most important, far less economic need than black women had to challenge men's attempts to define bartending as inappropriate work for women.

Politics of Struggle and Discourses of Gender

Discourses of gender were always entailed in trade union struggles, as workers sought to justify their demands to each other, to a general public, and to potential allies in the middle class. Strategies of self-representation are political choices, sometimes self-conscious, sometimes unreflective, but always choices. Differing modes of making a case are always available. How male trade unionists represented themselves or women workers shifted depending on how necessary they thought it was to appease middle-class allies and how pressured they were by their female colleagues who had a different vision of how they wished to be spoken of and seen.

For example, throughout the late nineteenth century and into the 1920s, the majority of the female factory labor force remained young and single. Male trade unionists and middle class reformers, male and female, attempted to win support for striking women workers by drawing on anxieties about young women's sexuality, an intense focus of public discourse in the period. Trying to picture factory girls as sympathetic victims, these discourses emphasized the differences between working men and women by defining women's low wages as a problem of sexual victimization (the cause of the working girl's "fall" into prostitution). When working women could make their voices heard, they strongly objected to this line of defense, rejecting its patronizing tone and advancing very different images. Shifting attention away from the issue of their virtue, young women strikers asserted their similarity with men, appealing for support on the ground of their breadwinner roles, their reliance on wage-earning to support themselves and their families.[10]

The process of choosing organizing strategies is both conscious and unconscious. Men and women's individual identities as workers are created, then reproduced and solidified, in daily life in informal workgroups and formal workers' organizations producing deep commitments to ways of understanding oneself and feelings about others. Defining the boundaries of "us" and "them" is part of everyday resistance to managerial authority on the job and certainly crucial to all kinds of confrontational challenges to management. While necessary for protection, group boundaries have their own rigidities and defensive sides.

The passionate feelings that leak through the minutes of both nineteenth and twentieth century union meetings where the employment of women was discussed demonstrate that craftsmen experienced lower-waged women's entry into their workplaces as an attack on their masculinity, their sexual and social selves. The economic threat that lower-paid women workers represented was certainly real. But much more than wage levels was at stake. Women's presence also threatened the practices, feelings, and relationships through which men had constructed a culture of solidarity within their organizations.

Solidarity involves defining and maintaining group loyalties to defend against the threat of both real and imagined betrayals. Organizing against a powerful (and seductive) enemy can be frightening. Gender difference (the obsessive demarcation of masculinity) could be, and often was, mobilized to manage these anxieties. But a defensive masculinity was only one strategy, and not the only one possible. Where the turn of the century Cigar Makers' Industrial Union (CMIU) pursued exclusionary strategies and very reluctantly organized women workers into a separate and secondary section of the union, male Cuban emigres in Tampa's cigar industry, radicalized by the struggle for independence, rejected craft organization in favor of an anarcho-syndicalist union, La Resistencia, which sought to organize all workers throughout the city. Prominent among them were women tobacco strippers who represented over one-quarter of Resistencia's membership. Attacked as both un-American and unmanly by the CMIU, the male leadership of La Resistencia characterized the CMIU as "a barn of white livered dung hill cocks," proclaiming themselves "the voice of virile labor."[11] In the context of a politicized community and an industry where men and women labored in the same factories and received equal pay for the same work (although men tended to monopolize the most highly paid jobs), strategic choices required working men to redefine the boundaries of gendered work and the meaning of masculinity.

Periods of labor radicalism and mass struggles were the most hospitable environment for challenges to hegemonic cultural constructions of gender. The movements' radically democratic ideology encouraged claims for gender equality and respect for women as partners, not subordinates. The actual organizing and solidarity of workers in conflict with employers encouraged women workers to organize and encouraged working-class men to support them. Organized feminism, while predominantly middle-class in membership, helped working-class women to develop the language and political resources to articulate demands for political and economic equality within their trade unions and communities. (The contrast between the 1930s and earlier moments of widespread class mobilization is especially striking along these lines.)[12]

In the nineteenth century, when labor radicalism was tied to a broader political movement and goals of revolutionary change such as the vision of cooperative commonwealth at the heart of Owenite socialism in England in the 1830s and the Knights of Labor in the United States in the 1880s, women could be full members of organizations, participating not only as workers but as members of working-class communities. This was especially important because women were a numerical minority in the paid workforce. Insofar as women were included, there was at least a potential base of support for feminist ideas. At the height of their militance, and responding to pressure from women delegates (mostly textile operatives and shoe workers), the Knights' national convention endorsed woman suffrage in 1886.[13]

Greenwald's comparative study of conflicts over women's entry into male jobs during the First World War suggests how men's strategic choices were affected by generalized class struggle and middle-class feminist alliances with working-class organizations. In Kansas City, a city-wide and week-long general strike in support of striking men and women laundry workers preceded the introduction of women as conductors on the streetcars. A strong branch of the Women's Trade Union League (WTUL) had cooperated with the union movement around the laundry strike, proving their reliability as working-class allies. When the streetcar company sought to hire women as conductors for lower pay, the Amalgamated Transit Union went out on strike, with newly hired women, demanding equal pay for equal work. Their strike won the support of the Kansas City labor movement and the WTUL. In Cleveland and Detroit, by contrast, the male dominated unions struck against the employment of women.[14]

The conditions that encouraged challenge to gender norms were not part of everyday life and organizing. Radical movements' defeat brought demoralization about the possibilities of broad-based challenges to capital, encouraging better-placed workers to fall back onto more narrow, sectorial forms of trade union organizing, and prompting others to seek more privatistic routes to economic survival.

Implications for the Present

Today the lines of conflict and solidarity between men and women workers have shifted in profound ways. The question of women's place in trade unions, of women's ability to labor and to lead, is, if certainly not settled, no longer the fundamental axis of gender relations. Forty percent of all trade union members are women, and their representation within leadership, especially in unions with large numbers of women, is growing significantly.[15] With feminism a strong current in the trade unions, women workers have organized for new bargaining issues like comparable worth, family leave, sexual harassment policies, and to redefine the scope of trade union politics, forcing their unions to take positions on abortion rights and lesbian and gay rights.

Unfortunately, these gains are outweighed by the sustained corporate assault against all workers' wages and working conditions. The unionized portion of the labor force is at its lowest point in fifty years, mainly because men's rates of unionization have fallen dramatically. Unions are on the defensive economically and politically. As various forces search for strategic counter-of-fensives, the drumbeat against "special interests" and "identity politics" has become very loud, expanding well beyond the right and the center. There is, of course, something real here: working people's distress and the concentration of wealth have become too great to ignore. However, this particular rediscovery of workers as a forgotten middle has counterposed "identity" to class politics, even holding the left responsible for the current weakness of progressive forces.[16]

Here, I think, is the new "fault line" of gender (and racial) conflict, posing the question of whether working-class institutions of struggle will adopt inclusive political strategies. Tragic losses suffered by blue-collar men threaten to overshadow, politically, the double day, the low wages, and the job insecurity faced by many working women. Broad political support for Clinton's assault on single mothers in the name of welfare reform reflects deep divisions within the working class between employed workers and chronically unemployed and underemployed workers, between married women with children and single mothers.

The history I have outlined demonstrates that how trade unions will respond to the employers' offensive depends, at least in part, on the political self-organization of marginalized groups. Declining male wages in the context of a hyper-competitive labor market, pervasive economic insecurity, and disappearing public services have destabilized the old gender order, but not in ways that clearly improve the lives of working-class women and men. Whether men will respond in a defensive reassertion of their lost male privilege depends on whether women will have the political resources to challenge men, forcing them to redefine masculinity in more egalitarian terms. In turn, how women come to define their own gendered interests depends on whether men and women together will opt for more collective rather than individualistic solutions to current dilemmas. Counterposing "identity" to "class" politics, therefore, is absolutely mistaken. Rather, as many movement activists and trade unionists are already doing, we have to build a coalition politics through struggles that creatively address (instead of wishfully disregarding) divisions within the working class and support (rather than undermine) the efforts of oppressed people to represent themselves, their interests, and their needs.

Notes

I would like to thank Ellen Meiksins Wood, Christopher Phelps, Aaron Brenner, and Bill Resnick for their helpful comments on this piece.

1. Ava Baron, "Gender and Labor History: Learning from the Past, Looking to the Future," in Work Engendered: Toward a New History of American Labor, ed. Ava Baron (Ithaca: Cornell University Press, 1991), 31.

2. Mary H. Blewett, *Men, Women and Work: Class, Gender, and Protest in the New England Shoe Industry, 1780-1910* (Chicago: University of Illinois Press, 1988), chapter. 8, esp. 242-49.

3. Dorothy Sue Cobble, *Dishing It Out: Waitresses and Their Unions in the Twentieth Century* (Chicago: University of Illinois Press, 1991), 192-200.

4. Ardis Camerion, "Bread & Roses revisited: Women's culture and working-class activism in the Lawrence strike of 1912," in *Women, Work & Protest*, ed. Ruth Milkman (Boston: Routledge, 1985); Karen Brodkin Sacks, *Organizing at Duke Medical Center* (Chicago: University of Illinois Press, 1988), chapter 5.

5. Elizabeth Faue, *Community of Suffering and Struggle* (Chapel Hill: University of North Carolina Press, 1991), chapter 5; Carol Turbin, *Working Women of Collar City* (Chicago: University of Illinois Press, 1992), chapter 3.

6. Eileen Boris, " 'A Man's Dwelling House Is His Castle': Tenement House Cigar Making and the Judicial Imperative," *Work Engendered*, ed. Ava Baron, 139.

7. Mary H. Blewett, *Men, Women & Work*, 123-33.

8. Ruth Milkman, *Gender at Work: The Dynamics of Job Segregation by Sex during World War II* (Chicago: University of Illinois, 1987), 145.

9. Cobble, *Dishing It Out*, chapter 7.

10. Mary H. Blewett, *Men, Women & Work*, 284-85; Jacquelyn Dowd Hall, "Private Eyes, Public Women: Images of Class and Sex in the Urban South, Atlanta, Georgia, 1913-1915," in *Work Engendered*, ed. Ava Baron, 260-69.

11. Patricia A. Cooper, *Once A Cigar Maker: Men, Women and Work Culture in American Cigar Factories, 1900-1919* (Urbana: University of Illinois Press, 1987), esp. 114-17, 151-52; Nancy A. Hewitt, " 'The Voice of Virile Labor': Labor Militancy, Community Solidarity, and Gender Identity among Tampa's Latin Workers, 1880-1930," in *Work Engendered*, ed. Ava Baron, 142-67.

12. For a fuller discussion of this point, see Johanna Brenner and Barbara Laslett, "Gender, Social Reproduction, and Women's Self-Organization: Considering the U.S. Welfare State," *Gender & Society* 5 (1991): esp. 323-27.

13. Susan Levine, *Labor's True Woman: Carpet Weavers, Industrialization, and Labor Reform in the Gilded Age* (Philadelphia: Temple University Press, 1984), chapter 5.

14. Maurine Weiner Greenwald, *Women, War, and Work: The Impact of World War I on Women Workers in the United States* (Ithaca: Cornell University Press, 1990), chapter 4, esp. 172-80.

15. Cynthia Costello and Barbara Kivimae Krimgold, eds., *The American Woman, 1996-97* (New York: W. W. Norton, 1996), 69.

16. See, for example, Richard Rorty, *Achieving Our Country: Leftist Thought in Twentieth Century America* (Cambridge: Harvard University Press, 1998), and Todd Gitlin, *The Twilight of Common Dreams* (New York: Metropolitan, 1995).

II
THE AMERICAN SCENE:
PROBLEMS AND PROSPECTS

American Labor: A Movement Again?

Kim Moody

Things are changing in the American labor movement, and at last they are changing for the better, despite setbacks and continued problems. The most visible symbol of this change is the new leadership at the AFL-CIO. The energy and high profile displayed by the New Voice team of John Sweeney, Rich Trumka, and Linda Chavez-Thompson are a welcome change. Even more important is the commitment of the new leaders to reverse labor's long decline by shifting enormous resources to organize the millions of low-wage workers that are the U.S. labor market's growth sector.

This was the major theme of the New Voice team, and the new leaders have tackled this job forthrightly by pouring big bucks into the project. They proposed $20 million for their first year in office and $30 million for 1997. The Organizing Institute, a small sideshow under their predecessor, Lane Kirkland, has become the federation's centerpiece. The O.I., as it is known, has recruited scores of young people and has helped kindle an interest in unions among the young and not-so-young of both working-class and middle-class backgrounds. In 1996 and again in 1997, Union Summer provided what the *L.A. Weekly* called "Class Struggle 101" for a thousand or so young people, many of whom said their lives were changed forever. In 1997, senior citizens joined the Summer campaign. The targets of the new organizing efforts taking shape in some of the AFL-CIO affiliates are low-wage workers, mostly women, people of color, and immigrants. This is a change that was almost unimaginable just a few years ago.

The promise to reverse labor's long decline was reaffirmed at the AFL-CIO's 1997 convention in Pittsburgh. In his keynote address, Sweeney asserted that "everything we do is connected to organizing." To dramatize this theme, some eighty union men and women, most of whom were recently organized rank-and-filers, lined the stage to give testimony to the cause of union growth. Even the successful 1997 UPS strike was seen as a sort of promo for unionism, which it was.

Delivering on this promise will not be easy. While the AFL-CIO claimed a net gain of 12,000 members for its affiliates in 1996, total union membership dropped by another 91,000 members that year. In 1997, it claimed that 400,000 workers joined unions and that federation membership held steady, but unions still experienced a net loss of 159,000 members, according to government figures. Many of the affiliated unions that must ultimately carry out the organizing are rusty at best. For example, despite the drop of union members from 75 percent of the country's auto parts industry in 1978 to 25 percent or less today, the United Auto Workers (UAW) spend very little on organizing—and then it is usually among workers safely outside the globally challenged U.S. auto industry. In 1997, they once again took on Nissan at its nonunion plant in Tennessee, but the campaign seemed lackluster and was abandoned early.

In addition to years of neglect, there has been an accelerating form of pseudo-organizing. Mergers or, more typically, absorptions of smaller unions are the universal response of the labor bureaucracy. Of the 120 or so mergers and absorptions since 1956, half took place after 1980, and half of those since 1991. Until recently, much of what was called organizing was actually big unions swallowing little ones. Breaking this habit will not be easy, particularly since the AFL-CIO is, as one labor insider in Washington put it, "conducting a virtual auction" in the race to reduce the number and increase the size of affiliated unions.

The push from the top to recruit new workers, however, is encouraging change in some national and international unions. The Communications Workers of America (CWA), for example, voted in 1996 to direct 10 percent of its budget toward new organizing. Other unions like the Teamsters, the Laborers, and Sweeney's home union, the Service Employees International Union (SEIU), have also upgraded their organizing programs. In 1996, the SEIU voted to raise the proportion of its budget that it spends on organizing from 20 percent to 30 percent—the highest of any union. By 1998, it claimed it was spending 40 percent of its budget on new organizing. There is controversy over how best to organize, but few would question that any new organizing is better than none.

The new leaders have also dismantled that most shameful of U.S. labor's institutions, the government-funded, CIA-influenced, overseas institutes that had carried the message of business unionism and anti-Communism to the third world since the early 1960s. These Cold War relics have been collapsed into a single American Center for International Labor Solidarity (ACILS). Barbara Shailor, a progressive from the Machinists union, now heads the federation's Department of International Affairs, ending the thirty years of unaccountable, monopoly rule by the cold warriors of the Social Democrats-USA.

John Sweeney's January 1998 trip to Mexico is another positive sign of a new international direction for American labor. Although he met with Mexican President Zedillo, he also met with leaders of Mexico's new independent labor federation, the National Union of Workers (UNT), and the older independent federation, the Authentic Labor Front (FAT). This is a sharp break from the alliance pursued by George Meany and Lane Kirkland with the corrupt, government-dominated Confederation of Mexican Workers (CTM). Sweeney established an agreement with the independent federations to fight for revision of NAFTA. Sweeney's presence lent support to other attempts at cross-border solidarity, such as the coalitions of U.S., Canadian, and Mexican unions supporting struggles at Han Young in Tijuana and Echlin's ITAPSA plant outside Mexico City.

Reflecting the undeniable ambiguities in Sweeney's world view, however, was his trip only a couple of weeks later to Davos, Switzerland, to hobnob with the world's financial and business elite. There he joined George Soros, finance capital's bad boy of the season, to plea for moderation in capitalist market excess. At about the same time, the federation gave a boost to the market by quietly endorsing the extension of NATO to Poland, Hungary, and the Czech Republic, for which they received a grateful note from the State Department. This was not simply a Cold War relapse, but an economic move that helps maquiladorize Eastern Europe. These actions reflect Sweeney's desire to aid corporate America while simultaneously restraining its excesses, a contradictory practice and outlook rooted in his nostalgia for the alleged labor-management "accord" of yesteryear.

To their credit, the new AFL-CIO leaders show a certain flexibility in the way they manage change. For example, in 1996 Rich Trumka casually suggested that since the good guys were in charge now, maybe the AFL-CIO no longer needed the semi-autonomous, action-oriented coalition Jobs with Justice (JwJ). When this brought an uproar from JwJ activists, the federation leaders backed off and eventually agreed to fund JwJ. Then, too, Sweeney did not intervene to dissuade a few of his affiliated unions from founding the new Labor Party in June 1996. Sweeney simply said he thought the timing was bad—coming just as the Clinton-Dole duel loomed on the horizon.

Despite this apparently laid-back posture, politics is also a priority for the newly re-elected leaders. During their first term, the "New Voice" team spent over $100 million on politics, mostly in the 1996 elections. In spite of talk of new approaches, $66 million went directly to candidates and the rest ($35 million) to media ads. Indeed, a media blitz was to be part of the new organizing efforts as well. The federation would spend $40 million on TV time to soften up targeted markets for organizing. On the one hand, the AFL-CIO could take credit for the intense effort that defeated the 1997 "fast track" trade legislation backed by Clinton and Republicans alike. On the other hand, they seemed asleep on their watch as Clinton prepared his stealth strategy for the globally sinister Multilateral Agreement on Investment being negotiated by the OECD nations, the $18 billion IMF funding package, the Free Trade of the Americas Area, and the African Growth and Opportunity Act.

The processes that are reshaping unions, however, run far deeper than leadership changes or the proliferation of institutes and centers at the AFL-CIO. The roots of labor's reawakening lie in the same trends that explain its downfall. All the forces routinely called on to explain labor's decline—industrial restructuring, downsizing, lean production, racial and gender recomposition, and, of course, the mother of all explanations, globalization—have forced workers and their organizations to seek new ways to act and organize.

Like all processes of change, this one is messy and contradictory. Some of its overlapping features include the toppling of national and local union leaderships, movements for greater union democracy, challenges to the regime of lean and mean production, and a return to militancy and direct action in several corners of the labor movement. In various ways, these unfolding trends made the more visible changes at the top possible.

Layered Labor and the New Satanic Mill

Sometime between George Meany and John Sweeney, when most of today's top leaders took office, the brave new co-managed workplace of the future turned into a top-down, well-lit satanic mill. Whether you work in a hospital or an auto plant, a post office or a post-industrial techno-office, more than likely your job is worse than it was a decade ago—if you had one that long. It is certainly more stressful, probably harder, and definitely more dangerous. U.S. injury and illness rates in the first half of the 1990s were running anywhere from 9 percent to 100 percent higher than in the first half of the 1980s after falling for a decade and a half since the implementation of OSHA in the 1970s. Though there was a slight drop in 1996, some observers attribute this to a growing reluctance to report minor injuries. Among major industry groupings, only construction workers and miners work at safer jobs.

When measured by the number of days lost for injury or illness, the difference is even greater through the early 1990s, running as high as 500 percent in auto assembly plants despite the declining number of workers. Not surprisingly, the Department of Labor stopped publishing the number of lost days in 1993. Contributing to this rise in occupational illness and injury are changing work-time patterns. Chances are your work hours are drastically longer if you're full-time. If they are shorter, it is because you are part of the precarious workforce that fills the country's growing number of part-time, temporary, or casual jobs.

What became equally evident by the mid-1990s was the decline of real wages: 12 percent since 1979 despite a productivity increase of 21 percent for the same years. Also highly visible is the incredible redistribution of income in favor of the wealthy. This trend is well known, but it is worth mentioning the recent *Business Week* cover story, "Two-Tier Marketing," that gave this rising inequality a practical twist.[1] Calling it the "Tiffany/Wal-Mart" marketing strategy, they note that more retailers are targeting either well-to-do or low-income markets, bypassing the middle. It seems that America's merchants have discovered there is more money being spent by the top 20 percent these days, while the great middle class (read working class) is up to its eyeballs in debt. The denizens of the economic lowlands, on the other hand, may have poor and declining incomes, but there are more and more of them.

The rise of the labor-management "partnership" has also been accompanied by a decline in benefits. Overall pension coverage at large and mid-sized firms fell from 91 percent of all workers in 1985 to 80 percent in 1995. Among that group, those with defined benefit plans, which guarantee a certain level of benefits upon retirement, fell from 80 percent to 52 percent during those years. Medical coverage shrank from 90 percent of full-time workers in 1988 to 77 percent in 1995. The proportion of health care recipients covered by managed-care plans rose from 26 percent in 1988 to 61 percent in 1995.

Even more visible these days is the blatant hold-up in progress by those most senior of partners, American CEOs. The stick-up artist of the year in 1997 was Sandy Weill, CEO of Traveler's Group insurance, who pulled down $230.7 million. This was the reward for cutting Traveler's workforce by a third since 1987. This sort of job-cutting not only brings outrageous executive salaries and bonuses, but propels the Dow Jones to unparalleled heights. This financial space shot, combined with stagnant wages and respectable productivity, has flooded company coffers. *Business Week* warns, "The worry is that many companies are taking in cash so fast they can't spend it efficiently."[2] No doubt the IMF aftermath of the East Asian financial meltdown and possibly the Multilateral Agreement on Investment being negotiated by the OECD nations will provide some outlet for all this cash.

All of this has not gone unnoticed by the majority that compose both the shrinking middle-income and the growing lower-income working class—and they are angry. Whatever glow may have accompanied the early days of partnership or participation faded rapidly for many workers, as their jobs were cut or intensified to boost profits, stock prices, and top salaries. Contesting with this anger and disillusionment, however, is fear of job loss by the same forces: downsizing, outsourcing, facility closures, or scab herding. As a *Multinational Monitor* editorial put it recently, "A ruthless employer class blends these multiple sources of job insecurity into a whole greater than the parts."[3]

Fear of job loss might well be the strongest emotion in most working-class families these days. Its hold on the vast bottom layer of organized labor has been strong for almost two decades now. Strike figures have plummeted as a result. So for a long time the mass of union members have been more or less passive. While there are plenty of exceptions, this fear-driven passivity has tended to reenforce the labor-management partnership agenda of the top officials. The members appear to accept the new workplace regime and go about their jobs silently, so all is right in this brave new world.

The other side of the downsized coin, however, is work intensification. If no one with power listened to the workers who complained about this, at least a few ears perked up when Wall Street insider Stephen Roach was quoted in the *Wall Street Journal* (June 17, 1996), "The so-called productivity resurgence of recent years has been on the back of slash-and-burn restructuring strategies that have put extraordinary pressures on the workforce." Roach predicted a "worker backlash."

There comes a point, after all, when the pressures of intensified exploitation outweigh the fear of job loss, as it did in the Great Depression. First one group, then another, tests the waters, and open conflict returns to labor relations—despite the trimmings of company unionism (1930s) or labor-management cooperation schemes. That is the meaning of the bitter strikes of the past couple of years in the United States. Some lose, as at Caterpillar and A. E. Staley. Others win, as in the dozen or so local GM strikes, the sixty-nine-day Boeing strike, the week-long general strike of Oregon state employees, the on-again-off-again strike at Yale, the seventeen-day strike at UPS, and the fifty-four-day confrontational struggle at WCI Steel in Warren, Ohio. Still others drag on, like the Wheeling-Pittsburgh strike, finally settled in 1997, and the Detroit Newspaper lockout, still not settled in 1998.

Then there are the massive strikes of immigrant and Latino workers in California: janitors, drywallers, carpenters, and waterfront truckers. To these should be added the struggle to organize 20,000 strawberry pickers in California, the smaller number of apple pickers and processors in Washington state, and farm workers in Oregon. These and similar struggles of immigrant and Latino workers around the country also point to something new: the rise of Latinos not only in the workforce but also in the unions. While union membership continued to decline from 1992 through 1997, the number of Latino union members grew by 13 percent.

After dropping for a decade to an all-time low in 1995, strike statistics rose in 1996. The number of major strikes (one thousand or more workers) rose to thirty-seven in 1996 from thirty-one in 1995. The number of workers involved grew from 192,000 in 1995 to 273,000 in 1996. Only the total number of days spent on strike by all workers dropped. More important than the figures, which are still very low, is that these are not the routine wage and benefit strikes of 1950 through 1979. For the most part, they are defensive struggles over issues associated with "lean production" and the workplace of the future: staffing levels, outsourcing and subcontracting, workload, health care, and pensions. They are outbursts of accumulated anger. In some cases, they draw on support from other unions or the communities in which the workers live. The massive confrontations that took place at WCI and the Detroit Newspaper strike in the beginning were symbols of a new consciousness. So, in a different way, were the series of strikes at GM, Chrysler, and Johnson Controls in the auto industry. Here, workers long afraid to buck the company-union love fest that was eroding jobs and conditions found their sea legs again. In a jujitsu-like flip of just-in-time production, these workers discovered you could close down much or all of a giant like GM or Ford—and in the case of supplier-firm Johnson, just by striking one or two plants. The 1996 strikes against GM alone cost that company $1.2 billion in lost production. As each of these strikes brought new hires into the plants, other local unions plucked up their courage for a shot at relief from leanness. In 1997, five more strikes hit GM, seeking more jobs and curbs on contracting out. If these strikes caught the attention of the country's working people, the stirring strike by 185,000 Teamsters at UPS in August 1997 caught their imagination.

There are, then, signs that a leaner, meaner capitalism is bringing with it and new labor consciousness and militancy. But if the whole labor movement is changing, it's changing in complicated and uneven ways. Unions in the U.S. today resemble geological layers in motion. At the top of most unions are yesterday's modernizers, officials whose upward career paths ran through the 1970s and 1980s and whose ideas were formed in that era of quality circles, teams, joint programs, and labor-management partnerships designed to make the employer competitive. The public image of the labor leader as a cigar-smoking pudge, *à la* George Meany, always an exaggeration, is way out of date. So, too, is yesteryear's opposite—the courtly social unionist in the Leonard Woodcock-Doug Fraser mold. Gone too are the last of the cranky, self-described socialists, William Winpisinger of the Machinists and William Bywater of the International Union of Electrical Workers (IUE).

For some time now, the upper stratum of the unions has been the terrain of a slightly slimmer, though still largely male and white, breed that speaks the lingo of human resources management, labor-management partnership, and worker participation. While these leaders sound state-of-the-art, they are themselves already living in the past. There are some important exceptions, leaders with feet in the future, like Bob Wages of the Oil, Chemical, and Atomic Workers (OCAW), the "outsiders" (that is, not AFL-CIO affiliated) at the United Electrical Workers (UE), and reform leaders in the Teamsters, who reject the partnership approach.

The majority, however, are leaders like Morty Bahr of the Communications Workers and Steve Yokich of the Auto Workers who enthusiastically embrace elaborate top-to-bottom versions of "jointness." As *Business Week* reported (April 7, 1997), the Steelworkers, Machinists, and Laborers, and the AFL-CIO itself have followed with elaborate training and consulting programs to help unions help companies in the race for market share. SEIU's new president,

Andy Stern, expresses a typical view when he says, "If we're going to be partners, we have to be equal partners." The problem with this is that employers have been seeking "partnership" schemes to weaken, not strengthen, unions.

Overall, the picture is one of jilted jointness guys who sincerely committed to cooperation with management in the 1980s only to have their membership, contracts, and unions downsized in the 1990s. The new AFL-CIO itself contributed to this portrait when it formed its misnamed Center for Workplace Democracy in 1997 to promote employee participation and labor-management cooperation schemes. In that same year, it went even further and, along with the SEIU and other affiliates, signed a partnership pact with the nation's largest and oldest HMO, Kaiser-Permanente. This act was all the more cynical because it occurred after Kaiser imposed concessions on the SEIU and while the California Nurses, who rejected the partnership, were in a bitter fight with Kaiser. Sticking to their guns and showing that there are alternatives to partnership, the nurses won a stunning victory in 1998, including the right to independently monitor the quality of patient care.

Most of this new consciousness and sometimes desperate militancy comes from the activists, the thin, middle, geological layer of the unions. These are workers, workplace representatives, and local union officials who keep America's unions going from day to day. They work between the upper layer of career officials and staffers and the majority of members on the lower level. Some are full-time, paid officials; many are not. They are forced to confront the reality of the workplace, as opposed to its ideology, whether or not they bought into this ideology in whole or in part. A significant minority of this layer, however, rejects the labor-management ethos that comes from employers and career union officials alike. It is in this layer that the return of resistance has gathered the greatest force and now and then breaks through the passivity of the members and the backward-looking immobility of the top officials.

This geological look at labor sometimes has the feel of colliding tectonic plates, to mix geological metaphors a bit. Labor's three layers are linked institutionally, so that the differing directions necessarily produce clashes. The forms of this clash are many. Pressure from the activist layer to act is one form, a major factor in the GM and Boeing strikes. Another form is turnover at the top. The Association for Union Democracy (AUD) estimated that about a dozen union presidents were ousted in contested elections from the late 1980s through the well-known 1991 victory of Ron Carey in the Teamsters.

Labor democracy attorney Paul Levy summarized the struggle in a speech to the National Lawyers Guild in the fall of 1996 when he said:

There is extensive intra-union activity in a large number of national unions, much more than ever before: in service unions such as the Food and Commercial Workers, the Service Employees and the Hotel Workers, construction unions such as the IBEW (Electricians) or the Bricklayers and the Carpenters and the Laborers, government unions like the Letter Carriers, the AFGE (Federal Employees) and the Treasury Employees, industrial unions like the Machinists and the Auto Workers.

To this list of challenges in national unions can be added similar movements in large local unions, such as the Members for Members caucus that took over the 40,000-member California State Employees Association; the New Directions caucus in the 30,000-member Transport Workers Union Local 100, in New York's transit system, that had its election stolen in 1997 but almost reached victory in 1998; or the reform group in the similarly large union of New York City janitors and doormen, SEIU Local 32J/32B—John Sweeney's home local. Even the famous Justice for Janitors local union, SEIU 399 in Los Angles, saw a massive opposition movement of Latino and African-American workers, called the Multicultural Alliance, replace the old-guard executive committee—only to be placed in trusteeship. The split of the militant California Nurses Association from the more conservative American Nurses Association in 1996 represents another form of rebellion from below.

There are also rebellions that have not yet focused on leadership challenges. Delegates to the 1996 IBEW convention, for example, voted over their union leaders' objections to make the future elections of top offices by secret ballot of convention delegates. The membership of the Laborers Union went even farther, with a 3 to 1 referendum vote to elect top officers by a direct vote of the membership in the future, also against the opposition of top leaders. Then, there were the reformers in the Machinists who went from successfully challenging restrictive candidate requirements in union elections to organizing a rejection of a settlement with Boeing recommended by the union leaders. The issue there was the massive outsourcing of work. The reformers forced the union and the company to return to the bargaining table and come back with an improved offer.

Two Steps Forward, One Step Back: The Teamsters

Nowhere was the challenge from below more successful, the return of struggle or the process of union reform deeper, than in the Teamsters. The election of Ron Carey in 1991 and his victory over Jimmy Hoffa "Junior" in 1996 opened a new phase of transformation. As Ken Paff of the Teamsters for a Democratic Union (TDU) explained, "We won the political battle over the value of a clean, democratic union. Hoffa had to adopt our program and promise to do even better at it. But we have not yet won the battle over the need for a new kind of union that derives its power from a mobilized and involved membership."

This was a major theme when 140 Teamster activists gathered in Detroit in February 1997 to discuss the future of the reform movement that had brought Ron Carey back for a second term as reform leader of the AFL-CIO's biggest union. The meeting, called by TDU, reflected some of the ambiguities of success in the new "clean, democratic union." Among the activists were a few international vice presidents, some Teamster staffers, a significant number of local union officials, and a majority of rank and filers. This crowd, reflecting every level of the union, not only discussed what a "new kind of union" might look like and do, but how TDU officers would relate to rank and filers, and how TDU as a whole would relate to Carey and the International Union staff. If the built-in tensions between labor's different layers were not entirely absent, the fact that within this reform movement representatives of all three were pulling in the same direction presented a ray of hope. Of course, the high-level officers in TDU were among those who fought to eliminate the multiple salaries and pensions that had made old-guard Teamster leaders wealthy men. Movements, after all, change not only institutional arrangements, but also people.

The dynamics of the Teamster "revolution," as many at the meeting called it, had brought TDU a long way from its fifteen years in the wilderness as the clear-cut opposition and its five years on the front lines defending the reform regime and attempting to defeat the old guard. Now the most difficult question of all was posed: how to go beyond the norms of "clean" American business unionism? Ideas ranged from the very practical to the highly visionary, but one theme ran throughout the entire meeting: the key to anything new was an informed, activated membership. Whether speaking of winning a strike at UPS later that summer, organizing the unorganized, or building broader coalitions for greater social goals, success would depend on mobilizing the tens of thousands of workers on whom the real power of the union rests.

This was no small task. More Teamsters voted in the 1996 election that kept Carey in office than in 1991, but the turnout was still only 34 percent of the members, and Carey took only 52 percent of those. For the majority of members, apathy and confusion remained the norm in the Teamsters, as in other unions. While Carey's bargaining record was far better than anything the Teamsters had seen since the days of the original Jimmy Hoffa, the reformed union was still fighting the uphill battle that all of labor faced. For many members, change was too marginal to inspire. Though Carey had stopped, even reversed, decades of downward motion in bargaining, in only five years he could not undo a thirty-year legacy or sweep aside the damage done by deregulation.

Even this heritage seemed on the verge of being overcome with the fifteen-day strike at UPS in August 1997. Against the predictions of the company, this highly diverse, 60 percent part-time workforce of 185,000 struck together and brought the "tightest ship in the shipping business" aground. This strike, more than any before in recent times, caught the working public's imagination—and that of tens of thousands of Teamsters as well. A Gallup poll showed public support for the strikers at 55 percent, while only 27 percent stood by Big Brown's management. The strike was also a symbol of the type of relationship that existed between TDU and Carey: sometimes at arm's length, but always mutually dependent. The grassroots campaign TDU had waged against UPS's "team concept" program since 1995 had helped to shape the UPS workforce into a fighting force. Carey's determination to win tangible gains on full-time jobs and contracting-out, issues of interest to million of workers in the U.S., and his nod to both official and TDU mobilization efforts before the strike put the union in place to win.

The ink was not dry on the new contract, however, when the court-appointed election officer declared the 1996 election invalid due to financial wrong-doings by the Carey campaign. In the weeks and months that followed, the details came out and the big-time press, notably the *New York Times* and *Wall Street Journal,* joined Congressional right-wingers in a feeding frenzy that attempted to throw the public image of the Teamster back to the Fitzsimmons-Presser-Mob era. Carey went from being the patron saint of labor to being a mere mortal-in-question.

The Teamsters, however, were not back to the old mob days. The record of reform and achievement by Carey and the reform movement as a whole was astonishing. Double-dipping of officers' salaries had been eliminated and a whole layer of useless bureaucrats removed; more than seventy locals had been put under trusteeship and, for the most part, on the road to democratic self-management; and the union was winning strikes and preparing for others. The "Donorgate" consultants, with Carey looking the other way or not even knowing, brought this to a screeching halt, but the accomplishments were not undone. The reform movement was, to be sure, confused about how to approach the election rerun and who to run, but the movement was still there, and above all, TDU was still fighting and organizing. By spring of 1998, the reform forces had rallied behind Ken Hall, one of the leaders of the UPS strike, as their candidate for president in the election rerun. Even if the old guard wins the election and Hoffa Junior assumes the presidency, the union will never be the same again.

The question that faces the Teamster reformers is essentially the same question that faces the entire labor movement: what kind of labor movement can be built that is adequate to the challenges of corporate power, international competition, and the dominance of conservative politics? It is here that the limitations of change at the top of the AFL-CIO become most evident.

Pressure From Above

Although the changing of the guard at the Teamsters and some other unions made the challenge at the AFL-CIO possible, it would be stretching the point to say that the force behind the "New Voice" team was rank-and-file rebellion. The chain of causality was more indirect and largely within the upper stratum. Probably more than anything, the New Voice challenge was a belated response to inaction in the face of labor's institutional decline. Mergers might solve the financial problems of one or another union, but declining proportions of union members in industry after industry spelled lost bargaining power; meanwhile, overall decline had seriously weakened labor's political clout.

While it is impossible to say precisely what set the rebels at the top in motion, the shocking retreat and defeat of the UAW at Caterpillar, first in 1992 and again in 1995, certainly sounded alarms in some high quarters. Caterpillar was a classic example of jilted jointness (as were Staley, GM, Boeing, AT&T, etc.). It had been a model of cooperation by the UAW since the late 1980s. But in 1991, CAT forced the UAW on strike with a list of concessionary "lean" demands that would have shattered the long-established pattern for the industry. This the union could not swallow in one gulp. The strike was on. Then in 1992, CAT threatened to bring in scabs. The UAW called off the strike in April 1992 in what most people saw as a serious (though some would say necessary) retreat for one of America's strongest unions. The strike was resumed in 1994, but called off in December 1995. The workers returned to work without a contract to face a vicious campaign of speed-up and repression that has not ended to this day. It is a tribute to the resolution of the rank and file of the UAW's Caterpillar locals that they ratified an unpopular "flexibility" contract in March 1998 only after forcing the union and the company to bring back all those fired for strike activity by first rejecting it in February.

Caterpillar represented not only the failure of "jointness," but also the price to be paid for allowing a growing nonunion workforce. During the years of cooperation, the company had invested hundreds of millions in new nonunion facilities, among them thirty-one components plants, while closing many older unionized operations. The union made no real effort to organize these new plants. By the time the strike began in 1991, UAW members composed only about 25 percent of CAT's total workforce. With nonunion parts plants and a scab workforce in the unionized assembly plants, the company was well positioned to outlast the union. By the time the UAW ended the second strike in December 1995, of course, the "New Voice" team had already been elected. But the whole Caterpillar saga, from 1991 on, was a clear reminder that not even the strongest of unions could exist successfully in a nonunion sea.

Another rude awakening was the political lockout of organized labor staged jointly by the reigning Democrats and Republicans. For nothing cushioned the half-century-long Meany-Kirkland dynasty so much as the belief that politics, that is, the Democrats, would save the day—some day. Can't organize? Get labor law reform from the Democrats. Can't strike? Get anti-scab legislation from our well-funded "friends." While this notion lingers on in the collective subconscious of the labor bureaucracy, it is no longer operable. Not only has the price of a White House luncheon or dinner risen since the Clintons took over the concession, but the menu for labor officials is thin gruel at best. The austerity triple play of Gingrich to Greenspan to Clinton is simply a further humiliation for Democrat-loyal labor.

In the realm of politics, as in that of union affairs, the new leaders saw a wing of their own supporters go off in a new direction to found a Labor Party in the United States. Led by the OCAW, a coalition of small unions that included the UE, the International Longshoremen's and Warehousemen's Union (ILWU), and, later, the United Mine Workers and the American Federation of Government Employees, took up this task. In addition, regional unions like the California Nurses and the California Carpenters and dozens of locals of major unions endorsed the effort. In June 1996, the founding convention attended by 1,350 delegates launched the new party. While the Labor Party was not to become an electoral challenger in the immediate future, its founding alone was a statement that some unions and many workers were prepared to go beyond the old AFL-CIO–Democratic Party bargain. In 1998, the Labor Party's leaders took this sentiment farther by proposing limited electoral intervention, with an eye to getting a small piece of the AFL-CIO's plan to run 2,000 union members for various offices in the year 2000.

So, labor's more aware leaders had plenty of motivation for change apart from the rumblings below. This explains not only the why of the challenge at the top, but also the limits and problems inherent in the process of change in the first two and a half years of the New Voice regime as well. Sweeney, for example, continues to plead for a business-labor partnership and to genuflect before the altar of competitiveness. Speaking to the National Press Club, he said, "We can no longer afford the luxury of pretending that productivity, quality, and competitiveness are not our business." He reiterated this outlook even more explicitly at the 1997 AFL-CIO convention: "One of our paramount goals is to help the companies we work for succeed, to work with our employers to creatively increase productivity and quality and to help American companies compete effectively in the new world economy and create new jobs and new wealth for our families and our communities to share." This embrace of the business agenda *du jour* certainly compromises the crusade against corporate greed Sweeney also calls for at times.

Indeed, the changes at the top of the AFL-CIO are limited by an obsession with technique, media dependency, and the proliferation of institutes. As Suzanne Gordon noted in *Labor Notes* on the eve of the New Voice ascension into office, "For every union problem there's a new Washington solution—an institute, a task force, a monitoring project, a clearing house, a policy center, a training center, a center for strategic campaigns, a new organizing department (with an office of strategic planning, a strategic planning process (Committee 2000), two or three campaign funds, a labor council advisory committee, and a 'strike support team of top people' from various union staffs. . . ." The promise made in the New Voice platform has been carried out with a vengeance. Rather than opening things up, the new leaders simply consolidated their regime and top-down style in 1997 by lengthening their term of office from two to four years.

To make matters worse, while many top union leaders talked revitalization on the AFL-CIO Executive Council, they practiced increased bureaucratization in their own unions. For example, more and more unions were signing longer contracts. Back in the 1940s, most unions had one-year contracts for which the members continuously debated demands and strategies, and there was still much vitality in the day-to-day life of the industrial unions. By the mid-1960s, three-year contracts with automatic "productivity" and COLA increases were the norm. Longer contracts and "automatic" gains meant less debate and increased bureaucratic control. With the crisis of the 1970s and the impact of globalization, deregulation, and concessions in the 1980s, things got worse. From 1985 through 1997, the percentage of union contracts longer than three years rose from 4 percent to 37 percent, while the percentage of employers surveyed by the BNA who said they would demand longer contracts in the following year's bargaining rose from 10 percent in 1985 to 20 percent in 1997.

While the new leaders correctly insist that "America Needs a Raise," some questions are simply not on their agenda: the brutal new workplace regimes and union democracy, to mention two. The significance of these last two unaddressed problems is that they are part of the more molecular process of change occurring beneath the surface. But these missing points also reflect both a lack of contact with the day-to-day issues of most working people and the low place on the lean-production learning curve so common to the current generation of top labor leaders.

They also represent barriers to the central goal the Sweeney team has set for labor: the massive escalation of organizing. First of all, in many industries, from health care to cars, it is doubtful whether unions that ignore working conditions will get very far. Building unionism on economic issues alone in the era of lean production, reengineering, casualization, and gendered and racial recomposition of the workforce is not likely to create the sort of momentum the leaders of the AFL-CIO talk about. Yet, very little on these crucial issues has come from the New Voice team, or from much of the rest of the labor bureaucracy, beyond blanket condemnations of downsizing.

Somewhat more subtle but no less important is the relationship between union democracy and mass organizing. Organizing on the scale needed to make the labor movement grow again has never been done primarily by professional organizers. It has always been a matter of workers organizing other workers, as it was in the industrial upsurge of the 1930s and when public-sector workers joined unions in large numbers in the 1960s.

Not surprisingly, the Teamsters have been using members to organize workers at Overnite Transportation, one of a number of nonunion freight and package firms that grew during the old-guard regime. Whereas the old guard's attempt to organize Overnite using its little army of time-serving "International Organizers" was a bust, Carey's use of rank and filers is working. In 1997, Teamster volunteers from Southwest Air helped organize five thousand mechanics at Continental. That year, the CWA had a similar victory when ten thousand reservation agents at USAir voted union after a campaign waged by CWA members from various sectors volunteered their time and effort.

A study of organizing strategies conducted by Kate Bronfenbrenner and Tom Juravich and published in *Organizing to Win* concluded that "union success in certification elections and first-year contract campaigns depends on using an aggressive grassroots rank-and-file strategy focused on building a union and acting like a union from the very beginning of the campaign." This rank-and-file approach included a representative committee of members from the bargaining unit, direct actions, and the use of ten or more rank-and-file volunteers from already organized workplaces. For every "rank-and-file intensive tactic" used in the organizing drives surveyed, the chances of victory grew by 9 percent.

In 1997, Carey called on the members to raise a volunteer "army of ten thousand member-organizers." This will be hard enough for the reforming Teamsters and could be precluded by a Hoffa victory in 1998. For unions where democracy, membership control, and leadership accountability are stifled, the likelihood of such a sustained mobilization is slim. Although the AFL-CIO is experimenting with member organizers and several unions employ this approach to one degree or another, going beyond marginal experimentation to mass mobilization cannot be separated from the question of internal union regime.

To put it bluntly, members who have an influence on the objectives, strategies, and tactics of their organizations are far more likely to devote their scarce free time to organizing others. Unions, of course, can and do mobilize members for specific events or actions even where there is little or no democracy. But to sustain such mobilization over time requires rank-and-file involvement in decisions as well as specific actions. This kind of mobilization cannot be turned on and off like a water faucet or run by remote control from headquarters.

The debate over this question is often characterized as being between the "service model" of unionism versus the "organizing model." The "service model" is the classic American business union practice of bargaining for and representing the membership (well or badly) without demanding (or wanting) their participation in the union's business. It is a passive form of unionism that bears much of the responsibility for the passivity of workers in the U.S. The "organizing model," by implication, calls on the members to play a direct role in defending their interests. In arguing for this approach, Michael Eisenscher makes the point that "democracy is an instrument for building solidarity, for establishing accountability, and for determining appropriate strategies—all of which are critical for sustaining and advancing worker and union interests." As reformers in Transport Workers Local 100 in New York's Transit Authority put it, "democracy is power" in relationship to both the union leadership and the employer.

The emerging practice today, however, is a sort of hybrid of the organizing and service models in which new members are recruited using radical mobilization techniques, then subjected to a service model unionism once they have won a contract. Sweeney's SEIU is the exemplar of this hybrid: tactically radical in organizing, but staff-driven and hierarchical in operation. Sweeney himself presents an almost colonialist view of democracy as something that is always down the road. He told the *Wall Street Journal* just before taking office, "I'm very interested in union democracy and rank-and-file involvement, but it can't be accomplished overnight." As though the problem only appeared the day he assumed the top place in the movement.

The views of Sweeney and many other labor leaders on the marginal importance of union democracy, on the one hand, and the continued adherence to labor-management partnership and bureaucratic solutions, on the other, are at odds with their own desire to organize the unorganized and tame the employers. The power to reach these goals must come from sustained mass mobilization, but distrust of the members runs deep at the pinnacle of labor's hierarchy.

Still, it seems clear that the changes taking place at various levels of the labor movement, along with the pressures on working people, are conspiring to bring about changes that may well be beyond the control of labor's managers of discontent. If a strategically placed union the size of the Teamsters pulls itself out of its momentary crisis and really does unleash an army of several thousand member-organizers, it is certain to be contagious. If rebellion continues to percolate at the base of many unions, and new members with high expectations join in large numbers, there may just be a new social movement and a new unionism in our future.

Notes

1. Leonhardt, David, "Two-Tier Marketing," *Business Week* no. 3518 (17 March 1997): 82-90.
2. Reinhardt, Andy, "An Enormous Temptation to Waste," *Business Week* no. 3513 (10 February 1997): 42-43.
3. "Class War in the USA," editorial, *Multinational Monitor* 18, no. 3 (March 1997): 5.

Organizing the Unorganized: Will Promises Become Practices?

Fernando Gapasin and Michael Yates

The New Voice leadership that captured power in the AFL-CIO in 1995 promised nothing less than the re-creation of a labor movement. This will be a daunting task. One measure of the strength of a labor movement is union density, that is, the fraction of the employed part of the labor force that is unionized. Union density in the United States is remarkably low, both in comparison with other countries and with what it once was. Densities between 60 percent and 80 percent exist in the Scandinavian nations, and in the other advanced capitalist states, they range between 10 percent in France to 40 percent in Great Britain and 33 percent in Germany. In Canada, with many similar economic features, density is around 30 percent. Even in New Zealand, which has experienced a profoundly antilabor legal restructuring, 23 percent of employees are union members.

U.S. union density has been declining since the mid-1950s and in free fall since the early 1980s. In 1955, the year of the merger of the AFL and the CIO, it was more than 30 percent. By 1980, it had fallen to 23 percent, and today it is a mere 14.1 percent. What is more, the general figure masks the remarkable fact that density in the private sector of the economy is now a paltry 9.8 percent, less than what it was in 1930. The only thing that has saved labor from a complete rout has been the robust growth of unionization in the public sector. Union density in the public sector is 37.7 percent, and this density actually increased slightly during the 1980s.[1]

Even total union membership has fallen. In 1983, union membership was approximately 17.7 million, but it was only 16.4 million in 1995. In 1997, it fell further, to 16.1 million. The AFL-CIO's own data on paid membership indicate that the federation has no more members now than it did in 1957, and it has one million fewer members today than it did in 1975. Some individual unions have lost hundreds of thousands of members.[2]

73

While a number of unions have increased their memberships, those numbers must be interpreted with care, because some of the increases are not due to organizing efforts but to mergers with other unions. AFL-CIO President John Sweeney's own union, the Service Employees (SEIU) has shown a dramatic increase in membership, from 480,000 in 1975 to 688,000 in 1985 and more than one million in 1995. But since 1985, SEIU has merged nine times, accounting for nearly one-fifth of all union mergers. Almost 100,000 members were added to SEIU as a result of these mergers.[3] While mergers may strengthen unions, they do not add to the union base. What is more, mergers such as that proposed between the United Steel Workers of America (USWA), the United Auto Workers (UAW), and the International Association of Machinists (IAM) may do little to encourage rank-and-file participation in unions already known for their top-down organizational structures and hostility to opposition movements.

The following comment by Richard Rothstein succinctly sums up the membership crisis now facing organized labor:

In 1994, the American economy added three million new jobs, while shedding a third as many in downsizings and closures—for a net gain of two million. But successful organizing drives enlisted just 72,000 potential union members; and not all victories led to union contracts. In order to hold the current 10 percent union share of the labor force, let alone increase it, organizing victories must add a quarter million new members a year; one-tenth of the two million net new jobholders, plus some—because jobs lost in economic churning are disproportionately in union firms. To reverse the pattern of decline, union organizing rates would have to increase many times over.[4]

It might be objected that union density is not an accurate measure of the power of organized labor. After all, public employees in France, a nation with a union density comparable to that of the United States, conducted a strike that paralyzed the economy and forced the government to roll back a series of assaults on the French working class. And the history of our own labor movement provides many examples of big results from small numbers. Actual union membership in the automobile industry was minuscule when the great sit-down strikes in the Great Depression brought General Motors to its knees.

Unfortunately, the United States of 1998 is not the France of 1996, much less the United States of 1937. Despite the increasing Americanization of Europe, workers there are still to some degree class-conscious, and the French working class stood solidly behind the striking public employees. Nothing comparable is likely in the United States now; organized labor itself would not support the air traffic controllers fired by Ronald Reagan.

The diminishing union densities and memberships accurately indicate declining power for organized labor in the United States. Not only have unions been forced by employers to give up hard-won gains such as cost-of-living adjustments, regular wage increases, equal pay for equal work, limits on subcontracting, holidays, and employer-financed health care, but they have also suffered a long string of political defeats, begining with the passage of the Taft-Hartley Act in 1947. Labor failed to get labor law reform in 1977 despite a Democratic Congress and a Democratic president.[5] It could not win passage of situs picketing rights,. Neither could it get Congress to limit the right of employers to permanently replace strikers. It failed to stop NAFTA, and it has been incapable of preventing the general attack on worker rights and security that have marked the past twenty-five years. It has watched the National Labor Relations Board (NLRB) and the courts nullify many of the rights the labor laws presumably granted. Even labor victories such as the Occupational Safety and Health Act have been tainted by the utter lack of enforcement of such laws.

The AFL-CIO spent over $30 million supporting Democrats in the 1996 elections, but the return on this investment has been meager. President Clinton, the recipient of a significant share of this money, responded by completely ignoring labor's candidates for Secretary of Labor. Bills introduced in the House of Representatives and in nineteen state legislatures to make it much more difficult for unions to use dues money for any political purposes have not encountered aggressive opposition from labor's "friends."

It is worth examining this most recent political assault on labor in more detail. Remarkably, it is wrapped in democratic cloth and euphemistically called the "paycheck protection" campaign by its supporters, most of whom are on the far right. There are presently state initiatives in Arizona, Nevada, Oregon, Florida, and California and "antiworker" legislation in many more states. There is federal legislation (S. 9, S. 497, and HR 2608) that threatens to choke labor's political voice. In Michigan and Washington, where legislation has been passed, union political funds have been cut by 90 percent. Based on data from the Federal Election Commission, corporate interests and their political action committees (PACs) outspend organized labor by eleven times. If all of this antiworker legislation passes, labor won't be able to spend a single cent, and the imbalance will be even more absurd.

In California, where the labor movement and the Latino community have been successful in returning the state legislature to a more "labor friendly" majority, labor's enemies have implemented a four-part strategy to defeat the labor movement, largely by scapegoating immigrants and minorities. Proposition 187 blamed undocumented workers for California's economic problems, and Proposition 209 blamed affirmative action for the inability of white people to get jobs and education, ignoring historic discrimination against racial minorities and simultaneously protecting the real cause of unemployment and underemployment—corporate restructuring. Two additional pieces of their legislative strategy are to limit the ability of non-English-speaking people to participate in the political process by implementing an English-only education system with Proposition 227, and to kill the political power of unions in California with Proposition 226.

At a time when the labor movement must take the offensive, it is being compelled to expend precious resources defending the status quo against a complex and multilayered right-wing strategy. And even before this offensive, the house of labor was in disrepair, subject to the roof caving in at any minute. Labor must organize on a massive scale if it is to defeat its enemies and become relevant both in the nation's workplaces and in the larger political world. The question is: can it do this?

Barriers to Organizing

Many argue that it will not be possible for the labor movement to rebuild itself, given the barriers to organizing. Four are frequently cited.

First, it has been argued that the labor laws are stacked so heavily in favor of employers that it is extremely difficult to organize workers into a union. Employers have virtual carte blanche for the tactics they may use to combat unionization.[6] They may interrogate workers concerning their union sympathies. They can compel workers to attend captive audience meetings at which they attack unions, while unions do not have the right to respond inside the plant. In fact, any union presence on company property has been severely curtailed by the NLRB and the courts. Employers routinely use consultants in organizing campaigns, and these consultants have perfected a combination of legal and illegal techniques that are hard for a union to successfully counteract. For example, employers frequently fire union supporters, knowing that even if they are found guilty of violating the law, they will not suffer an unduly burdensome penalty and, in the meantime, the chilling effect of the firings will erode union support.

Should a union manage to win a certification election, the employer can simply refuse to bargain seriously. Consultants have mastered the technique of "surface bargaining," that is, giving the impression of good-faith bargaining but having no intention of reaching agreement. A union can file an unfair labor practice against such practices, but the usual penalty for a guilty employer is merely an NLRB order to return to the bargaining table. Only in cases of egregious bad-faith bargaining can an employer expect to face a court order to bargain or face contempt charges. As a rule, there is no monetary penalty for refusal to bargain. These days the NLRB has become much more willing to agree with an employer that there is an impasse in the bargaining, giving the employer the right to simply impose its last contract offer on the workers. Of course, a union is free to strike and picket to force the employer to bargain, but it cannot organize any type of secondary boycott. If it strikes, the employer can permanently replace the strikers, and the police will stand ready to make sure that the scabs can do their work.

Two consequences of the collapse of legal protection for workers are the rapid increase in unfair labor practices and the reduction of the union victory rate in NLRB elections. The unfair labor practices most germane to union election campaigns rose fourfold between the early 1950s and 1990, and employer refusals to bargain increased eightfold during the same period. In the period from 1950 to 1954, unions won 72.1 percent of NLRB elections, but today it is closer to 45 percent, and the number of employees in newly certified bargaining units has steadily decreased, from more than 500,000 in the early period to fewer than 80,000 now.[7] Empirical studies indicate that the tactics utilized by employers, including illegal tactics, have a negative impact on union success rates.[8]

Some researchers have argued that an important reason for the increasing inability of unions to organize workers is the decline in the demand for union services by workers themselves. However, this is difficult to square with poll results, which consistently show that a much higher fraction of workers than the fraction now in unions would vote for a union if given a chance. African-American workers, especially, have shown a very strong demand for unionization.[9]

A third claim is that the rapid globalization of business has made it much more likely that employers will evade unions by moving to other countries. Trade agreements such as the North American Free Trade Agreement (NAFTA) have made it more profitable for some companies to move to Mexico. These days, it is not uncommon for employers to openly threaten to close their plants or move them when their workers try to unionize. Some managers place maps of North America with arrows pointed to Mexico around the workplace; one company actually took equipment from a closed plant, put it in trucks in lots at the plant at which an organizing campaign had begun, and put fake labels on the equipment indicating that it was going to Mexico.[10] However, there are good reasons to believe that the globalization threat has been exaggerated. For one thing, nearly 80 percent of all employment is in the service-producing industries, many of which (restaurants, janitorial services, etc.) cannot move. Further, most manufacturing still occurs in the high-wage capitalist nations, meaning that a lot of manufacturing takes place in the United States and will continue to do so in the foreseeable future. With union densities in service industries very low, there are plenty of opportunities for successful organizing. If the service sectors of Sweden are overwhelmingly unionized, why cannot the same thing be true in the United States?

A final argument frquently made is that employers have radically structured their workplaces and in the process have effectively immunized them from unionization. Employers have, for example, instituted a "team concept" of

production with greater emphasis on employee empowerment and involvement in decision-making. If such changes did indeed empower workers, they
would no doubt reduce the desire of workers to form unions. However, as much
research indicates, "team" programs give workers little real power and are just
a way to gain a more sophisticated control over them by their employers.[11] This
is not to say that some workers do not buy into such schemes, but only to
suggest that these same workers could be made to see the real nature of these
schemes, and probably will see it through their own experiences.

Along with the team concept, employers have been able to restructure in
such a way that they are able to use a variety of so-called contingent workers
in place of long-term, full-time employees. These types of workers—part-time,
temporary, leased, at-home, and independently contracted—are undoubtedly
more difficult to organize. But, as history shows us, it can be done. For instance,
migrant farmworkers required unions to follow them from camp to camp or
even country to country (between the United States and Mexico) in order to
become organized. Constantly laid-off garment workers remain organized and
unionized through the use of community "worker centers." And irrespective
of these possibilities, recent research by the Bureau of Labor Statistics indicates that contingent workers do not constitute nearly as large a share of
employment as previously thought (6 percent as opposed to 25–30 percent).
So while temporary workers and the like will present serious organizing
problems, the general phenomenon of contingency does not preclude the
rebirth of the labor movement.[12]

The Ball Is in Labor's Court

We certainly do not want to underestimate the severity of the barriers to
organizing unions. Any labor organizer will tell you that the pains are many
and the pleasures few. Certainly the legal climate is thoroughly pro-employer.
Yet it is no worse than it was when the CIO was on the march. And in the
United States it is assuredly more benign than in South Korea, where, despite
police brutality and the illegal status of independent unions, workers have been
organizing and demonstrating on a massive scale.

Workers do organize despite the barriers, legal and otherwise, which
confront them. It may be instructive to look at these organizing successes for
guidance. Let us look at two examples: the ingredients for victory in traditional
NLRB types of union elections and the activities of what we might call
"organizing" Central Labor Councils.

Research by Kate Bronfenbrenner and Tom Juravich indicates that when
organizers slowly build a democratic and class-conscious rank-and-file organization, they can win NLRB elections despite the anti-union efforts of employers and the weaknesses of the labor laws.[13] In fact, they say that "[such] union
tactics as a group played a greater role in explaining election outcome more

than any other group of variables, including employer characteristics and tactics, bargaining unit demographics, organizer background, or election environment." Some of the best tactics include forming a broadly representative rank-and-file organizing committee; house-calling by workers, organizers, and workers from already-organized workplaces; holding frequent mass and small group meetings which serve informational, strategic, democratic, and social functions; using solidarity days in which workers take some action to confront managerial authority; and forming bargaining committees before any election is held. Further, they discovered, "Unions which focus on issues such as dignity, justice, discrimination, fairness, or service quality were associated with higher win rates than those which focused on more traditional bread and butter issues, such as wages, benefits, and job security."

The focus on such issues is a part of the development of a "culture of solidarity" that must permeate every aspect of the union drive. The employer must be understood as the class antagonist of the workers, only defeatable if the workers stick together, acting as if "an injury to one is an injury to all." The union should encourage a gradual escalation of solidarity actions through which the workers can see for themselves that it is both possible and beneficial to act collectively. For example, once an internal organizing committee is formed, its members can begin to have informal meetings with other workers outside of the plant or arrange to visit workers at their homes. Then a petition of union support might be circulated. Signing a petition might be the first step in getting a person's commitment; once it is obtained the worker's further commitment should be sought or demanded. Once sufficient numbers have signed a petition, a rally might be organized; an open rally makes people stand up for what they have done and makes further actions easier. Regular events, from meetings with speakers to social gatherings, can further solidify the workers. People must be made aware at these events of what the employer is doing or will be doing to undermine the union effort; it will be relatively easy for the union to predict the employer's tactics, because they all use basically the same ones. In addition, the workers' families and the larger working community must be brought into the campaign from the beginning. Workers at other union facilities can be excellent organizers because they speak from direct experience. As soon as possible, workers should begin to formulate the demands that they will take to the bargaining table when their union drive succeeds. Perhaps demands can be presented to the employer before the election.

It is possible to organize unions outside the NLRA electoral framework, through more direct mass actions that force employers to recognize the union. This has become increasingly common, and it is estimated that some seventy thousand workers were organized without elections in 1996.[14] Organizing workers through mass picketing, demonstrations, civil disobedience, boycotts, and strikes usually requires unions to cooperate with one another and to build various types of alliances with community organizations (of course, traditional organizing through elections can use all these tactics, too). In February 1997, the AFL-CIO launched a large-scale "Road Map to Union Cities" to do all these things, in the process rebuilding union membership and creating a radically new labor movement, one aimed at "organizing for change, changing to organize, mobilizing against anti-union employers, building community and community coalitions, promoting economic growth, protecting [working-class] communities, educating union membership in pocketbook economics, generating support for the right to organize, making sure that union leadership mirrors the face of the membership, and encouraging all local unions to increase their membership."[15] The key element in these efforts will be Central Labor Councils (CLCs) committed to creating union cities. CLCs are the local analogue of the AFL-CIO, that is, local federations of member unions. Currently there are 572 in the United States. At different times in history, CLCs were the centers of union-organizing activities. However, since the formation of the AFL-CIO in 1955, CLCs, for the most part, have left organizing to the national unions and concentrated upon political lobbying and getting out the vote for labor-friendly candidates. As radicals of various stripes found their way into the labor movement during and after the 1960s, a few CLCs became actively engaged in organizing, not just at work sites but in communities as well. Today, 23 percent of the CLCs engage in organizing activities that go beyond support work and transmitting information to national unions.

The CLCs that have successfully engaged in organizing activities have three main characteristics: leadership that believes organizing is a priority of the CLC, at least one affiliated union that is willing to dedicate resources and staff to organizing, and support within the community. In addition, the "organizing" CLCs usually exhibit seven distinguishing behaviors: (1) they have leadership that can visualize goals, such as coalition building, political power, and organizing; (2) they provide opportunities for affiliates to mediate differences between themselves; (3) they position themselves so that they can mobilize around specific issues for different groups within a community; (4) they frame the major concerns of working people within their community in a way that allows delegates, affiliates, union workers, nonunion workers, and different community organizations to take action that is consistent with their perceived interests, thus helping to foster the image that labor is a positive part of the community; (5) they communicate the CLC's "message" effectively to these same groups; (6) they build the capacity of the CLCs by developing activism and new leadership, increasing affiliations, maximizing the use of existing resources, and creating new resources, i.e., money and people; and (7) they plan and evaluate activities that concern all of the above.

Put simply, "organizing" CLCs have a vision of the labor movement as not just organizing workers and fighting for traditional bread-and-butter gains but also creating vibrant working-class communities and a working-class culture. They work actively with community groups and academics to educate working people, to create jobs (often for women and people of color, as in Atlanta during the 1996 Olympics), to improve community life (unionists and environmentalists have cooperated in Los Angeles to stop corporate outlaws from polluting working-class communities), and to organize workers (as in Las Vegas, now the strongest union city in the nation, and in the strawberry-growing areas of California). The leaders of some of these CLCs also train cadres of secondary leadership, which then organize groups of volunteers available for mass actions. Borrowing from the practices of a few CLCs, the AFL-CIO has reintroduced the concept of "Street Heat" to CLCs throughout the U.S. Street Heat is simply the ability of local CLCs to mobilize significant numbers of people to take militant action on behalf of workers and their communities. Some CLCs have obtained funding from various sources to hire special staff and attack special problems, such as plant closings and worker retraining. They also research their areas for new organizing opportunities, and they sometimes initiate the organizing.

What is most exciting about these "organizing" CLCs is that they create the local structure for building a social justice movement. CLCs are the logical foundation within the AFL-CIO for multi-union organizing drives. Rather than organizing one employer at a time, they can organize them all at once—as have janitors in Los Angeles and the Silicon Valley, and hotel workers in Las Vegas. CLCs can also organize contingent workers, who might have to be organized on a geographic, industrywide basis. They can develop strategies to organize the contractors and the firms simultaneously, coordinate the use of technology to organize a dispersed workforce (i.e., visualize cyberspace as a cyberworkplace), promote associate member programs, and even create minority unions. And they do not act like individual unions competing against one another; they organize workers jointly. Most important, rather than unionized workers isolating themselves from their communities as special interest groups, they can become vital parts of communities that are rebuilding themselves and gaining control over their own fates. For example, when the K-Mart in Greensboro, North Carolina, refused to bargain with the employees' union (UNITE), black workers held a series of demonstrations and conducted a boycott, eventually forcing the company to settle and encouraging other groups to turn up the heat on the employer. Later the union donated money for the rebuilding of black churches that had been burned in South Carolina.[16] Mass actions build solidarity and class consciousness as workers come to see the true functions of the police and the state, which invariably oppose their efforts.

Education programs can further strengthen their understanding of the nature of our society.

The Missing Link: Political Ideology

We have, then, a labor movement that has suffered a long period of decline but has new leadership pledged to reverse labor's fortunes. We also have a lot of research that suggests that grassroots, democratic, class-conscious organizing campaigns can succeed, not only in increasing union membership but also in beginning to transform the entire society. And we have some evidence that the New Voice leadership has already launched such a campaign by transforming the culture of the labor movement. As AFL-CIO Executive Vice President Linda Chavez-Thompson has said, "We're aiming to create a culture of organizing throughout the union movement. . . ."

Yet much remains to be done. First, national and local unions must allocate their resources so that organizing is a priority. While there are some notable exceptions, the average union today spends a mere 3 percent of its budget on organizing. This is especially vital at the local level because approximately 70 percent of union revenues are held locally. Most local unions do not do much organizing; they exist to protect what their own members have won. However, given the size of the nonunion workforce, this focus is insufficient; in order to create more maneuvering space for local unions, the unorganized must be organized. Unfortunately, the AFL-CIO, given its structure, cannot force national and local unions to devote more resources to organizing. The AFL-CIO's new and dynamic Organizing Institute can train new organizers, but it cannot force the unions to use them. Like most CLCs, local unions will have to be won over through the process of planning, leadership development, economic education, and collective action.

Second, the AFL-CIO program for rebuilding the labor movement, for all its good features, is still a sort of "revolution from above." Many new programs have been launched as the result of studies and committees sponsored at the top, but these have to filter down to the rank and file. There are a number of militant local and regional organizations, with significant female and minority memberships, that champion the rights of workers and actively help them to organize, and to protect and improve their communities. Over the past nine years, Jobs With Justice (JwJ) has been doing just the type of work (coalition-building, demonstrating and picketing in support of workers and their communities, forming "Workers Rights Boards," etc.) that the new leadership says must be done. Yet the AFL-CIO, while praising JwJ, has not given it much financial support. Similarly, Black Workers for Justice has been doing yeoman work of a similar nature in the South. Again, however, the AFL-CIO has not done enough to support this group or kindred organizations, such as the Korean Immigrant Workers Association in Los Angeles, the

Chinese Progressive Association in Boston, the Chinese Staff and Workers Association in New York, the Asian Immigrant Women Advocates in Oakland, and the Pilipino Workers Center in Los Angeles.

Third, as many others have noted, a reborn labor movement must be absolutely committed to racial and gender equality. This, in turn, means more than opportunistically organizing women and minority workers. It means a commitment to an end to women's "double day," opposition to racism and sexism within unions, relentless antagonism to the dismantling of the welfare state, and a demand for the demolition of the structure of racial oppression that permeates this country. So far, the AFL-CIO has said some of the right things, but here more than anywhere else, actions will speak louder than words. A real commitment to organizing the economically dynamic South and Southwest (the historic homelands of African Americans and Chicanos, respectively) has not yet been made; until it is, a labor movement will be hard to build. The vast majority of CLCs are still run by white males. This is ironic, given that some of the most militant mass organizing campaigns have been those of people of color, including Latin American immigrants steeled in against political repression and intense exploitation in their homelands.

Similarly, the AFL-CIO has a responsibility to support international trade unionism. In addition to simply supporting the economic and social struggles of other trade unionists around the world, the federation has the duty to support and initiate legislative action in the United States to forcefully support worker's struggles, e.g., the worker protection provisions provided under NAFTA. The AFL-CIO can lead the charge for cross-border organizing and coordination of organizing efforts with unions from other countries. Some unions, such as the USWA, the Communication Workers of America (CWA), and the United Electrical Workers (UE), are actively working with unions in Mexico to strengthen the ability of Mexican workers to fight back, particularly in the border developments known as the *maquiladores,* as in the recent victory of Han Young (Hyundai) workers.

What all these shortcomings have in common can be summed up with the words "political ideology." A labor movement cannot be constructed on the basis of pocketbook economic issues alone. Of course, it is good for workers to improve their standard of living, and AFL-CIO President Sweeney's slogan, "America Needs a Raise," resonates strongly among working people, but these things alone are not enough, as the conservatism of many well-paid union members in the period following the Second World War attests. A labor movement based upon consumption is doomed to fail because it accepts the ideology of its class enemy. In such a movement, workers will judge things according to a crude "what's in it for me?" calculus guaranteed to eventually pit worker against worker, workplace against workplace, and union against union.

To avoid this, the labor movement must unabashedly champion class-unifying themes: everyone has the right to a decent job; everyone has the right to decent housing, publicly-funded health care, education at all levels, day care, paid family leaves, and vacations; racism and sexism must be eradicated now; every institution in the society must be democratically controlled, including workplaces, unions, and all levels of government; work must become an end in itself and not just a means to the end of more private consumption; workers everywhere in the world are exactly the same as those here, with the same rights. And labor activists must understand clearly that the present economic system is utterly incapable of satisfying these demands.

In other words, a labor movement needs a labor ideology, a worker-centered way of seeing the world and interpreting what happens in it. This implies, in turn, an independent labor politics, distinct from the corporate-financed parties. With such an approach, fights for higher wages and union democracy will occur within a radically different context than is now the case. Members imbued with such a way of thinking will not so readily oppose spending union money on organizing, because they will realize that they are helping to build a new society. Higher wages will not just be an end but one among many means of creating a just world. An independent and oppositional politics, combined with aggressive organizing, is also more likely to achieve the political reforms needed by workers to organize further.

The organizing strategies that seem to work are based, although not explicitly, on just such a way of thinking and acting. In addition, local union leaders who have a worker-centered world view are most likely to fight for the interests of women and minority workers and to encourage them to take leadership roles. Unfortunately, it is just here that the AFL-CIO most obviously fails. Labor does not have an independent politics; quite the contrary, it is tied tightly to the Democratic Party, a party wholeheartedly committed to capital that now seldom gives even lip service to the interests of workers.

If the labor movement does not assert a political program of social and economic justice, it will have great difficulty mounting an effective challenge to the control that corporate America exerts over our lives. Nor will it easily build solidarity with workers in the rest of the world, who, as some of the articles in this book show, are far more radical than workers here. Only when labor does develop an independent politics will it be able to become a movement. The AFL-CIO as currently structured is not likely to do this, although it must be said that its new leadership has not opposed the independent Labor Party or the New Party, both of which hold great promise for working-class politics. Nor has it opposed fusion politics, in which a major and a minor party both run the same candidate. (Unfortunately, the Supreme Court just ruled that state anti-fusion laws are not unconstitutional.)

This said, what should radicals do? The AFL-CIO's new emphasis on changing to organize obviously has important cultural and ideological implications for the entire labor movement. There is an opportunity for radicals, along with more traditional labor bureaucrats, to redefine the U.S. labor movement. The traditional model of "business unionism" is based upon the assumption that labor has a guaranteed "piece of the American pie." However, as U.S. capitalism continues to prosper, American workers work more and earn less. Of the industrialized nations, only Japanese workers work more hours, and only workers in Canada and the United Kingdom earn less money per hour. Business unionism does not prepare unions to develop a strategy that effectively deals with the corporate strategies that have caused this gap: deregulation, privatization, casualization of the workforce, and de-unionization.

The New Voice focus on organizing the unorganized, economic strategies, community alliances, and political accountability provides an opportunity to change the demographics of unions (increasing the possibility of involving more minorities and women), integrate the labor movement with other important social movements, change local economies, and develop a unified political agenda for the labor movement. This means that "other" models or ideologies may have a voice in the struggle to redefine the U.S. labor movement. And, in the course of debate, at the national, state, and local levels, different, more effective cultural and ideological models may emerge.

Thus, the opportunity presents itself for an alliance among left intellectuals, community activists (especially racial minorities), and leftists within the labor movement. Hopefully we can build organizations that demographically represent all workers, develop radical analyses of our society, and help to make these available to the rank and file. It is striking, even in the literature of the New Voice programs, how little space is devoted to a frank statement of what labor stands for in this country. Perhaps we can push and prod labor into making such a statement, one which must by necessity distance labor from the bland pro-corporate platitudes of the Democratic Party. And, of course, we must continue to support existing left structures that are active in the labor movement (and help to create new ones), foster the continued growth of a leftist culture, and continue to develop an ideological alternative that challenges the existing capitalist power structure.

Notes

1. Barry T. Hirsch and David A. Macpherson, *Union Membership and Earnings Data Book* (Washington, D.C.: Bureau of National Affairs, 1996); Clara Chang and Constance Sorrentino, "Union Membership Statistics in 12 Countries," *Monthly Labor Review*, Dec. 1991, 46-53; the data for New Zealand were provided to me by Ellen Dannin, who is writing a book about labor law in New Zealand. The most recent data are taken from the BLS Website at *http://stats.bls.gov/newsrels.html*.

2.   "AFL-CIO Statistics on Paid Membership of Union Affiliates Prepared for Federation's 21st Constitutional Convention," Bureau of National Affairs, 12 October 1995.
3.   Lisa Williamson, "Union Mergers: 1985-94 Update," *Monthly Labor Review,* February 1995: 18-24.
4.   Richard Rothstein, "Toward a More Perfect Union," *The American Prospect,* May-June 1996: 47. Rothstein's 10 percent figure uses the labor force rather than employment as a denominator.
5.   Michael Yates, *Labor Law Handbook* (Boston: South End Press, 1987), chapter 5.
6.   Michael Yates, *Power on the Job: The Legal Rights of Working People* (Boston: South End Press, 1994).
7.   U.S. Deptartment of Labor, *Fact Finding Report: Commission on the Future of Worker-Management Relations* (Washington, D.C.: Government Printing Office, May 1994), 81-87.
8.   Kate Bronfenbrenner and Tom Juravich, "The Impact of Employer Opposition on Union Certification Win Rates: A Private/Public Comparison," Economic Policy Institute, Working Paper No. 113, February 1995.
9.   Richard Freeman and Joel Rogers, "Worker Representation and Participation Survey: First Report of Findings," *Proceedings of the 47th Annual Industrial Relations Research Association Meeting* (1994): 336-345.
10. See Kate Bronfenbrenner, "Organizing in the NAFTA Environment: How Companies Use 'Free Trade' to Stop Unions," *New Labor Forum,* Fall 1997: 51-60.
11. Mike Parker and Jane Slaughter, *Working Smart: A Union Guide to Participation Programs and Reengineering* (Detroit: Labor Notes, 1995).
12. Anne E. Polivka, "Contingent and Alternative Work Arrangements, Defined," *Monthly Labor Review,* October 1996: 3-9.
13. Kate Bronfenbrenner and Tom Juravich, "Union Tactics Matter: The Impact of Union Tactics on Certification Elections, First Contracts, and Membership Rates," Institute for the Study of Labor Organizations, Working Paper, n.d. The two quotes in this paragraph are from this paper.
14. Marc Cooper, "Labor Deals a New Hand," *The Nation,* 24 March 1997: 11-16.
15. Most of the rest of this paper is based upon work by Fernando Gapasin and Howard Wial, "The Role of Central Labor Councils in Organizing in the 1990s," in Kate Bronfenbrenner and others, eds., *Organizing to Win* (Ithaca, N.Y.: Cornell University Press, 1997).
16. Manning Marable, "Black (Community) Power!," *The Nation,* 22 December 1997: 21-24.

Race and Labor Organization in the United States

Michael Goldfield

In the United States of America, the fate of labor—its ability to win lasting gains, its success in sustaining solid organizations, and its episodes of class consciousness, as well as its brief flirtations with broader class and independent political organizational forms—has always been closely tied to the issue of race. This is not only true today but from the nation's earliest colonial beginnings.[1]

Throughout most of U.S. history, despite a wide range of resistance, nonwhites have been discriminated against, excluded, and denied equal access to political, social, and economic opportunities. Although employers and the ruling class in general have been responsible for the racial subordination of nonwhites, most majority white labor organizations—with a few important exceptions—have participated in this oppression.

There have, however, been several brief periods when large numbers of whites, perhaps majorities, have supported or at least tolerated equality for nonwhite minorities: the years immediately preceding the American Revolution of 1776-1783, the early part of Reconstruction after the Civil War (1867-1874), a stretch of the 1930s and 1940s, and a few years in the middle 1960s at the height of the civil rights movement. Solidaristic labor struggles and organizations have often emerged, not merely in hospitable situations, but even in the most unlikely times and places, including the Deep South during the most racially oppressive periods.

This contradictory history argues against the assumption, traditionally common on the left, that unions will inevitably evolve toward nonracist, egalitarian positions as the numbers of African-American workers increase. But it also suggests the inadequacy of the currently fashionable view that all whites (and especially all white male workers) are inevitably and incurably racist—whether for deeply rooted psychological or cultural reasons or, in a more materialist version, because of the compulsions of labor market competition.

We need to assess the current situation of race in the labor movement against the background of this complex history, in the hope of reviving some of that movement's better traditions and finally eradicating the racism that has consistently weakened the movement and eroded its class solidarity. This history should also make it clear that, just as an anti-racist commitment is vital to the success of the labor movement, an anti-capitalist class politics is the best hope for the anti-racist struggle.

The 1930s

To understand today's situation, we must go back at least to the 1930s and 1940s, when there was a tremendous upsurge of interracial industrial unionism and a new, broader culture of solidarity. That trend has to be situated in the context of certain economic and demographic developments. While economic development and changes in industrial and occupational structures, as well as the racial, ethnic, and sexual composition of occupations and industries, are never the whole story, they are the indispensable starting point.

From the time of the Civil War through the first three decades of the twentieth century, U.S. industry underwent relatively continuous, rapid expansion, and the industrial workforce grew rapidly. In the North, industrial employment before the First World War was overwhelmingly white, while in the South, African Americans had gained important footholds in many industries during the late nineteenth century—notably coal and metal mining (especially in Alabama), iron and steel, longshore, railroads, tobacco, food processing, and wood. Before 1900, 90 percent of African-Americans lived in the South and worked mainly in agriculture. With the expansion of northern industry at the beginning of the First World War and the cutoff of European immigration, black workers began to migrate to the industrial cities of the North in large numbers as well as to southern cities. By 1940, more than 6 million African Americans, almost 48 percent of the total black population, were classified as urban.

Mexicans and Chicanos were drawn in large numbers into southwestern and West Coast agriculture and food processing during this period, and to metal mining throughout the Southwest. Puerto Rican workers increased their employment in New York City, while Asian Americans made further inroads in canning and other industries on the West Coast. The militant sugar plantation workforce in Hawaii, numbering tens of thousands by the 1920s, was overwhelmingly nonwhite, with Japanese and Filipinos making up the largest groups.

Facing this new industrial configuration with its multiracial, multiethnic workforce, the CIO, from its beginning in 1935, not only advocated inclusive interracial unions but also espoused an egalitarian rhetoric. A question arises of whether this represented a real break from AFL racial policies, or merely a continuation of AFL racial practices in a new industrial setting—a setting in which white workers, who could not control the labor market for themselves in unskilled industrial workplaces without enlisting the support of their fellow black and other nonwhite workers, made the necessary opportunistic overtures.

The answer to this question is not simple, because the CIO and its various component unions had a wide range of racial practices. Individual unions were at times and in some places quite forthright in asserting the rights of their nonwhite members. At other times and places, CIO officials and particular unions hardly seemed different from the AFL. And there are some unions that began as racially progressive and later became quite backward, and there are one or two examples of the opposite trend.

The range of CIO practices was particularly striking in southern industrial cities such as Memphis. There the Communist-led United Cannery, Agricultural, Packing, and Allied Workers of America (UCAPAWA; after 1944, the Food and Tobacco Workers of America, FTA) began organizing black workers who were previously considered unorganizable. UCAPAWA Local 19 in Memphis was very militant and had black leadership, including its president. Its almost unbroken string of organizing successes stimulated the organization of white workers in both integrated and overwhelmingly white workplaces, showing that the fears of racially conservative CIO leaders—that organizing blacks first would alienate the white workers—were, at the very least, exaggerated. Yet at the same time, for example, the conservative Memphis CIO director W. A. Copeland (who owed his position largely to national CIO leader and Philip Murray ally John Brophy) opposed integrated meetings of black and white workers and expressed special venom for FTA's racial policies.

If "moderates" in the CIO national office supported racist leaders, it was not necessarily because they completely agreed with their racial attitudes. It was largely because their commitment to building interracial solidarity, or even to building a dynamic growing labor movement, was outweighed by their desire to eliminate communist influence and to achieve respectability among business leaders and national political elites. This is a legacy for which today's dwindling union organizations are still paying dearly.

Left-led unions were generally committed not only to integrated unionism but to varying degrees of racial egalitarianism. Some were majority white unions with significant numbers of non-white workers, such as FTA, the United Packinghouse Workers, and the Mine, Mill, and Smelter Workers (which in addition to its black membership in Alabama had significant Mexican and Chicano membership in the Southwest). These unions fought aggressively for job rights for their members, engaged in anti-racist education, and were deeply involved in fighting Jim Crow practices outside their workplaces. There were also certain left-led unions with only small percentages of black and other nonwhite workers who engaged in similar activities. These unions included the Farm Equipment Workers (FE), the Fur and Leather Workers, and the National Maritime Union. The latter union, with barely 10 percent black membership, had a black man, Ferdinand Smith, as its secretary-treasurer. Other left unions were not so exemplary,[2] but with a few exceptions the left-led unions were far better than their non-left counterparts.

Left and racially egalitarian unionism was largely defeated during the late 1940s. The CIO right, in the guise of anticommunism, destroyed and undermined the most promising bulwarks of interracial unionism. FTA's largest local, Local 22 in Winston-Salem, North Carolina, was attacked so badly by the national CIO in a racist, redbaiting campaign that the local not only was decertified in a National Labor Relations Board campaign, but could never be reorganized by the AFL-CIO.[3] The Steelworkers, who had shared some of the racially egalitarian perspective of the United Mine Workers in their initial organizing, soon solidified as an organization whose department seniority system served to protect the better paying, higher-skilled jobs for white workers. Under their president, Philip Murray, they took the lead in destroying the interracial Mine Mill locals in Alabama by openly appealing to the racism of white workers. Years later, the CIO was still trying to figure out why the black community in Birmingham would have nothing to do with them.

The Post-Second World War Period

The anti-racist promise of the 1930s and 1940s died in the anticommunist and generally anti-left climate of the postwar period. The years after the Second World War are correctly seen by many on the left as a period of bureaucratization and retreat by the CIO, a loss of militancy and grass roots democracy, and a drawing closer to the capitalist class on both domestic and foreign policy. All of this is true. What is not sufficiently emphasized in such accounts is the degree to which their retreat on racial issues was at the center of these trends.

With the defeat of the left unions and the abandonment by the national CIO of basic commitments to civil rights for minorities in the workplace and in the society at large, the possibilities for racially egalitarian unionism diminished greatly. Nevertheless, the CIO, especially the more liberal anticommunist unions like the UAW, maintained an undeserved reputation on civil rights. The huge postwar housing boom, largely financed by government loans (in particular, VHA and FHA), completely excluded nonwhites, especially African Americans. Skilled construction jobs for housing and the massive federally-funded highway system also excluded minorities. Hardly a peep was heard from the politically sanitized, bureaucratized CIO. Within the individual CIO unions themselves, the situation of minorities was hardly more salutary, as unions in major industries like steel, mining, and auto allowed the conditions of their black members to deteriorate.

What the large CIO unions might have done in fighting against racial discrimination is suggested by the struggles of black workers and the remnants of the labor left during the 1950s. The UPWA, the FE, Mine Mill, the less radical Brotherhood of Sleeping Car Porters, remnants of the United Public Workers, and the several-hundred-member Local 1199 continued successful civil rights activity. The CP-supported National Negro Labor Council (NNLC)—subpoenaed, harassed, and redbaited by the government and the national CIO, with support from only a small segment of the labor movement—carried on many labor-related civil rights activities in the early 1950s. For example, in December 1952, the NNLC in Cleveland mobilized 1,500 pickets to protest the refusal of American Airlines to hire blacks in any but the most unskilled positions. Twenty percent of the demonstrators were white. In Louisville in 1953, the NNLC engaged in a yearlong campaign to get the new General Electric plant to hire and upgrade black workers; in that city they put similar pressure on Ford and GM and on the railroads, with the support of the large FE International Harvester local union in Louisville.

While African Americans were generally excluded from more skilled jobs during the postwar period, and even from some less skilled jobs, as in southern textile, and driven out of certain industries where they had been a large percentage of the labor force (e.g., southern sawmills, tobacco manufacturing, and mining), they were hardly marginalized in the economy. In meatpacking, steel, auto, farm and construction equipment, transportation, and hospital work, African-American workers were heavily concentrated in the lower-paying occupations, while disproportionately employed in the industries as a whole.

Despite their greater representation in many of the old CIO unions, black worker influence did not translate into greater militancy by their unions for civil rights. CIO unions had been at the head of the battles for racial equality during the 1930s and 1940s. Yet as the new civil rights movement emerged during the 1950s and 1960s, unions were at the margins. The sit-in movement that began in February 1960, had as its leadership and foot soldiers African-American college and high school students. When working-class people became involved—in Montgomery, for example, cooks, housekeepers, and other African-American workers were the vast majority of those who boycotted the buses—it was not generally under union auspices.

With some notable exceptions, labor struggles by blacks for equal rights were not led by unions; rather, blacks often targeted white-led labor unions as part of the problem. Black workers and civil rights organizations repeatedly picketed publicly-financed construction sites around the country that refused to hire nonwhite workers. In one celebrated instance in 1964 at the city-financed Bronx Terminal Market, New York City officials intervened to force the hiring of one black and three Hispanic plumbers. When nonwhite plumbers who had previously been refused membership in Plumber's Local 2 arrived for work, all the union plumbers, supported by their former business agent, George Meany, then president of the AFL-CIO, walked off the job. Black caucuses existed during the 1960s and 1970s in thousands of workplaces and made demands for equality that should have been made before by their unions. In steel, both the companies and the unions resisted the demands for equality for black steel workers. Both were the target of large numbers of suits under Title VII of the 1964 Civil Rights Act.

Certain unions, however, briefly used the impetus of the civil rights movement to aid in the organizing of African-American workers. The American Federation of State, County, and Municipal Employees (AFSCME) was among the most prominent. Their successful campaign to unionize the overwhelmingly black Memphis garbage-collection workers was made famous by the assassination of Martin Luther King, Jr. there in 1968.

The Present Situation

Over the past several decades, women and nonwhites have become an increasingly large percentage of the labor force. Where in the economy are the growing numbers of nonwhites located? It has been argued that minorities, African Americans in particular, are becoming increasingly marginal to contemporary U.S. society. There is, to be sure, important evidence to substantiate this argument. For several decades, unemployment rates for Latinos (with the exception of Cubans, who stand midway between other Hispanics and whites) and blacks have been double that for whites. Surveys taken among the unemployed and discouraged workers (those who are out of work but are not currently looking for a job, and are thus not counted among the officially unemployed) suggest that several times as many members of minority groups than whites say they would take a job if they could find one. The prison population of 1.5 million is heavily minority, approximately one-half African-American. Poverty and unemployment go a long way toward explaining why the U.S. military is disproportionately nonwhite. In 1995, African Americans made up 19.4 percent of all enlisted personnel but only 11.4 percent of all officers. And there are many industries, including high-paying ones like steel, auto, and meatpacking, with disproportionate numbers of African-American and other nonwhite workers, that have dramatically cut back their labor forces in recent decades.[4]

Yet these facts, though important, are not the whole story. On the one hand, there are a number of industries whose workforces are declining (including mining, agriculture, and petrochemicals) and in which minorities are underrepresented. On the other hand, minorities, particularly blacks, are disproportionately represented in some sectors that have grown the most, including transportation, communications, utilities, government employment, social services, hospitals and health care, cleaning and building services, protective services, prison personnel, and the military. African Americans have also gained increasing employment in certain sectors that were previously closed to them, including wholesale and retail sales and certain areas of manufacturing, most notably textiles. Thus, African Americans and other minorities are heavily concentrated in sectors that are not only crucial to the production of surplus value and the maintenance of capitalism today, but in those sectors that will undoubtedly remain vital in the foreseeable future.

In virtually every industry (whether they are overrepresented or underrepresented) African Americans and other nonwhites are disproportionately located in the lower-pay and lower-status, although still highly essential, occupations. In the growing and important health care industry, for example, African Americans are concentrated in the lowest-ranking occupations. While in 1994 they made up only 4.2 percent of doctors and 3.7 percent of dentists (a slight increase from 1983), they made up 9.3 percent of registered nurses, 18.7 percent of licensed practical nurses, and almost 30 percent of nurses' aides, orderlies, and attendants.

The same story can be told not only within but across various industries, with blacks in 1995 making up 24 percent of telephone operators, 29 percent of postal clerks, 29 percent of bus drivers, 34 percent of garbage collectors, and 28 percent of correctional officers in the nation's prisons, one of the fastest growing of U.S. industries. With the exception of social work and a few other occupations, minorities are grossly underrepresented in a number of higher-level occupations. Among airline pilots, tool and die makers, and aerospace and petroleum engineers, they represent one percent or less. And there are only small percentages of minority workers among auto mechanics, electricians, carpenters, construction superintendents, and architects.

There is some debate about whether the present situation of minorities in the labor force is due largely to present discrimination or is rather the result of historic discrimination combined with recent large-scale changes in the domestic economy. There is further debate about whether blacks as a whole are better off or worse off since the civil rights movement of the 1960s. Finally, and related to this, is the question of whether racial discrimination has lessened or grown (and the associated question of whether whites, particularly white workers, will ever change). An increasing number of liberals and putative leftists are very pessimistic. These pessimistic conclusions are unwarranted in the long run, but the situation is deeply contradictory, and the evidence is open to a wide variety of interpretations.

On the one hand, there have been vast changes as a direct result of the civil rights movement. Many changes in the harsh system of white supremacy that existed, particularly in the South before the 1960s, cannotsimplybe dismissed. The repressive and extremely violent system of racial oppression that existed in the southern rural areas before the 1960s, supported by the state (including the federal government), has been mostly dismantled. Many parts of the South seem to display far more interracial activities and institutions, from schools and neighborhoods to beaches, than much of the North. Certain white attitudes for the country as a whole, at least as expressed in public opinion polls, have changed substantially. By the 1980s, white Americans overwhelmingly responded favorably to integrated schools and transportation, equal access to jobs, open housing, and even the right of people of different races to intermarry. Several decades earlier, most whites rejected these views.

It is tempting to argue that much of this attitudinal change is superficial. Yet there have been some striking transformations. Before the 1960s, interracial couples in most parts of the country were subject to violent attack and universal condemnation. Today, interracial intimacy is just another piece of the complex landscape, belying the claim of many who look to the primacy of psychology and culture and argue that a deep-rooted sexual jealousy is at the root of racial discrimination. The civil rights movement successfully exerted enormous pressure to gain access to large areas of U.S. society previously unavailable to middle-class and working-class minorities. Educational opportunities opened up. Public employment opportunities grew. Many formerly all-white occupations that involved face-to-face contact with whites, including bank tellers, store clerks, and bus drivers, have become disproportionately nonwhite.

Because of these many changes, conservatives often argue that there are no more discriminatory barriers, only a debilitating ghetto culture and a lack of individual will. This argument is not new and has been asserted by conservatives and other bigots throughout U.S. history. Many liberals and social democrats, on the other hand, have minimized the existence of current discrimination and attributed the plight of minorities, particularly the most impoverished people in inner city areas, to structural changes and historic discrimination, problems that could conceivably be overcome by broad social-democratic policy initiatives.

Neither of these views can stand up to scrutiny. In a stagnant and highly dislocating capitalism, racist attitudes find fertile soil among those who feel most insecure. This phenomenon is visible all over the world. Without a solidaristic labor movement that takes aim at the cause of people's problems— the nature of capitalism itself—many will always go looking for scapegoats. The same public opinion polls that show many whites becoming more liberal on certain racial issues also show them having racist, factually incorrect, and hostile views about welfare and affirmative action, just as they did earlier about busing. Overwhelming numbers of whites in Louisiana voted in two major elections for David Duke, the former Ku Klux Klan leader and proto-fascist racist. Others across the nation might have done likewise, given the same chance.[5]

Despite the highly contradictory nature of the present period, which includes the enthusiastic, if often strained, acceptance of African Americans and other minorities in music, literature, sports, and other cultural spheres, there is much that signals retreat, often seemingly orchestrated by those in power. There is a tendency among many liberals to see this retreat as largely the province of the Republicans. This claim is simply wrong, since Republicans have no monopoly on racism, although they are clearly at the cutting edge of racial retreat.

The signals are striking. In 1995, when the new Republican majority Congress took over, they brought in sixty-five new pages, sixty-four of whom were white, the other an Asian American. In previous recent sessions, fifteen to twenty were Latino, African-American, or other minorities. Presidents Reagan and Bush made a concerted effort to reduce the number of black federal judges. From 1980 to 1992, only 2 of the 115 judges appointed to the U.S. Courts of Appeals were black (one of whom was Clarence Thomas). And, of course, there was the infamous Willie Horton episode in the 1988 campaign.

But if Republicans have been more guilty of playing the racist card, the Democrats, too, have made their symbolic, though necessarily more subtle (since they, unlike the Republicans, rely on a substantial black vote), appeals to white racism. Bill Clinton's snubbing of Jesse Jackson, for instance, and his calculated attack on hip-hop singer Sister Souljah at a Rainbow Coalition meeting during the 1992 campaign were clearly meant to reassure whites.

Beyond these signals of racism are the irreducible facts of the labor market. There can be little doubt that, despite the high-profile publicity given to affirmative action, women and racial minorities still face enormous discrimination in the labor market. In addition to the underrepresentation of minorities in upper-level working-class occupations and their disproportionate numbers at the lower end of the spectrum, the picture is even more extreme in professional and executive occupations.[6] For instance, 97 percent of senior-level male managers are white, while .6 percent are African-American, .3 percent Asian, and .4 percent Hispanic. African-American men with professional degrees earn only 79 percent of the amount earned by their white male counterparts, while African-American women with professional degrees earn only 60 percent. And on all fronts, there is ample evidence of overt discrimination in hiring practices, as well as the de facto discrimination that results from the fact much hiring is done through informal networks that are almost always all-white.[7]

Unions and Race Today

The number, location, and conditions of minority workers make one thing very clear: organizing minorities, as well as women, has to be at the center of the labor movement today. Not only should the movement's values require it, but the strength and success of labor depend on it. African Americans and other nonwhite minorities are a large and growing part of the labor force. They are heavily concentrated both in those occupations and industries that are already highly unionized and also in those areas where the labor force is expanding most rapidly: health care, services in general, government, communication, and transportation. Minority workers represent both a tremendous reservoir of support for labor unions and a great potential for new organizing.

A look at some statistics is revealing. In 1995, 14.2 percent of whites in the nonagricultural civilian labor force were members of unions, while 19.9 percent of African Americans were members. Hispanics and other minorities were slightly more unionized than whites. Surveys taken since the 1970s have also shown that black workers who were unorganized were more than twice as likely to say that they would join a union if one began to organize their workplace. Women, Hispanics, and southerners in nonunion workplaces also responded more favorably than white males in general.

Aside from the more complex reasons of political consciousness, there is an economic basis for these pro-union attitudes among minority workers. Economic studies have shown that unions have a dual effect on wages. On the one hand, they tend to raise the average wage significantly, thus raising the pay of all employees. On the other hand, they narrow the wage dispersion between the top and the bottom. Since women and minorities tend to be among the lowest paid, union organization tends to raise their wages by a greater proportion than those of white males. The AFL-CIO unions have increasingly become more diversified by sex and race, with women and racial minorities making up a larger percentage of their total membership. In addition, the best prospects for current organizing appear in those venues where women and minorities are heavily concentrated. These related factors are among the more important reasons why at least some unions have developed a more diverse leadership group, with increases in women and minorities in top, visible leadership positions.

The response of unions to continuing discrimination in the labor force, its changing demographic composition, and the changing complexion of union membership has varied greatly. Many unions, of course, have responded by doing nothing at all. They have neither attempted to organize new segments of the labor force nor altered the complexion of their leadership nor made any efforts to fight discrimination in the workplaces they represent or the society at large.

In other unions, the situation is different. Between 1960 and 1975, the public sector at the federal, state, and local level went from barely 5 percent to almost 40 percent of the workforce organized. A disproportionate number of the workers organized in this sector were female and minority. The main public-sector unions, including the postal unions, whose organization came much earlier, thus have not only a disproportionately minority and female membership, but also an increasingly diverse leadership body at both the national and local levels. These unions include the American Federation of Teachers (AFT), the National Education Association (NEA), the American Federation of Government Employees (representing federal workers), and the American Federation of State, County, and Municipal Employees (AFSCME), representing state and local government workers. Each of these unions has substantial representation of women and minorities in national and leadership bodies, with the NEA and the AFGE having had African-American presidents. AFSCME's executive council of thirty-three members in 1997 had nine women members and approximately a dozen minority-group members (of whom ten are African-American, one Asian-American, as far as can be detected from their names and pictures). Other unions, including most of the old CIO unions and almost all the old AFL unions, have been much slower to change their leadership composition, even when their membership base has changed substantially. The 1982 Civil Rights Commission report on equal employment opportunity and unions paints a fairly dismal picture, at both the national and local levels.

Yet the composition of leadership bodies and their degree of diversity, while important, hardly tell the whole story. In the battle to gain equal employment opportunities in the wake of the civil rights movement of the 1960s, very few unions—the exceptions being several former left-wing unions—took the lead in fighting for the rights of minority workers. Despite rhetorical stances in favor of civil rights, most unions, including the UAW, the Teamsters, and the Steelworkers, were the object of struggles by black worker caucuses and of massive antidiscrimination suits. In general, these unions defended existing discriminatory arrangements rather than playing a role in fighting against them. The best that unions during this period and at the present time have done is to make their leadership bodies more diverse.

Some unions, together with the new AFL-CIO leadership, have trumpeted this diversity. But, with the exception of certain campaigns of equal pay for equal work, their record in fighting for the rights of women and minorities on the job is rather weak. Little has been done to open up hiring and to integrate white male preserves, except in token numbers. The initial impetus for such change mandated by the federal government under Title VII of the 1964 and 1972 Civil Rights Acts has receded, and few unions are willing to pick up the baton.

There is little evidence of the type of campaigns that left unions waged during the 1930s and 1940s on behalf of nonwhite workers, or even the hiring and upgrading campaigns by the labor left in the early 1950s. Today's unions play little role in mass protests against housing and mortgage-lending discrimination, neighborhood and school issues, protests against police brutality, and other issues of importance to minority communities. Unions today have done little to combat the racial attacks on welfare and affirmative action, although unions on the West Coast have had an important involvement in fighting anti-immigrant hysteria.

In general, today's unions, with or without the current change in leadership at the top of the AFL-CIO, seem quite hesitant to confront issues of racial inequality. Even when unions themselves are directly victimized, they receive little publicity. An example of the latter is the selective racial hiring by management at the Cannon Mills textile plants in North Carolina. As black workers became increasingly pro-union, employers began hiring more whites and Hispanics. When Hispanics became pro-union, employers began hiring non-English-speaking Asians. Such racial tactics should be publicly exposed to the maximum degree. While the greater diversity of today's union leadership is certainly a change for the better, as other articles in this issue have suggested, their commitment to racial equality has been more a matter of talk than of action. The failure to organize the South is particularly symptomatic.

Race and the Politics of Labor

It should be clear from the history of the U.S. labor movement that the rise and fall of anti-racist unionism has been closely tied to the fate of the American left. Although there are no doubt many economic, social, and cultural reasons for the current situation, a major factor in determining the less than glorious recent record of the labor movement has been the legacy of the anti-left hysteria which dominated the post-War era. The retreat of the left in the unions, and the attempts by many union leaders to prove their "respectability," had lasting effects that have not been overcome to this day. They will not be overcome without a new political alignment in the labor movement.

The assertion of an aggressive, racially egalitarian policy by unions is virtually impossible as long as they stay tied to the Democratic Party. As the Democrats have moved more into line with racial conservatives (the ending of welfare, abandonment of affirmative action, support for more repressive anti-crime legislation, including more police and the extension of the death penalty), the AFL-CIO under the Sweeney leadership has extended its embrace of the Democratic Party. What the labor movement needs today is independent, aggressive, class-based action against racial subjugation, and that is impossible without a rejection of the Democratic Party.

It needs to be emphasized that the object of mobilizing class solidarities across racial divides is not only necessary to strengthen the anti-racist struggle for its own sake but also to strengthen the labor movement itself in its struggles against capital. A change in policy by unions is essential to achieving broader class goals, but it is also vital for the attainment of the minimal goals in which mainstream labor leaders claim to be interested. The labor movement will not be invigorated without aggressive appeals to and representation of the interests of female and minority workers.

Having a diverse face and stressing merely lowest-common-denominator issues without also confronting sexual and racial inequalities will not lead to a dynamic labor movement. And without stressing broad class issues, including the grievances of those most excluded and oppressed, the labor movement will never project the broad socially progressive image that will win the support of much of the working and middle classes. The historical record shows that no radical social change or broad class mobilization in the United States has ever had even a chance of success without doing this to some degree.

A revitalized labor movement must break with the business-dominated two-party system, take broad aim at the capitalist system, lead struggles around a wide range of class issues in society at large as well as at the workplace, and place the demands of racial and sexual equality at the top of its marching banner.

Notes

1. For a detailed discussion of this history, see my book, *The Color of Politics: Race, and the Mainsprings of American Politics from Colonial Times to the Present* (New York: New Press 1997). The book should also be consulted for more complete citations of other works on which I have drawn.

2. For a discussion of left-led unions, see my "Race and the CIO: The Possibilities for Racial Egalitarianism During the 1930s and 1940s," *International Labor and Working-Class History* (Fall 1993).

3. Goldfield, "Race and the CIO."

4. *Statistical Abstract of the United States, 1995* (Washington, D.C.: U.S. Department of Commerce), 400-401.

5. For more on this, see my *The Color of Politics*.

6. See the Glass Ceiling Commission report: *Good For Business: Making Full Use of the Nation's Human Capital* (Washington, D.C.: U.S. Government Printing Office, 1995), 12.

7. On hiring practices, see George Galster, "Polarization, Race, and Place," *North Carolina Law Review* (June 1993); and Harry Cross *et al.*, *Employer Hiring Practices: Differential Treatment of Hispanics and Anglo Job Seekers* (Washington, D.C.: The Urban Institute Press, 1990).

Class, Community, and Empire: Toward an Anti-imperialist Strategy for Labor

Eric Mann

The left and labor—will they ever meet again? In my view, new political movements in the United States, in explicit opposition to imperialism, offer the best chance for a refusion of the socialist project with the workers' movements. The central strategic premise of this proposal is the construction of a broad anti-imperialist united front led by the multiracial, multinational working class that recognizes the right of self-determination of oppressed nations and peoples both inside and outside the United States.

The U.S. labor bureaucracy has a history of complicity with U.S. imperialism. This was especially true during the Cold War, but the collaboration with imperialism has not ended. Today the Clinton administration is building its foreign policy strategy on two explicitly stated objectives: the penetration of U.S. capitalism into every market in the world—the destruction of what is left of self-determination in third world nations under a repackaged "open door policy"—and the rebuilding of NATO into a world military alliance to police those economic arrangements.

Yet organized labor has not opposed this new imperialist tactical plan, and there is a clear connection between transnational capitalist corporations, the Democratic Party, and the AFL-CIO bureaucracy. This became apparent at the 1997 AFL-CIO convention. President Clinton, knowing that many delegates opposed his fast-track proposals for the next round of NAFTA, went on the offensive. He justified his trade policies to the delegates by explaining, "This is how 4 percent of the world's people can continue to hold 22 percent of the world's wealth." To its credit, the Sweeney wing of the AFL-CIO united with House Minority Leader Richard Gephardt to defeat the fast track. But overall, the convention delegates engaged in a love fest—yelling "Four More

Years" to a president who had just thrown women and children into the streets to "end welfare as we know it."

Where was the left in the AFL-CIO? Where were the insurgent demonstrations against Clinton, the motions to withhold support for his candidacy, the floor fights over U.S.-supported torture in Indonesia, and the Clinton administration's refusal to sign virtually every binding ecological and human rights agreement at the UN? Where was the criticism, let alone the outrage, that once even liberals would have expressed?[1]

U.S. imperialism's far-reaching and aggressive actions are shaping the entire context of the world today, from corporate board rooms to factories, workplaces, and communities throughout the world. It is penetrating nation states and mass organizations, and colonizing minds by means of a pervasive culture industry. So analyzing domestic class struggles as component parts of an anti-imperialist struggle has never been more important than it is today in the last remaining superpower. Yet the U.S. left has never been less conscious that imperialism is the context in which strategies for class struggle must be constructed.

Debates on the left about whether struggles should be local, national, or international are missing the point. There are obviously many sites of struggle: the workplace, the community, the nation, and the international arena. But in today's conditions, more than ever, it is impossible to detach even the most local struggle from its global setting, and the real test of a political strategy for labor is its capacity to integrate the various levels of struggle. There can be no effective color-blind class struggle, and certainly none that is complicit with, or even neutral toward, imperialist domination. This is especially true in the U.S., where domestic class struggles occur within the framework of racism and national oppression.

Again, the message here is a strategic one, as much as an ethical one. Just as struggles in the workplace spill over into the surrounding community, even the most local domestic struggles today are likely to implicate much larger international forces, and workers are likely to need the solidarity and support of other labor movements in other countries. Besides, even to forge alliances within their own local communities, especially in typically multiethnic communities in the United States, workers also have to recognize that community support involves a more profound understanding of and empathy for the struggles of others, often far beyond their own borders. It is ultimately suicidal for the organized labor movement to treat other working people as competitors and to pursue their objectives at the expense of other workers, at home or abroad.

From Workplace to Empire: The Case of GM in Van Nuys

The benefit of an anti-imperialist strategy was demonstrated in United Auto Workers (UAW) Local 645's Campaign to Keep GM Van Nuys Open.[2] From

1981 to 1987, as an auto assembler at the General Motors plant in Van Nuys, California, and a member of the League of Revolutionary Struggle (Marxist-Leninist), I served as the coordinator of this campaign to stop GM from permanently laying off 5,000 workers, of whom 2,500 were Latino, 750 were black, and 750 were women. We organized perhaps the only successful campaign to prevent a plant closing in the United States by uniting the multiracial, multinational working class and the oppressed nationality movements rooted in L.A.'s black and Latino communities to take on the transnational General Motors Corporation. Our main tactic was to project the economic struggle into the political and ideological realm, initiating the threat of a preemptive boycott of GM products in Los Angeles if General Motors ever closed the plant. We created the Labor/Community Coalition to Keep GM Van Nuys Open and forced then-GM president F. James McDonald to negotiate with a political movement—located in but not confined to a labor union local—and kept the plant open for ten years.

Throughout this period our strategy was in direct conflict with the strategy of the leadership of the UAW international. During the 1980s, the UAW and most of the Democratic Party leadership explained the massive loss of unionized jobs as a bitter but necessary "downsizing" so that the U.S. could compete in the brave new world of Japanese, German, and Mexican imports. As we tried to organize a movement against the automakers, the international countered with a war against the Japanese. At the 1986 UAW convention, large posters proclaimed: "Unemployment—Made in Japan." UAW workers bashed Toyotas in parking lots, and at the height of the frenzy, I feared for the safety of Mark Masaoka, one of the most popular left organizers in the plant. We were able to convince the most progressive workers in the plant that at that time in history, the central issue of the class struggle was to directly challenge anti-Japanese xenophobia in the working class. We explained to our co-workers, often in fear for our physical safety, that the international union was using the anti-Japanese campaign to deflect the struggle from the U.S. capitalists and, through more than a year of organizing, were able to at least beat back that wave of mass and reactionary hysteria. Who would argue that avoiding that struggle and focusing instead on "shop floor" or self-interested campaigns alone could have unified the working class?

The integration of rank-and-file insurgency in the union local, black and Chicano national liberation movements, and an anti-imperialist strategy with left leadership, led to one of the labor movement's few victories in the 1980s. Even then, the opposing strategy of labor-management cooperation between the UAW international and General Motors and their joint attacks against our local led to the eventual closing of the plant in 1992.

The L.A. Bus Riders Union: Multiple Sites of Class Struggle

In response to the situation in Van Nuys, we organized in 1989 the Labor/Community Strategy Center, a multiracial "think tank-act tank," first, to continue the Campaign to Keep GM Van Nuys Open in a context independent from and therefore more protected from the repression of the UAW international and, second, to expand this experiment in new forms of multiracial labor-community working-class insurgencies to other sites of struggle against transnational corporations and the capitalist state.[3]

One of the Labor/Community Strategy Center's test-case campaigns to build the interconnections between class, community, and anti-imperialist struggle is an experimental political working-class union, the Bus Riders Union/Sindicato de Pasajeros in Los Angeles, a mass, antiracist organization fighting against the government for civil rights in the form of a first-class, clean fuel, public transportation system in the most air-polluted, auto-dependent region in the United States. The BRU was organized from the ground up by activists trained at the Strategy Center's National School for Strategic Organizing: Kikanza Ramsey, Chris Mathis, Rita Burgos, Martin Hernandez, and Ted Robertson, who have now been joined by BRU members Lupe Rivera and Mari Aguirre. The Union/Sindicato is a new form of working-class union—a mass political organization of low-wage workers, particularly women, people of color, and immigrants in both manufacturing and service industries as well as the most unemployed and underemployed sectors—focusing on mass campaigns against transnational corporations, the corporatization and privatization of government, the racism of domestic public policy, and increasingly, the role of the United States in the third world.

The BRU is a democratic organization. It is run by an elected Planning Committee of twelve members, and the grassroots direct action work is led by an Organizing Committee of another fifteen members. We have an active general membership of 200 people, of whom 50 to 75 usually attend monthly meetings. We have a dues-paying membership of 1,500, and at least 35,000 bus riders read our news leaflets, wear our buttons, and identify as BRU members.

The immediate focus of our class and race struggle is our demand that virtually all the Los Angeles Metropolitan Transit Authority's $3 billion annual budget go to rebuild the bus system, and that the MTA place a moratorium on all construction of light rail and subways. This "Billions for Buses, Fight Transit Racism" campaign is based on the analysis that the bus system, serving 94 percent of all the MTA's riders, is a segregated, discriminated-against system, with 350,000 riders, most of whom are from minorities, yet it receives only 30 percent of all MTA's funds, while the rail system, serving a small, suburban, more affluent, and chiefly white ridership—and the profit objectives profit objectives of contractors and developers—steals 70 percent of the MTA's funds to serve only 6 percent of its riders.[4]

Sometimes there is the sense that the work of the left is inherently outside mass consciousness and only in the realm of criticism, whereas the Riordans, Clintons, and Sweeneys are in the "real world." In this case, however, the Bus Riders Union is understood as even broader than its name. It is a very militant, visible, influential, and political force fighting for the rights of the low-income working class, Latinos, blacks, Asians, the elderly, students, the disabled, the unemployed, and welfare recipients in a world urban center. We have managed to develop a high-visibility media strategy, with frequent features in the *Washington Post,* the *Christian Science Monitor,* and ABC's *World News Tonight;* weekly and sometimes daily stories in every major L.A. newspaper and television station; our own guerrilla postering campaign; and a forthcoming documentary by the Academy Award-winning cinematographer Haskell Wexler.

To achieve our goals, the BRU has used a number of tactics. We are known as a militant organization that engages in direct action, such as taking over intersections to block traffic for hours, and sit-ins in which many of our members have been arrested. In addition, as a result of a civil rights lawsuit, we became the "bargaining agent" for L.A.'s bus riders. Through a consent decree we signed with the MTA to settle our lawsuit, they agreed to major improvements for L.A.'s bus riders—reduced bus fares, many new buses, reduced overcrowding, and service to new areas to overcome the racially discriminatory impact of L.A.'s separate and unequal transportation system. Moreover, the courts established the BRU as the "class representatives" for 350,000 bus riders, functioning in an adversarial relationship to the MTA for the next decade in an institutionalized Joint Working Group (JWG), of which I am co-chair in tandem with a representative of the MTA. The JWG meets weekly to struggle over future bus routes, funding for bus stations, reducing overcrowding, and every other aspect of the future of mass transportation in Los Angeles. Needless to say, our new role as bargaining agent has made the construction of democratic, working-class structures of initiative and accountability within our own union even more crucial.

The Bus Riders Union/Trade Union Connection

The Bus Riders Union is unique, because it is a community-based, regional political movement with strong support for, and participation in, the trade union movement. We are experimenting with multiple sites of working-class organization.

The BRU/Sindicato has many members, many of whom are Latino immigrants, who are also active in struggles of their traditional labor unions: the Hotel and Restaurant Workers, UNITE, and SEIU's Justice for Janitors. While we sometimes have differences with the local union leadership over their willingness to take on, for example, powerful Latino politicians who are good on most union issues but reactionary on public services issues, the BRU's well-publicized fights for late-night bus service for janitors, maids, and garment workers, and our own members' participation in those unions, has led to a constructive and often very positive alliance.

Nonetheless, on almost every major political issue facing the working class as a whole (for example, immigration, affirmative action, crime, police, prisoners rights, and tax policy), the BRU often takes more progressive political positions than the existing trade union leadership and many look to the BRU as an alternative and competing political center to the AFL-CIO.[5]

For example, the Los Angeles County Federation of Labor and Hotel and Restaurant Workers endorsed conservative Republican, pro-corporate Mayor Richard Riordan (just as the AFL-CIO endorsed Riordan's twin, Rudy Giuliani, in New York) on the basis of the self-defeating, realpolitik argument that they were "the only game in town." The BRU did not endorse either Riordan or Senator Tom Hayden, out of our general neutrality about the two dominant parties, but also out of our many disagreements with Hayden.

Similarly, the BRU has taken a strong position against the privatization of bus lines, while the United Transportation Union (UTU) has signed contracts allowing the MTA to privatize up to 13 lines, and in their last contract, signed what we call a "self-privatization" agreement in which the UTU will compete with nonunion, privatized bus companies and, if necessary, work for significantly lower wages to keep the jobs in the union. Several militant bus drivers approached the Strategy Center, and we helped them organize a rank-and-file caucus to oppose privatization and more explicitly ally with the BRU.

At the same time, the BRU has excellent relationships with the rank-and-file bus drivers, members of the United Transportation Union. Our organizers do most of their organizing right on the buses, and the first order of business is always to check in with the drivers, who are usually harried, with buses so overcrowded they can barely drive, let alone think. Most bus drivers love the BRU—we are, after all, fighting for more buses, more drivers, more mechanics, more maintenance people, clean fuels, better wheelchair lifts, and (of course) more jobs! Many drivers take the microphone and tell the passengers, "The Bus Riders Union is here. Give them your attention, they are fighting for all of us." Still, for many years the leadership of the UTU refused to meet with us. According to their more militant members, it is because "they are threatened that you are fighting harder for the drivers than they are."

Another example occurred in our organizing work in Wilmington, California, where the Strategy Center built a watchdog environmental organization to fight for the public health of a very low-income, Latino working-class community exposed to astounding levels of toxic emissions. In the struggle against Texaco and other polluting refineries, we made many overtures to ally with the Oil, Chemical, and Atomic Workers Union, only to have them oppose our campaign and even threaten to march against us, on the grounds that if the community had the right to know about the chemicals to which they were exposed and demanded a massive reduction in toxics, the company might shut down the refinery and they would lose jobs.

We have had high-visibility battles with the bureaucratic leadership of Service Employees International Union (SEIU) Local 660, the L.A. county workers' union, when we opposed their raiding of bus-eligible funds from the state legislature—which pitted one social service against another. SEIU's leadership, in a desperate effort to find funds for deteriorating hospitals, refused our offer to work with them to demand new taxes on corporations and a reduction in prison construction. Instead, they tried to raid bus funds, thinking the bus riders were a weaker constituency than the prison guards' unions and the large corporations. The Bus Riders Union countered with a "Don't Tear Us Apart Campaign," arguing that our members needed more funds for both hospitals and bus service, and chastising SEIU's leadership and the Democratic Party for orchestrating a divisive campaign in which either outcome hurt working people. We were able to kill most of the bill and reduce the raid from $350 million to $50 million. Then the courts overturned the entire bill as an illegal raid on transportation funds. These splits are tragic: the refinery workers are exposed to hazardous chemicals, and the county workers are now forced to conciliate with a new wave of privatization schemes in a desperate effort to keep their jobs—when a more militant, pro-active strategy was offered to them and is still available.

From Local Class Struggle to Anti-Imperialist Internationalism

A great deal of our work goes into struggles for the daily class needs of our members—on-time bus service, workable wheelchair lifts, dramatic reductions in overcrowding. This focus on the daily needs of the low-income working class may seem to make us very similar to a traditional, albeit more than typically militant and democratic, labor union. However, as we grew and expanded, it became clear that our daily class struggles intersect with larger political issues, especially those revolving around U.S. imperialism. This gave rise to intense internal conflicts.

The first political challenge came in the debate over immigrant rights, when the Republicans, in 1996, put on the ballot their latest in a series of racist propositions, this one cleverly called the "Save our State" initiative, Prop. 187, that would force the state to eliminate the medical, educational, and food benefits of "illegal immigrants."

The Democratic Party and the trade union bureaucrats tried to find ways to go on record against the initiative while downplaying their opposition, focusing instead on the election of Kathleen Brown, running for governor against Pete Wilson, one of the sponsors of the initiative. The Brown camp, along with the Latino and trade union establishment, put forth the view that "187 is not the best way to solve the immigration problem," while liberal Democratic Senators Boxer and Feinstein proposed to criminalize the international mobility of labor by placing more INS agents at the Mexican border. The Strategy Center wrote a polemic, "Immigrant Rights and Wrongs," in which we argued for full rights for immigrants and chastised many of the labor unions for conciliating with nativism in a pathetic effort to elect Democrats on the backs of immigrants. But how would our BRU members react?

In October 1996, as many immigrants' rights groups organized a "No on 187" rally, several of our Salvadoran and Mexican immigrant members initiated a motion that we organize a large BRU delegation to the march. This led to a turning-point debate in the development of our organization. Other members, mainly black and white, argued that while they opposed 187, we should not get involved in divisive issues, in that "immigrant rights has nothing to do with improving the bus system." Some Latino members threatened not to work with a Bus Riders Union that defined its cause so narrowly as to turn its back on the human rights of its own members. Other white and black members implied that if we did endorse the march, they would leave. Pat Elmore, a black woman from a communist and black nationalist background, argued that if the BRU turned our back on any member, it didn't deserve to exist. She had not risked her life in the fight for civil rights to listen to black people attack Latinos for "stealing their jobs."

I watched the room as the votes and minds of many members changed. The final vote was seventy-five in favor of endorsing the march and ten against. Most of the members who voted against the motion never came back. But the organization was shaped and, in my view, saved by that vote—it represented a commitment to working-class politics beyond immediate self-interest. Now we have principles of unity as well as the bylaws of the Bus Riders Union/Sindicato de Pasajeros that include immigrant rights. The entire organization is going through a major expansion of our international understanding and disposition of forces.

In 1997, we invited Jorge Cuellar Valdez, the international representative of the independent, left labor union, SUTAUR 100, in Mexico City, to speak at a mass BRU meeting in which we discussed the struggle against privatization in Los Angeles and Mexico City. Soon afterward, Martin Hernandez and I went to Mexico City to attend an international meeting, sponsored by SUTAUR, against privatization and neoliberalism, in which we worked with forces all over the world to stop the Mexican government's efforts to break that amazing union.

At that meeting, in which every independent union in Mexico was represented, along with representatives from the Zapatistas (EZLN), the lack of
support from the AFL-CIO was painfully apparent. In my remarks to the
plenary session, I criticized the Clinton administration for its strong pressure
on the PRI to privatize the bus system and other public services to protect the
interests of U.S. transnational investors. I also criticized the AFL-CIO for its
lack of intervention in this important struggle (it had sent only a rather pathetic
letter of support from Linda Chavez Thompson) and asked why the AFL-CIO
did not organize a demonstration and bring at least hundreds of delegates to
this important international meeting—when a real-life struggle was in the
balance. Several of the Trotskyist organizers felt that while my statements were
true, they were not tactically appropriate. They explained "off the record" that
I had no idea how hard it had been just to get that simple letter of endorsement.

That day, as we brought a delegation to the Zocolo in Mexico City to
demand the release of eight SUTAUR leaders who had been imprisoned for
one year for their refusal to go along with privatizing the bus system, our bus
was surrounded by Mexican police, and we were detained for two hours—until
long after our press conference. That night, at a rally of more than 25,000 bus
drivers and their families, we participated in a truly international event of
solidarity. This time a battalion of more than 2,000 Mexican police attacked
our demonstration, at which time we took to the streets in an orderly and
militant extension of the protest. Throughout the time the police were chasing
us, I asked myself a question I understood the answer to only too well—where
the hell are the U.S. labor unions?

Within a week, after more than a year on strike, the SUTAUR movement
had to accept a massive defeat. With its leaders still in jail, and its members
literally starved back to work, it agreed to disband its labor union and accept
the government's offer of reconstituting itself as a workers' "cooperative" to
run three bus lines—with the loss of half its members and its union altogether.
Even then, it took the election of the moderate progressive Cuauhtémoc
Cárdenas in Mexico City's federal district to restore the union's seized treasury
and finally release its leaders from prison.

In addition to our participation in the struggles of Mexican workers, we are
involved in other international actions. Rita Burgos just returned from Cuba,
and we are trying to find resources to spend more time on antiblockade work.
Many Strategy Center and BRU members are working with the National
Committee for Democracy in Mexico (NCDM), focusing on support for the
Chiapas struggle, and many of the NCDM members are joining the BRU, both
as bus riders and because of our politics.[6]

At the Strategy Center, we are engaging in discussions with organizers
throughout the United States about campaigns based on a working-class
internationalism: the repeal of the Helms-Burton Act, in which President

Clinton allowed Congress to tighten the embargo on Cuba; bills to oppose all Congressional contributions to the International Monetary Fund and reverse the structural adjustment plans for third world nations, including the forgiving of third world debt. We are trying as explicitly as we can to formulate the entire theory of our work in an international context.

Conclusion

The benefits of empire run deep, and we all have to confront our own ideological and material stakes in the existing order of things. But that kind of searching criticism is what a transformative left politics is supposed to represent. Progressives, socialists, and trade union, civil rights, and community activists who desire a new vision for a left working-class politics will have to combine opposition ti imperialism with commitment to labor if they hope to advance either cause.

Notes

1. See Eric Mann and Lian Hurst Mann, "How to Stop the Clinton Assault" in *Z Magazine,* September 1997, and an expanded version in *AhoraNow* no. 3 (October 1997), in which we argue that the frontal opposition to Clinton's center-right transnational capitalist politics was the greatest challenge to a new left.

2. For a detailed discussion of this struggle against GM, see Eric Mann, *Taking on General Motors: A Case Study of the UAW Campaign to Keep GM Van Nuys Open* (Los Angeles: UCLA Center for Labor Research and Education, 1989).

3. For a more complete understanding of the work of the Labor/Community Strategy Center see Eric Mann, *LA's Lethal Air: New Strategies for Policy, Organizing, and Action* (Los Angeles: Strategy Center Publications, 1990); Urban Strategies Group, *Reconstructing Los Angeles—and U.S. Cities—From the Bottom Up* (Los Angeles: Strategy Center Publications, 1993); Urban Strategies Group, *Immigrant Rights—And Wrongs* (Los Angeles: Strategy Center Publications, 1994); and *AhoraNow,* the periodical publication of the Labor/Community Strategy Center.

4. See Eric Mann, *A New Vision for Urban Transportation* (Los Angeles: Strategy Center Publications, 1996), and Eric Mann and Chris Mathis, "Bus Rider Organizers Meet the Law: Legal Tactics for Left Strategy," *AhoraNow* no. 4 (1997).

5. See Eric Mann and Kikanza Ramsey, "The Left Choice is the Best Choice," *AhoraNow* no. 1 (1996).

6. In the hope of forging international alliances, we participated in the Paris conference on the 150th anniversary of the Communist Manifesto, in May 1998. See my paper for that conference, "The Struggle Against Imperialism is the Key to Socialism's Reconstruction," in *Le Manifeste Communiste: 150 ans apres,* 5e dossier (March 1998), reprinted in *AhoraNow* no. 5 (1998).

Labor Education in the Maelstrom of Class Struggle

Bill Fletcher, Jr.

Labor education is unfolding within the context of dramatic changes in organized labor and the conditions of class struggle. The assumption of AFL-CIO leadership by John J. Sweeney, Richard Trumka, and Linda Chavez-Thompson must be set against the collapse of the truce between sections of northern and western capital and the leaders of organized labor in the period after the Second World War; against the end of the Cold War, and its implications; and against activity at the base by left and progressive trade unionists in local unions, central labor councils, and pro-worker, community-based organizations.

Although there has been some debate over whether the term "truce," "social contract," or "social compact" appropriately characterizes labor-management relations in the post-Second World War period, it is clear that the nature of labor-management interaction shifted dramatically after the war. After a series of defeats and the purging of the left, the relationship between organized labor and northern and western capital changed. Organized labor conceded to management the control of production, sales, and basic hiring decisions, while correspondingly, it accepted that its own role was to protect wages, hours, and working conditions. Labor-management conflict was moved into the arena of industrial jurisprudence, and workplace injustices were resolved through legalistic channels.

None of this means that class struggle ceased. Rather, the leadership of organized labor in the United States negotiated itself into respectability with leaders of northern and western capital, content to accept the confinement of class struggle to industrial enterprise conflicts.[1] In exchange for accepting this role and for advancing the objectives of the Cold War, the leaders of organized labor believed that they had a permanent deal with capital so that the living standard of unionized workers would improve, tied to improvements in productivity.

By the 1970s, the truce had unraveled. With its economic hegemony challenged by increasing competition, economic problems heightened by the Vietnam War, a decline in the rate of productivity and growth, the oil embargo, and the 1973 recession, U.S. capital faced a "profit crisis." In response,

110

corporate America initiated an offensive against labor. Waves of plant closings and the shifting of industry to the South and Southwest became characteristic of the 1970s. Shortly thereafter, the growth of Thatcherism in Britain and Reaganism in the United States signaled a new approach of major sections of capital on matters ranging from economic recovery and development to relations with organized labor. Though not recognized at first, these ideologies were symptomatic of a global realignment within capitalism that came to be known as neoliberalism.

Unfortunately, organized labor did almost nothing to resist. By the early 1980s, most sections of organized labor were willing to admit that the situation was deteriorating, but they were, by and large, unwilling or unable to understand the depth of the crisis and the terms of a possible response. As neoliberalism grew in both scope and intensity, organized labor declined and, with it, the political influence that its leaders had taken for granted since the end of the Second World War.

The full implications of this became evident with two events: the end of the Cold War and the 1994 midterm U.S. Congressional elections. With the end of the Cold War went any illusion of a payback to organized labor for its faithful service to U.S. foreign policy and the objectives of corporate America. The midterm Congressional elections and the Republican capture of both houses of Congress shocked the leaders of organized labor. Their political strategy had proven itself to be not only ineffective but, on the whole, incompetent. This reversal of the political situation was acute, given the new batch of Republicans and their virulent, antilabor, antisocial, neoliberal program.

These factors helped to influence the discussions and struggle at the top. They also shaped important strategic debates, most clearly illustrated by the now famous exchange between contending AFL-CIO presidential candidates Tom Donahue and John Sweeney, which raised the difference between building bridges and blocking bridges.[2] It would be incorrect, however, to see the changes as only the result of external factors influencing movement at the top of organized labor. Years of struggle at the base, often led by forces on the left, contributed significantly to changes at the top. There are numerous examples of this, including the multiyear struggle against concessions in Watsonville, California, by the largely Latino cannery members of a Teamsters local; the mid-1980s formation of groups such as the National Rank and File Against Concessions initiative, sparked by the struggle of UFCW, Local P-9; the *Labor Notes* magazine conferences and networks; the various pro-Jesse Jackson initiatives among labor activists; and the creation of groups such as Jobs with Justice. In addition, several Central Labor Councils came under the leadership of progressive forces, thereby helping to influence both labor solidarity and political activity.

The existence and interaction of these various forces and factors helped to propel the struggle which had been simmering in the AFL-CIO. It would be a mistake to assume that the Sweeney-led forces were united behind much more than the need for a change. Although the New Voices ticket had a platform that called for greater resources for organizing and out-front labor activism, the unions and union leaders endorsing the New Voices ticket had a variety of reasons for looking for a new direction. Indeed, the reverse was true as well. Some of the forces that supported Donahue would have been expected to be on the side favoring change. In either case, the sides were set, but they were not consistent, and therefore were unstable. Nevertheless, they were sufficient to lead to one of the most significant changes organized labor has witnessed since the heyday of the CIO.

The Challenges Facing Labor Education

Today there may be a window of opportunity for the left. Declining union membership and the capitalist offensive have resulted in a willingness on the part of more centrist forces in organized labor to unite with sections of the left, as well as to experiment with alternative approaches to trade unionism. Labor education can be part of this process. There are four major areas in which labor education can be both useful and timely: leadership development, organizing, class consciousness, and the relationship between college-based and union-based labor education.

Leadership Development. Leadership development today must do two different but related things: (1) develop and consolidate a new echelon of labor union leadership and (2) open up accessible pathways for women and people of color to enter the leadership of organized labor.

At both the national/international[3] and local levels, organized labor is paying a very dear price for its failure to attend to developing new leaders. The top leadership of most national unions came of age in the 1950s and 1960s, a period of labor decline. The form of trade unionism that they learned, practiced, and taught—industrial jurisprudence, anticommunism, and traditional activities in the political-legislative arena—discouraged progressives from participation and are of limited use today. Local unions are more open to younger and more militant leaders, many of whom entered the labor movement from antiwar, civil rights, and women's struggles. Unfortunately, these new leaders often lacked administrative and managerial skills or got so involved in the day-to-day work of their unions and Central Labor Councils that they had no time to develop long-range progressive strategies. Many became demoralized or suffered burnout; without a supportive organized labor left, they drifted or became independent operators.

The civil rights movement demanded that labor open its doors to workers of color, but most unions were slow to respond. Some inroads were made in the 1960s and 1970s, but even these were limited. Workers of color and women workers were often appointed to positions as heads of civil and human rights committees or women's committees, which tended to represent both victory, because there was some measure of inclusion, and marginalization, because many of these positions had a limited role.

Some national/international unions began facing the question of leadership development by the 1980s. The example of the Service Employees International Union (SEIU) is noteworthy here. Spurred by women activists and activists of color and supported by then-president John Sweeney, SEIU decided at its 1992 convention to make leadership development one of its priorities, and a series of programs was established.

The SEIU Leadership Development Program (LDP) included an Officer Program (a weeklong program for leaders of local unions with more than 2,500 members; a weekend program for local unions with fewer than 2,500 members); a Staff Enrichment Program (a semi-apprenticeship and mentoring program for local union organizing directors); a Unity in Action program (study groups for rank and file members); a Collective Bargaining Internship Program (to train bargainers); Leadership Roundtables (two-day discussion circles for leaders of larger locals); and the Regional Women's Conferences and Civil and Human Rights Conferences. Through these the union was able to do something that had hitherto been quite difficult: bring together different departments in SEIU to coordinate a portion of their education and training objectives.

Several aspects of the LDP stand out. First, the LDP, by allowing local union leaders to shape the discussion, challenged the accepted view of leadership education. In the week-long officer training course, a major debate took place about whether the program should begin with an overview of the economic situation facing workers today. One side took the position that local leaders wanted skills and did not want abstract, academic lectures and discussions. The other side argued that the labor movement was in a defensive posture not, in the main, because local leaders had insufficient skills, but rather because the movement lacked strategy, vision, and analysis, the result of which was the undermining of labor's ability to fight back. The first week-long officer program did start with an excellent overview delivered by the president of the Economic Policy Institute, Jeff Faux. And every one of the participants expressed the view that more such discussions were needed. This experience was very different from prior educational programs, and some participants became outspoken advocates for labor education within SEIU.

A second important feature of the LDP was the politics involved in getting the program off the ground. Perhaps the biggest issue faced by labor education, particularly since the anticommunist purges in the late 1940s, is fear. The purges chilled labor education in the union movement. There was less experimentation, and an entire set of issues and subjects, such as capitalism, was off-limits to any rigorous analysis or discussion. Local union leaders were also often fearful that labor education was actually a means for the international to train insurgents who could run against them. Unfortunately, it is not uncommon in the labor movement to have leaders who are afraid of an educated membership.

These fears created difficulties for the Leadership Development Program. A program run by a national/international union faces the suspicion that its purpose is to overthrow local union leaders, so a pilot program had to begin with locals that were willing to cooperate and serve as an example to others.

The content of the programs admittedly pushed the envelope, at least by labor movement standards. The analysis tended to be left of center, and in all cases, the programs promoted debate. Although the participants in the programs tended to engage in more vigorous exchanges than might have been common in many other unions, the reality is that a new practice was being introduced that was not entirely comfortable for all. Some participants continued to hold back their views, particularly if SEIU staff were present. There were those who wondered, sometimes aloud, whether they were being set up to speak their minds and then later to be repressed.

A third and critical aspect of the LDP is that it helped to catalyze other changes in SEIU's educational efforts. Increasingly, education came to be factored into other programs of the union. The LDP helped to bring into being the Local Union Transformation Project, an effort to (1) identify, analyze, and popularize initiatives that were already being taken by local unions to alter their representational practices in a manner that saved resources and (2) work with willing local unions to help them place greater resources into organizing while not abandoning representation. This was a conscious effort to deal with some of the structural changes necessary for organized labor to address its own crisis.

Organizing. Unfortunately, organizing has seldom been a central part of labor education. Now the challenge for union educational programs is to reorient themselves to focus on organizing. The connection between organizing and education falls into three main spheres: (1) membership education, (2) organizational development (or what is currently referred to as "changing to organize"), and (3) organizer training.

Pro-organizing membership education is different from the skills-based training of organizers in that it aims to promote a discussion among the members of the importance and need for organizing. This kind of education has often been ignored by trade union leaders and educators, but there have been some successful examples, such as the Construction Organizing Membership Education Training (COMET) program in the building trades. This program, developed by the International Brotherhood of Electrical Workers

(IBEW) and Cornell University's labor school in New York City, sparked a membership discussion of why the building trades unions were losing density and what steps were needed to halt this decline. The success of COMET in the IBEW led to its use in other building trades unions, and it has become central to some of their major organizing programs, including their current efforts at multi-union organizing in Las Vegas.

The achievements of COMET encouraged the development of the Membership Education for Mobilization and Organizing (MEMO). Although MEMO began as the nonconstruction version of COMET, it evolved into one of the products that the AFL-CIO and affiliates are using as part of their Common Sense Economics Education. The Common Sense Economics Education program aims to promote dialogue among the members about corporate capitalism, the attack on workers, and the necessity for resistance. MEMO and the other materials produced in this project have encouraged a discussion about organizing and the need to conduct a different kind of grass roots political action.

Pro-organizing membership education is new, and it has aroused a fair degree of controversy. Some argue that such efforts are unnecessary, that the main problem in moving local and national unions to devote greater resources to organizing is a lack of will on the part of the leaders. But labor leaders do not exist apart from a social base. It is true that local and national/international union leaders must have the will to undertake organizing, but such efforts can be stalled or halted if the base is not there to support them. Pro-organizing membership education enters here, therefore, as a means of engaging the members in a discussion about their situations and what it will take to rebuild worker power in the United States.

It is only recently—since the 1980s—that several national-international unions have begun paying greater attention to organizational issues in general and strategic planning in particular. But the problem is that strategic planning can mean many things, not all of which contribute to building unions committed to organizing. Though the AFL-CIO and some of its affiliates have begun speaking about changing to organize, this effort is in its infancy.

It is worth giving attention to the sources of some of the difficulties unions are experiencing as they try to reorganize themselves, that is, as they try to change to organize. Today's union movement represents the fusion of the industrial unionism that grew out of the 1930s and the craft unionism that preceded it. Organizations were either created or transformed in order to deal with the capitalist industrial—"Fordist"—economy and a corresponding form of labor-management relations in the New Deal and postwar period. Unfortunately, this transformation included the purges in the late 1940s, which, more than anything else, stifled substantive internal union democracy. Anyone showing the slightest inclination to dissent could be quickly smeared as a "red," or just a troublemaker. This is not to say that the pre-purge union movement was particularly democratic, but at least there existed an organizational culture that permitted far more scope for debate.

Post-purge unionism also solidified a brand of business unionism commonly described as service model unionism. This model relied primarily on formal grievance procedures, depending not on rank-and-file activity but on union staff to handle all forms of workplace injustice. This brand of business unionism was reinforced by the organizational structure of the unions. External organizers, for example, did not hold a significant position in the organization, whereas "business agents" did. Staff received accolades for their handling of grievances and arbitrations more than they did for successfully organizing campaigns. Political action was reserved for either the top leadership or a political action committee, but rarely was it a field of activity for the membership, except when it was time to vote. A form of organization was created which, in essence, said to the members " . . . this is what we will do for you . . . these are the services that we will offer . . . we ask nothing of you . . . in fact, we ask only that you attend union meetings (if you can), but we do not need or want your involvement in the internal affairs of the union. . . ."

The most important consequence of this approach was the further bureaucratization of the unions. The principal objective of the union-as-organization focused more and more on getting along better with the employer and enforcing the collective bargaining agreement, rather than ensuring that the members were represented.[4] The other aspect of this, of course, was the decline in external organizing, with the corresponding decline in the percentage of workers represented by organized labor.

Given this history, the current concern with organizational change has pluses and minuses. The pluses are obvious: without significant attention to organizational change and development, organized labor will move closer to oblivion. Thus, a willingness to be creative and experimental is essential, particularly in response to the changes in strategy by neoliberal capital. On the other hand, changes in organizational forms and methods will not by themselves change fundamental problems facing organized labor. Without changes in the mission, vision, and strategy of organized labor, organizational improvements will not be enough in confronting our opponents.

There are several approaches to organizational change that are worth noting here. In each of them, labor education has played, and can continue to play, an integral role. Both the SEIU and the AFL-CIO, the former through its Staff Enrichment Program and the latter through its George Meany Center for Labor Studies, have begun training programs for lead organizers, persons who can be held accountable for local union organizing and to ensure that the local has a basic organizing plan. The Meany Center has sponsored the Turner

Scholarship Program to recruit trainees, and it has targeted women and workers of color. It has also been developing a course titled "Changing to Organize."

In the 1980s, some unions began to train new organizers, focusing on the training of rank-and-file workers as organizers. Volunteer Organizing Committees (VOCs), also known as Member Organizing Committees (MOCs), were established, sometimes by local unions and sometimes by national/international unions, as a way of institutionalizing this effort. For example, the Teamsters, in preparation for their 1997 contract battle with the United Parcel Service, conducted intense member education and organizing programs. Many affiliate unions and the Meany Center began training in what came to be known as one-on-one organizing. This is a method of getting local union staff and activists involved in talking with the members about issues. It is also a useful approach to internal organizing campaigns.

Less attention has been paid to the training of the existing organizing staff. The training of organizing staff should not be a task separate from the rest of the work of the union. Because organizers often lack an appreciation of the work involved after the organizing campaign is over, their training must not be limited to the skills of organizing a bargaining unit, but instead must be part of an overall plan. The timing of organizing must be viewed within the larger context of the organizing program,beginning with the pro-organizing member education programs and including the training of member and volunteer organizing activists and committees, staff organizers, and the local union organizing directors. It is vitally important that organizer education and training have what might be called a worldview or big-picture component. There has to be a deeper understanding of some of the great issues facing unions and of larger questions of trade union strategy.

Class Consciousness. Unions are not political parties. They are united fronts of workers who have come together to improve their conditions as workers, and those conditions will vary according to the degree of the members' class consciousness and political understanding.

Much, of course, depends on what we mean by class consciousness. Business unionism equates it with trade union consciousness, that is, with the willingness to fight for the demands of one's own union, or even the willingness to support whatever the leadership says. The limits of this approach are obvious when one sees unions raiding other unions, bargaining units at war with one another, and unions that face the same employer cutting deals at the expense of one another. The list could go on and on. Forget class consciousness—this isn't even good trade union consciousness.

The business unionist approach, however, has broader implications. With organized labor representing less than 15 percent of the workforce, who speaks for the unorganized? How and why should unions deal with issues such as welfare repeal and the workfare workers, whose conditions are like those of indentured servants? Is there an alternative to economism as workers attempt to unite across racial, ethnic, and gender lines against capital? These are the types of questions for which business unionism either has no answers or bad answers.

Labor educators can never replace the work of a political party in promoting social struggles and building class consciousness, but they can assist in the process, raising provocative questions and creating a dialogue through which workers begin to come to progressive conclusions regarding the conditions in which they live. They can help to challenge the view, held even by some leftists and progressives, that class consciousness arises simply through labor struggle and not through a synthesis of theory and practice.

Some consciousness-raising has been taking place through the institutions of the trade union movement over the past several years. One very important vehicle in helping to build class consciousness is the study of labor history, which is itself a terrain of struggle. By and large, unions ignore labor history in their training programs. Some unions, however, have supported labor studies programs at the university and college level. The Labor Studies Programs at the College of Public and Community Service of the University of Massachusetts-Boston and the University of Massachusetts-Amherst, which have received support from the Massachusetts AFL-CIO, have deeply involved themselves in popularizing labor history. This has been done through classes, exhibits, and literature. The New York-based American Social History Project has been another significant contributor. Their two-volume work (and CD-ROM) *Who Built America?* is a major contribution to the study of the U.S. worker and the reconstruction of U.S. history.[5]

Despite such excellent work, labor history has not, for the most part, been successfully integrated into trade union education. The task of integrating it into the work and practice of trade unionism represents the next big challenge for labor historians and labor educators. If we fail to utilize history, we fall into the typical U.S. pit of short-term pragmatism and empiricism. Consciousness will not arise or be able to sustain itself in the long run, without a historical analysis.

A second important intervention in the arena of consciousness-raising has been economics education. While economics education has been practiced, in one form or another, within the trade union movement since its inception, with the purges of the 1940s it became difficult to address the realities of capitalism and their impact on the U.S. worker without incurring the wrath of the anticommunist crusaders. Economics education, along with many other subjects relevant to workers, was exiled to labor studies programs. After the recent changes in AFL-CIO leadership, however, and with some unions feeling a need for a sound foundation for their political actions, economics education has become a project of the labor movement.

Without detailing the entire history of what has become known as the Common Sense Economics Education Program, there are a few points worth noting. First, this program emerged as a result of individual programs run by various affiliates, against the background of some basic problems in the movement as a whole: in particular, the fact that between 25 percent and 33 percent of union members regularly act against their own interests. Whether this takes the form of a formal vote on a tax initiative that will cut governmental jobs and services, or whether it takes the form of disengaging from the union and its activities, a significant proportion of workers either opt out of the political arena altogether or take conservative positions. The new AFL-CIO leadership recognized this problem and sought to solve it.

Second, there was a significant and largely successful effort to build a consensus among the affiliates of the AFL-CIO about the form and content of the project. Nine products were developed that could be used to promote a discussion with the members regarding how they experience the economy, what capitalism means for them, corporate America's anti-worker agenda, and the need to fight back, principally through unions. Each of the products, ranging from a 2½ hour workshop to study groups, aims not so much to teach economics, but to promote a dialogue among the members about the economy and to offer an analysis that might lead to progressive conclusions and action.

The emphasis on dialogue is essential. The aim is not to talk *at* workers, but rather to encourage debate. The object of debate is to promote the consciousness of workers, but here we come up against some fundamental problems. Some in the labor movement argue that workers must come to understand their economic interests as workers and must therefore not be distracted by "wedge issues," i.e., divisive issues around race, gender, and the like. Others argue that while economic interests are of critical importance, the working class does not see things only through the narrow prism of economics. Class itself is configured racially, ethnically, and by gender in the United States. So workers cannot be inoculated against divisive or wedge issues. Class consciousness cannot be built unless they deal with such issues and take a position on them. History demonstrates time and again the folly of attempting to live in denial of their centrality to the class struggle.

The Common Sense Economics Education program attempts to confront the issue of class within the parameters established by organized labor, while pushing the envelope a bit. It tries to address the so-called golden era of U.S. capitalism (how it came into existence, and why it ended), the objectives of corporate America, and the deteriorating conditions of workers. If connected to programs of action, this initiative may help to produce some unprecedented results: a growing political and class consciousness among a new set of labor leaders, the development of these new leaders, a real debate among worker-leaders about the future of organized labor, and a discussion of the interests of the working class in the era of neoliberalism.

What is also exciting about this initiative is the attempt to deliver it on a large scale, which requires hundreds of trainers and facilitators. Central Labor Councils, state federations of labor, and affiliated national/international unions are being asked to set up programs to develop cadres of trainers and facilitators to deliver these programs in local unions. These trainers will be well-informed, but they will not be "experts" or professional economists. (This was actually a point of some controversy. Some thought that only trained economists could run these programs. This view was defeated.)

As for the relationship between class consciousness and the divisions within the working class, some unions have undertaken efforts at diversity training, in some cases with programs that are explicitly anti-racist, anti-sexist, and anti-homophobic. Unfortunately, the calls for such programs often come in the midst of a crisis arising from such issues rather than before. In general, there is little understanding of what is involved in tackling the various sources of working-class division. The problem is rooted in the ideology of economism, or lowest-common-denominator trade unionism that tries to build unity on exclusively economic issues. Such unity more often than not shatters on the rocks of racism and sexism.

SEIU, inspired by the Doris Marshall Institute in Toronto, began turning their attention to this problem several years ago and borrowed from Doris Marshall the notion of social justice education, as distinct from diversity training. Social justice education is an approach to the divisions within the working class that focuses not just on their symptoms but on their root causes. This approach does not mirror corporate diversity programs but instead emphasizes understanding and overcoming obstacles to unity. This approach is still in its infancy. Many trade unionists are reluctant to tackle these issues in advance. This is a major challenge for labor education as we face the new century, and it is integral to the development of class consciousness.

Strengthening the relationship between university- and college-based labor educators and trade-union-based labor educators. After the purges of the 1940s, antagonisms developed between union-based and college- and university-based labor education. Higher education became somewhat isolated from organized labor, becoming the repository of an educational tradition, much as medieval monasteries preserved the knowledge of the ancients. Although the split was partly over turf, more fundamentally it concerned politics: to what extent a socioeconomic and political critique of capitalist society was to be permitted within labor circles. As might be expected, this struggle was marred by redbaiting of some labor educators in the colleges and universities. Yet university- and college-based labor education not only persevered but, in many states, cultivated strong relationships with the local labor movement. While many scholars had to tone down their critique of capitalism in order to survive, they still managed to accomplish a great deal.

With the change of guard at the AFL-CIO, these partnerships can now be expanded and new ones cultivated. However, the neoliberal offensive has limited the resources of many publicly funded colleges and universities. In both public and private schools, the free-market ethic has encouraged research directed by the demands and needs of corporate America. Even labor studies programs are under increasing pressure to serve the needs of capital, either directly or indirectly through corporate-influenced conceptions of labor-management relations.

This potentially catastrophic situation is not something that organized labor can afford to ignore. For organized labor, labor studies programs serve several purposes. They are outposts for a pro-worker viewpoint within the halls of academe, sources of important research that can assist organized labor, collaborators (particularly on matters concerned with organization), and providers of either formal or informal courses of study. It would be disastrous for these programs to close or to become increasingly dominated by a pro-corporate perspective.

Of course, in the final analysis organized labor cannot protect labor studies without strengthening its own hand. But there are immediate steps that can be taken to defend these programs and the individuals who participate in them. The relationship between organized labor and labor studies must also change. It must be approached as a partnership. This means that areas of common work need to be identified and an appropriate division of labor established. At the national level, a good working relationship exists between the AFL-CIO and the University-College Labor Education Association (UCLEA), but this does not necessarily translate into a corresponding relationship between the affiliate education programs and members of UCLEA. Some steps have been taken to address this through the work that led to the creation of the Common Sense Economics Education Program, in which some members of UCLEA and Local 189, Workers Education Local (affiliated with the Communications Workers of America), participated.

One specific step that should be taken is joint planning. Although some steps have been taken in this direction, they are few and inconsistent. On the state level, union-based labor educators and university- and college-based educators should meet to discuss their yearly objectives and how the work of each side can assist the other. In the Northeast, such discussions are being encouraged by UCLEA, the AFL-CIO Regional Director, and some state federation leaderships. Not only does this need to happen in other regions, but local union education personnel need to be drawn into these discussions as full participants.

Labor Education: The Thread Which Weaves the Fabric

The struggle within the ranks of organized labor over how to avoid oblivion is just beginning. The right wing of organized labor would like to build a consensus for New Deal nostalgia, believing that unions can be rebuilt on the basis of strong, well-publicized leaders, closer collaboration with and appeasement of corporate America, and greater care of their existing memberships. These forces have no interest in an expanded role for labor education, particularly a labor education that advances the notion of class and class struggle. We are in a race against time, a race to institutionalize a different practice of labor education that truly draws on the experiences of the members and helps them to translate those experiences into a progressive analysis and practice. Indeed, such a practice of labor education may play a role in building up the forces to defeat or restrain right-wing forces in organized labor.

This approach requires that labor education be woven through the fabric of the work of organized labor. Labor education and labor educators can no longer be educational technicians brought in at the last moment to implement someone else's ideas. Labor educators need to be at the table during the conceptual stage, and labor education needs to be factored into the original plans.

This also means that labor educators will have to see their roles in very different terms. No longer can the labor educator be the individual pulled out of the closet for this or that training program and then discarded once the task is completed. The labor educator has to see himself or herself as teacher, organizational consultant, facilitator, theoretician, and indeed, as organizer. Only organizers who have a larger vision of their job and see themselves as building a different kind of unionism will grasp our historical moment and understand the urgency of our mission.

Notes

1. The emphasis on northern and western capital is because conditions in the South and Southwest continue to be openly bitter and hostile, and labor there is badly divided along racial and ethnic lines.
2. This reference has to do with the alternative approaches of the two candidates. Donohue was a strong proponent of labor-management cooperation programs. He contrasted his stand with that of Sweeney, who, through initiatives such as the Justice for Janitors (JfJ) campaign to organize the building services industry, often found himself in confrontation with employers. In 1995, JfJ activists blocked a bridge in the Washington, D.C. area.
3. Some U.S. unions are called "internationals" because in the late nineteenth and early twentieth centuries they expanded into Canada, and later into the colonies and semicolonies of the United States. Organizing in Cuba was thwarted by the inability of the U.S. unions to distinguish who was black and who was white, reflecting the typical racism of trade unionism in that era. See Philip S. Foner,

Organized Labor and the Black Worker, 1619-1973 (New York: Praeger Publishers, 1974), 107.

4. See, for example, the contrast described in Victor G. Devinatz, "An Alternative Strategy: Lessons from UAW Local 6 and the FE, 1946-52," in *Beyond Survival: Wage Labor in the Late Twentieth Century,* eds. Cyrus Bina, Laurie Clements, and Chuck Davis (Armonk, N.Y.: M. E. Sharpe, 1996).

5. Bruce Levine and others, *Who Built America?* (New York: Pantheon, 1989). It is also worth noting the work of the University of Massachusetts-Boston professor and labor historian, James Green, whose book, *The World of the Worker: Labor in Twentieth-Century America* (New York: Hill and Wang, 1980), is widely read as a labor history primer.

3
A WORLD TO WIN?

Worker Insurgency, Rural Revolt, and the Crisis of the Mexican Regime

Richard Roman and Edur Velasco Arregui

We have prepared and achieved all through years of the silent accumulation of forces.

—Subcomandante Marcos

Images of Mexico, both positive and negative, rarely include the urban, industrial working class. Mexico is often still seen as a rural country, though 75 percent of the population lives in urban areas. Mexico is also seen as a peasant country, though 70 percent of the economically active population in urban areas and 50 percent of those in rural areas live through the sale of their labor power. Real unemployment is around 20 percent in urban areas and 50 percent in rural areas. Our purpose here is to examine the current conditions of the Mexican working class and the emerging modes of working-class resistance and struggle.

We argue that the democratic transformation of Mexico depends on the emergence of the working class as a central actor in the struggle for, and in the development of, an alliance with an exploding countryside. This alliance is the only bulwark against counterrevolution and a new and more savage dictatorship. Neoliberalism and the intensification of imperial aggression on the part of the United States have eliminated the viability of moderate and reformist solutions to the Mexican crisis. The existence of NAFTA, the increasingly direct role of the U.S. government in managing Mexican affairs, and the presence of great numbers of Mexican workers in the U.S. working class mean that the struggles in Mexico will not be confined to Mexico. International solidarity with Mexican workers, peasants, and indigenous peoples in their struggle for democracy, dignity, and justice is of fundamental importance.

Some History

The social contracts between capital and labor that emerged in twentieth-century capitalism are being dismantled everywhere, but in Mexico this process has a very particular and distinctive meaning. It amounts to a counterrevolution against the "revolutionary nationalist" road of capitalist development that emerged from the Mexican Revolution of 1910-1920. The vast mobilizations of peasants and workers forced the revolutionary leaders into a set of commitments and the ruling classes into a set of compromises with the popular classes. Some foreign enterprises, notably the oil companies, were nationalized and an anti-imperialist rhetoric was given expression by the government. Peasants and indigenous peoples were given some claim to the land, including communal holdings called *ejidos*.[1] These land tenure arrangements allowed much of the peasantry to survive on the land while providing cheap food for urban workers and a lower wage bill for Mexican capitalists.

Workers were incorporated into the revolution through a system of paternalistic and government-controlled labor relations, including government-dominated labor unions. While wages were kept low and workers were not free to form independent organizations (for example, the government controlled the registration of labor unions, and only registered unions could bargain with employers and file grievances), the social pact that arose out of the revolution allowed for some job security and social benefits for key sectors of the working class.

Union leaders were actually a part of the state bureaucracy, and in return for power, privilege, and opportunities to enrich themselves, were expected to discipline their members. But to maintain their positions, it was necessary for them to secure concessions for the workers, especially whenever workers threatened to act independently, either on the job or in the political arena. The pro-worker ideology of the revolution and some of its laws, such as the 1931 Federal Labor Law, provided leverage that could be used by labor leaders to wring higher wages or better benefits from the state (itself a major employer) and private employers.[2] In other words, if the labor relations system was a framework that allowed official union bureaucrats to achieve power and privilege as a part of the state-related elite, it was also a framework through which the discontent of union members could be contained by the achievement of wage gains or social benefits (such as housing or medical care) that came from the state and were controlled by these union bureaucrats.

This distinctive form of corporatism, dominated by a single political party, the Institutional Revolutionary Party (PRI), which maintained power by a combination of force and co-optation, began to unravel in the 1970s as world capitalism went into a prolonged period of crisis. Mexico, under pressure from both the United States and its own capitalist class, had begun to open its economy to the world market, borrowing large sums of money from foreign banks to build up its export industries and encouraging foreign investment. When the crisis hit, it found itself saddled with an enormous debt and a sluggish economy. The international lending agencies and their masters in the advanced capitalist countries began to turn the screws, pressuring Mexico to abandon what was left of its economic independence. Mexico's rulers, themselves largely trained in the United States, have been all too happy to comply. The results have been catastrophic for Mexican workers and peasants.

The Collapse of Living Standards

Throughout the capitalist world, the profit crisis of the 1970s was met by a fierce attack upon working class living standards as the owners sought to restore their profits. As the crisis generated massive unemployment and falling wages, Mexico's elites and their international allies began to destroy the corporatist structure that had afforded some workers and peasants minimal protection from the uninhibited rule of capital. During the 1980s, plants were closed and often relocated in areas "free of restrictive labor contracts;" there were mass firings of workers, and the agricultural subsidies essential to the survival of the ejidos and the small landholders were eliminated. One of the crowning achievements of capital was the passage of the North American Free Trade Agreement (NAFTA), which is speeding up the collapse of the living standards of workers and peasants.

To assess the precipitous decline in wages, we must look at both the "minimum salary" and the "industrial salary." The former is the legal minimum wage, and the latter represents the average pay of industrial workers, those typically laboring in larger establishments and under union contract. At the end of 1996, the average minimum daily salary in Mexico equaled 24.50 pesos, which is the equivalent of approximately $3.00 (about 40 cents per hour);[3] 17 million of the 33 million gainfully employed persons earn an income around the minimum wage.[4] Of the rural population, 75 percent have incomes equivalent to the minimum wage, and 54 percent of the population in urban areas have incomes that are in a narrow range just above and below the minimum wage. Fifty million people, half of the Mexican population, in turn, depend on the income of these 17 million minimum-wage workers. These 50 million inhabitants live on a wage mass of only $36 billion. To put this into perspective, the OECD estimated that the Mexican GNP in 1994 was $371 billion. Needless to say, therefore, the distribution of income in Mexico is highly skewed. Whereas 10 percent of all families have annual incomes of at least $100,000 (utilizing the technique of "purchasing power parities" of the OECD), 50 percent of the population finds itself immersed in profound misery, subsisting on a salary mass equal to 10 percent of the GNP.

The current minimum and industrial wages represent the nadir of a long period of decline. It is important to note that the most significant trend is in the minimum wage, which represents the condition of the working class as a whole. The minimum wage constitutes the floor of social rights and basic conditions of life and the possibilities for growth or decline in workers' collective share of the social wealth. The industrial salary measures the capacity of the national unions in the large enterprises to share in the growth of productivity (due largely to technological developments in specific industrial sectors) for their members. But contrary to some arguments that claim that these industrial salaries have become detached from trends in the minimum wage, the two are still closely related. Since the mass of workers earn the minimum wage, the condition of this majority affects the condition of labor in general, together with the influence of the unions. In any event, both contractual salaries and the minimum wage have suffered significant declines. The buying power of the minimum wage has fallen by 75 percent, while that of contractual salaries has diminished by 60 percent. Most significantly, the industrial salary in 1996 was for the first time below the minimum salary of twenty years ago!

The decline in working-class living standards was accompanied by a great wave that wiped out factories, buildings, labor contracts, and worker organizations, and by the collapse of agricultural production, the destruction of peasant farms, and the takeover of the Mexican economy by international financial capital and its internal creditors. At the same time, there has been a tremendous increase in the monopolization of the production and distribution of the goods and services consumed by workers. Globalization has translated itself in Mexico into a ferocious centralization of capital and a gobbling up of a good part of the wage bill as a base for capital accumulation. Contrary to the predictions of the politicians and the economists, NAFTA has led to an open, sluggish, and shrinking economy.

As in the United States, capital's attacks have decimated the unions. Unionism has lost ground in defining the economy as a whole, and unions now represent only a small fraction of the labor force. National industrial unions represent less than 10 percent of the country's labor force of 40 million persons, and, overall, 86 of every 100 workers lack any union organization.

The plunder of wages by capital has been aided by the cooperation of the official unions, which have not been able to find an effective way to adapt to the new rules of the game. Capital and the political rulers have decided that they no longer need the "social accord" in which some leaders were allowed to share government power and some workers were granted concessions in return for labor peace. But the official labor leaders weakly pleaded for the restoration of the old rules of the game while continuing to act—ineffectively—as if they still existed. The imposition of neoliberal economic policy was made possible by the continuation of the traditional collaboration of the union bureaucracy with a framework of negotiation that segmented the interests of the working people. The leadership engaged in private negotiations with employers, and "union discipline" was rewarded with concessions above the average. Bilateral negotiations, company by company, isolated and unconnected, signified a complete abandonment of even the pretense of class struggle.

In the process, the labor bureaucracy further isolated itself from its social base, sliding into a deepening political and ideological crisis, which had the effect of corroding the daily life of workers and of acting like a dead weight on the combative disposition of millions of workers. It is against this background that workers began to take independent actions.

The Chiapas Rebellion and Independent Worker Response

To an outsider, urban industrial Mexico seemed resigned to the destruction it was suffering. But this resignation was really not passivity and quietude. It was more akin to the calm before the storm. Two events that took place days before the Zapatista uprising illustrate this and give concrete meaning to the statistics of working-class decline described above. The dictatorship of savage capitalism is not limited to backward Chiapas but extends to all the modern territories of the republic.

The first of these events took place on December 11, 1993, when hundreds of fired workers from the sugar mill of Zacatepec, in the state of Morelos, were violently repressed by a military and police operation for demanding alternative jobs after two years without work as a result of the privatization of their old center of work. The second event, one of the direct consequences of the "growing productivity of privatized industries," occurred on December 22, when a spill of molten iron in the Altos Hornos de Mexico, in the state of Coahuila, killed two workers and gravely burned ten others.

This latter event was just one instance of the industrial terror on which Mexican manufacturing exports rest. As the official data of the Anuario Estadistico de Riesgos de Trabajo show, the number of accidents in Mexican factories has grown substantially in a period of six years. In 1988, the number of work accidents in the manufacturing industry was 97,000. In 1991, it rose to 266,000, then slowly descended to a level of 200,000 accidents in 1995, that is, an accident rate of 7 per 100 workers. An average of 2,000 workers were killed each year from 1991-1995 in work accidents, ground down by interminable "industrial competitiveness."[5]

The Chiapas rebellion of January 1994 acted as a catalyst for a growing insurgency of Mexican workers. The response of the workers of Mexico City to the Zapatista uprising during January 1994 paralyzed the iron circle of 60,000 soldiers that were mobilized by the Mexican state to smash the indigenous insurrection. On January 7, in commemoration of the Rio Blanco strike of 1907 (repressed by the army during the Porfirian dictatorship, 1884-1910), independent unions carried out the first large-scale mobilization against the military siege in the Lacandon jungle, while simultaneously demanding the meaningful implementation of the constitutional minimum salary and an end to the dismissal of workers and the jailing of union dissidents.[6] Tens of thousands of workers showed their solidarity with the radical challenge to NAFTA and the neoliberal program of the regime that came from the Mexican Southeast.

Five days later, on January 12, 1994, great columns of workers and students marched from the Monument of the Revolution to the Zocalo (central square) of Mexico City, demanding that the government stop its bloody offensive against the indigenous communities. In less than twelve days, electrical power workers, teachers, auto workers, and urban service workers in transportation, education, and health had meetings in their work centers in the principal cities of the country, demanding that the government stop its war machine and reverse the adverse effects on employment and conditions of work resulting from the policies of the Salinas regime of privatizing and squeezing workers.

On Sunday, January 16, thousands of workers took to the streets in Juchitan, Guadalajara, and Torreon to demand a political solution to the Chiapas conflict. On February 6, workers of the sugar mill of Puruaran, Michoacan, voted in a general assembly to unite with the EZLN. On February 14, striking trade unions in the centers of higher education seized for several hours the general headquarters of financial speculation, the sumptuous building of the Mexican stock exchange (Bolsa Mexicana de Valores) in the midst of a mood of generalized civil disobedience. In merciless assaults, the government succeeded in recapturing the municipal centers in the mountains of Chiapas, but it lost the political battle in the streets of the industrial zones.

In the months following the uprising, the Zapatistas held three national democratic conventions (between August 1994 and February 1995) in which hundreds of union committees were represented.[7] These conventions, with active solidarity from thousands of workers, sowed the seeds for a potentially powerful tie between the indigenous movement and the union movement. The rhythm of development of a worker and Zapatista movement has been uneven in these four years since the initial uprising. Great masses of workers have spontaneously taken to the streets in protest whenever the government has initiated full-scale assaults on the Zapatistas, but organizational forms of the alliance have been more difficult to consolidate.

Again, there were great mobilizations of workers in January 1998 to protest the massacre of Acteal.[8] In September 1997, 500,000 people, mostly workers, gathered to greet the peaceful and dramatic Zapatista march of 1,111 indigenous leaders as they entered Mexico City to demand the fulfillment of the San Andrés accords.[9] And all the oppositional May Day workers marches since 1995 have had a great presence of symbols of identification with the Zapatistas. In March 1998, the Frente Zapatista de Liberación Nacional (FZLN), the civilian wing of the Zapatista movement, convened a national convention in

Guadalajara to define a strategy and a program for strengthening the Zapatista presence in the union movement. The program adopted was the one that had been formulated in an earlier meeting between the EZLN and the CIPM in San Cristóbal, Chiapas. The strategy adopted in Guadalajara seeks to establish a Zapatista presence in the working class as strong as that which exists in the indigenous communities. (The Zapatista revolt has also had a great resonance in working-class movements in Italy, Argentina, Spain, and Brazil. In Rome, 60,000 marched in February 1998 in support of peace and the Zapatistas).

The Mexican government's abrogation of the San Andrés Peace Accords and the intensification of the ongoing low intensity war against the indigenous peoples have produced organizational responses as well as street responses. The Coordinadora Intersindical Primero de Mayo (CIPM), the Ejército Zapatista de Liberación Nacional (EZLN), and the Partido de la Revolución Democrático (PRD) called a National Peoples Assembly in Mexico City. On April 4, 1998, tens of thousands of workers and Zapatista supporters met and adopted a common platform of struggle against the brutal strategy of the government. They also agreed on a set of demands for May Day that have both indigenous rights and workers rights at their core.

The contrast with the official labor movement could hardly be sharper. Fidel Velazquez, the recently deceased leader of the official union federation (CTM/CT) and the main "labor representative" as defined and recognized by the government for the past 57 years, demanded a violent response from the government, "within or outside of the Constitution," as in its response in 1972 to the democratic insurgency within the unions. He called on the government "to exterminate" the indigenous uprising (the Chiapas rebellion) and, days later, opposed any truce. The official union bureaucracy, reliant upon armed gangs and shock troops for its control of the unions, and faced with resistance by its own members, became the most belligerent of the government forces. Velazquez stated that, "as in 1968, the CTM did not permit the student movement to infiltrate the unions, now it would impede any attempts in that direction.... [N]o worker," he added menacingly, "has participated in the Chiapas uprising, and the campesinos who had initially joined the revolt would leave it on seeing that it would lead to death."[10] This genocidal approach to indigenous demands and the indigenous movement has continued to this day as the CT/CTM continues to call loudly for repressive actions against the Zapatistas.

Three Currents of Response: CT, UNT, Intersindical

Neoliberalism has attacked the working class as a whole but has also threatened the power base of the official labor bureaucracy group. In very broad terms, it is possible to speak of three main currents of response to this assault. The first two currents come from the official labor bureaucracy. The third comes from a new attempt to form a rank-and-file workers' opposition based on democratic unions, democratic locals of official unions, and rank-and-file caucuses fighting for democratic and genuine unions within official unions.

Official unionism is in a deep crisis. Brutal restructuring has dramatically decreased its membership base and, accordingly, its revenues from dues and the sale of jobs. Four of the key unions in the original formation of the CTM and CT—the oil, railway, power, and mine and metal workers—have collectively seen their membership decrease by 40 percent in the period from 1988 to 1996. They have lost over 180,000 members from closings, privatizations, and downsizings.[11] The declining political leverage of labor officialdom in the PRI and in the state has removed their main source of leverage with management, as their bargaining power has not generally come from rank-and-file mobilization but from maneuvering among the rulers. And the demogogic nationalist discourse of labor officialdom has been sidelined by the regime's total rejection of it.

The old labor bureaucracy has been shunted aside. In the old system, as part of a powerful political machine and with great power over job opportunities, it had maintained its position by maneuvering within the state and ruling party apparatus, on the one hand, and containing worker discontent, on the other. Now, its old sources of leverage have been dramatically undercut by neoliberalism. Neither the state political machine nor management has much need for these labor bureaucrats as intermediaries, though they may be useful in the transition to the new systems of labor exploitation being brought in through the restructuring process.

This threat of extinction of labor officialdom as an influential and powerful stratum has led to two responses on its part. The main body of labor officialdom, the CT, continues in its path of defeat and demise. The opening volley of the presidency of Carlos Salinas was the military assault on the headquarters of "La Quina" (Joaquin Hernandez Galicia), the powerful boss of the oil workers union. La Quina was arrested and tried, and he spent almost nine years in prison. The selection of La Quina was a result of his flirtation with the candidacy of Cardenas in 1988 in an attempt to preserve the official empire of oil. The instant destruction of one of the most powerful charros in Mexico was an exemplary action that showed the charros that even the most powerful labor official could and would be broken by the state if he crossed certain boundaries or challenged the neoliberal restoration of the unbridled power of capital.[12] Thus did President Salinas make clear the content of his project and the cost of opposition to it.

These charros are an endangered stratum, no longer with maneuvering leverage in the state and ruling party apparatus, and no longer with the possibility of threatening to mobilize their members. For the state has made clear its willingness to ruthlessly dispense with their services. And this labor officialdom has become so fearful of losing control of its own rank and file that it has canceled the traditional massive May Day demonstrations.

May Day had been an official holiday, celebrated every year from 1925 until 1995 with gigantic marches of official unions to the Presidential Palace in Mexico City, with the President standing on the balcony greeting "his" working class. The CTM canceled these marches from 1995 through 1997, but in 1998 held a rally that, again, was greeted by President Zedillo in front of the Presidential Palace. The old labor bureaucrats protest government policies but are ignored by the government. They are an increasingly weak force and focus on survival of their power over their dwindling domains.

The second set of currents is grouped in a new labor federation, the Unión Nacional de Trabajadores (UNT). The UNT was founded in November 1997. This split in the official labor movement does not represent either independent or democratic unionism but a modernizing adaptation to the neoliberal restructuring of Mexican and world capitalism. The main leaders of the UNT were strong supporters of Salinas and his neoliberal restructuring. They, as well as the rest of the leadership of the CT, strongly supported NAFTA without protection for labor rights. They seek to moderate the consequences of neoliberalism without challenging the basic project.

The UNT seeks to substitute direct, unmediated collaboration of labor leaders with capital for the traditional tripartite collaborationist policy of the old social pact, This neoliberal project is dressed up in the costume of union independence, a historic demand of the Mexican working class. But it really is the substitution of dependent integration with big capital for dependent integration with the state. On February 11, 1998, the union FESEBES (whose top leaders are also the top leaders of the UNT) signed a pact with the notoriously anti-labor Confederación Patronal de la República Mexicana (Mexican Employers Confederation—COPARMEX) to propose changes to the labor law, in accord with the suggestions of the OECD and World Bank.[13] These UNT leaders described the signing of this agreement as follows: ". . . the labor and productivity reforms [proposed] represent a historic accord between businessmen and workers, elaborated without the tutelage of the government." Nevertheless, this "independence" from the government doesn't preclude the top leaders of the UNT from remaining key and loyal members of the corrupt, authoritarian government party, the PRI. Leaders of key unions in the UNT (telephone and social security) have supported privatizations and have proposed that wage recuperation struggles be conditioned to growth of productivity.

The UNT developed out of the Foro del Sindicalismo ante la Nacion. There were major defections when it formed into a new labor federation. The *charrista* teachers union (SNTE), led by government supporters, was not for a full break with officialist unionism but for its renovation. And the democratic power workers union (SME) feared that the formation of the UNT was a manuever in the struggle among *charrista* leaders and had not developed a process of rank-and-file involvement. The UNT is a very important regrouping of official and semiofficial unions (and a very small number of independent ones) that presents a moderate and ambiguous opposition to aspects of the labor policy of neoliberalism and to the old structures of statist labor control. Some small independent and democratic unions have been part of these developments in the hope that they will provide new possibilities for real unionism. But the odds are heavily against them, as the key unions are under *charro* leaders who use the old strong-arm and manipulative methods of control over the rank and file. The democratic currents are slight and the old mechanisms of co-optation and repression are still very much alive.

Some of the UNT unions, such as the union of telephone workers and that of the Institute of Social Security, have favored the partial privatization of social services and pensions, which opens the door to their destruction. They have also favored productivity pacts and competitive modernization of Mexican industry; some of these leaders were close to the Salinas government and are not different in their *charrista* undemocratic structure from the CT unions. But they see the CT unions as archaic in their modes of control and operation.

The UNT is seeking a new accommodation with the dominant project. It is maneuvering in the difficult, shrinking political space left by the power and policies of the government and the political and ideological bankruptcy of the CT. It seeks to modify the neoliberal project to protect the interests of its leaders, organizations, and membership while not taking actions that would challenge the basic project. It does not challenge the legitimacy of the authoritarian Mexican state but seeks to modify its policy and substitute itself as a better and more modern interlocutor for the archaic CT. It calls for professional, nonpolitical unionism and stays aloof from the critical struggle for a democratic transition. While not taking a position on the Zapatista struggle and indigenous rights, the key leaders of the UNT and its predecessor, the Foro, remain leaders of the de facto official party (PRI) of this authoritarian state, a state that is obstructing a democratic transition and is engaged in a genocidal, low-intensity war against the indigenous peoples of Chiapas.[14]

While the UNT is an organization of leaders, most of whom were selected undemocratically, it has also become an arena for rank-and-file pressure demanding the democratization of these very unions and a more effective and combative unionism. Some of these rank-and-file groupings overlap with the Intersindical, which belongs to the third set of currents in the Mexican labor movement.

These currents combine a number of old Mexican left perspectives (including anarcho-syndicalism, various Marxisms, and revolutionary nationalism of Cardenista inspiration) with new inspiration from the Zapatista uprising in

Chiapas and its proposal for a civil insurgency to force a democratic transition with social justice and workers dignity in Mexico. This collection of currents, organized now in the Coordinadora Intersindical Primero de Mayo, seeks to combine trade union struggle with class struggle and the battle for a democratic transformation of Mexico.

The Intersindical was formed in March 1995 to organize an independent and oppositional May Day demonstration. Its May Day 1995 demonstration drew an enormous multitude of over half a million workers, who overflowed the streets of Mexico City. May Day 1996 was even bigger and was extended to all the principal industrial zones of the country. And May Day 1997 witnessed the CTM/CT leadership booed by their members in their own indoor rally of 12,000, while the FORO and the Intersindical held separate but coordinated marches. May Day 1998 had three separate events. The CT/CTM held a friendly rally (no march), with the president once again greeting loyal unions. The UNT held a march that ended with no rally and did not enter the central plaza. The Intersindical held a march that entered the central plaza and a rally to express their opposition to the regime. The Intersindical, unlike the Foro, focuses on classwide and hegemonic issues, rather than operating within the dominant system exclusively for the sectorial interests of employed and unionized workers. Also, unlike the Foro, it is not looking for a new accommodation with the dominant project but is looking instead for the construction of an alternative project that would put people at the center of any proposal for the reorganization of material production.

The different currents within the Intersindical share the perspective that workers' rights can only be won as part of a bottom-up democratic transformation of the Mexican regime, which must mean the demise of the state-party system. The CIPM has therefore developed an alliance with the EZLN, and part of the civil arm of the EZLN, the workers committees of the FZLN, are members of the Intersindical.

The Intersindical draws its membership from democratic unions, democratic locals of official unions, rank-and-file caucuses in official unions, workers cooperatives, community movements, and parties of the left. While there is a range of views and perspectives with certain shared premises, the biggest divisions concern the interlinking of PRD moderate nationalism, with all its programmatic weaknesses, and more clearly class-based and socialist oriented projects. There is also a tension between the PRD commitment to an electoral transition and the view that a civic insurgency is a necessary condition for a democratic transition. The sorting out of these tensions and ambiguities is critical for the development of the movement and will determine whether the popular movements become an electoral and mass pressure base for reformist politicians or find their own voice and modes of struggle for a new society. This tension has been intensified by the PRD victory in the Mexico

City elections in the summer of 1997. This victory has increased the hope of an electoral transition at the national level in the year 2000. But at the very same moment of electoralist hopes, the national government is intensifying its war against the Zapatistas and putting large areas of the country under de facto military rule. The renewed attempts of the Zapatistas and the CIPM to deepen the Zapatista presence in the working class and to forge a more organic link between working-class struggles and indigenous and rural struggles is all the more urgent in the face of the escalating military assaults against the indigenous people of Chiapas.

Conclusion

The ferment in labor organizations and in the working class is taking place in the context of a countryside in a more advanced stage of protest and rebellion. We should remember that the recent neoliberal assault on rural peoples' rights and aspirations to land—the changes to Article 27 of the Constitution—was a key factor in the decision of campesinos and indigenous peoples to take the path of an armed uprising in Chiapas, leading to the emergence of thirteen guerrilla fronts in different states in the next few years.

This is what sharply distinguishes the Mexican situation from that of other countries—Spain, Argentina, France, and Korea—where a counter-reform of labor legislation has been carried out. In these countries, general strikes took place. In Mexico, the workers' rebellion could be much more consequential, because its context would be that of a growing rural rebellion.

Another point of great importance must be made. The ultimate success of the Mexican workers' movement will depend to a considerable degree upon the recognition that the composition of the Mexican working class is undergoing a profound change, the massive entry of women into the labor market. Thirty-five percent of women of working age are now in the labor force, and this proportion is growing rapidly.[15] The upheaval in practices and customs represented by this simple fact has not been systematically considered by analysts of Mexican society. With this development, the centuries-old division within workers' families between wage work in the hands of men and unpaid domestic work by women now rests on different and shakier ground. Whether these labor force developments will lead to a more egalitarian sharing of domestic power and chores or to a continuation of gender subordination marked by a double day of wage and nonwage labor will be determined by the manner in which the womens' and the workers' movements develop.

In the sphere of work, women live a profound contradiction between the emancipatory potential of their incorporation into the labor market and the miserable conditions in which they labor, most of the time with wages inferior to those of men, in unhealthy conditions, with neither benefits nor stability of employment. For the radical potential of the union movement—intuitively perceived by Zapatismo—to unfold, working women must be incorporated into all aspects and all levels: from the platforms of struggle, which must incorporate gender demands, to the eradication of traditional machismo in the rules, practices, and customs of the union movement, both written and unwritten. For the workers' movement to expand and deepen its role, women workers must demand, as the Zapatista women did in the months before January 1994, an adjustment of accounts, a new code of workers' and union conduct, granting equality of rights and condemning the everyday oppressions that women suffer at the hands of their own campañeros and, of course, at the hands of the bosses.

Subcomandante Marcos has never stopped calling on workers to become the subjects of their own emancipation and the fundamental allies of the indigenous peoples' cause. He has said, "We, the insurgent combatants, use the colors of red and black in our uniform, symbols of the working people in their strike struggles." The demand for work heads the list of the thirteen demands of the EZLN and of their "Revolutionary Laws," which include a section on work, in which the present Federal Labor Law is reaffirmed and to which is added the obligation of foreign companies to pay Mexican wages that are equivalent to what they pay in their home countries. This is an overt proposition to internationalize the union struggle. But it is their declaration on May Day 1994 that states most precisely and clearly the workers' program of Zapatismo:

> The struggle for organizational independence of the workers has made clear the triple alliance between the bad government, the corrupt union leaders, and the powerful men of money. Those who enjoy the ill-gotten gains have put a new label on them. Another mask hides our sadness from our own eyes. The new name of injustice, slavery, usurpation: neoliberalism....The workers who constructed our country are bleeding through their wounds: the powerful are bleeding the workers through unjust salaries, humiliations, and threats; the traitors that head the big government union federations are bleeding the workers with extortions, blows, and deaths; the sellers of the commonwealth are bleeding the workers from their usurped offices—with their prophetic version of the counterreform of the Federal Labor Law—and writing laws that are dictated to them.

Four years later the impoverished workers of Mexico are echoing the names of the guerilla heroes of contemporary Mexico. Fidel Velazquez was right. Zapatismo will not infiltrate the ranks of the workers because that very same spirit of rebellion against injustice and exploitation has already long been present in the working class. Zapatismo and the independent workers' movement are seeking new ways of organizing and mobilizing an alliance between the working class, the peasantry, and the indigenous peoples to build a new, just, and democratic Mexico.

Notes

1. The term *ejidos* refers to the communal holdings of land that, until the recent reform of Article 27 of the Constitution, could not be sold or alienated from the community. Land use could be collective or familial, but ownership was communal. The reform to Article 27 is intended to privatize communal holdings in the name of efficiency. It will lead to a further displacing of peasants and indigenous peoples from their lands.
2. Among other things, the Federal Labor Law provided a formal guarantee to permanent employment and made it difficult, in principle, to discharge workers.
3. *Diario Oficial,* 2 December 1996.
4. According to data in the *Encuesta Nacional de Empleo* (National Survey on Employment), INEGI (Instituto Nacional de Estadistica, Geografia e Informatica), Estadisticas Sobre Asentamientos Humanos y Medio Ambiente, 1996.
5. INEGI, 1995, 170.
6. Article 123 of the Constitution contains a clause stating that the minimum wage must be sufficient to satisfy the normal material, social, and cultural necessities and to provide obligatory education of children by the head of the family. The demand in January 1994 was for 90 pesos daily, the equivalent of $12 US at the then current exchange rate.
7. Delegates from democratic sections, such as SITUAM, SUTIN (nuclear power workers), the auto union local at the GM plant in the Federal District (closed two years later), workers at the Cooperativa de Refrescos Pascual, Sindicato de Costureras 19 de Septiembre in the Federal District; delegations of dissident caucuses in official unions, such as the Red & Black caucus in the Sindicato Nacional de Trabajadores de Seguro Social and the democratic currents in the rail workers union that publish "El Rielero."
8. Parliamentary forces slaughtered forty-five children, women, and men in the village of Acteal, Chiapas, on 22 December 1996. These paramilitary forces have been set up and armed by the feseral government to carry out terrot against the civilian population.
9. The San Andrés Accord was signed by the federal government and the EZLN on 16 February 1996. It promised to incorporate into the Constitution a set of indigenous rights, including indigenous self-government and automation within a framework of national unity. The government never fulfilled itd commitment, and in January 1998, President Zedillo repudiated it as he intensified the military attacks on the Zapatistas.
10. *La Jornada,* 12 January 1994.
11. Membership in the railway workers union at *Ferrocarriles Nacionales* (National Railways) declined from 95,000 members in 1990 to 35,000 in 1997. The oil workers union experienced a decline from 180,000 to 100,000 members in the same

period. And the miners and metallurgical workers union was reduced from 183,000 to 98,000.

12. The term *charrazo* was used to describe a coup by the state and some opportunistic leaders in the railway workers union against the elected leadership of the union in 1948. It has become a general term in Mexico to describe corrupt, undemocratic union leaders and practices. A *charro* refers to a leader and *charrismo* to the practice of state-linked, corrupt, undemocratic unions. The term *charro* derives from the highly stylized horsemen's attire worn by the imposed leader. It is now a term of opprobrium often chanted in labor demonstrations.

13. FESEBES (Federación de Sindicatos de Empresas de Bienes y Servicios—Federation of Goods and Services Unions) was created in 1990 with the backing of President Carlos Salinas. It consists of unions from telecommunications, airline, power generation, film and television and others.

14. Various labor leaders are also leaders of the PRI, including the telephone workers' pro-privatization head Francisco Hernández Juárez. Elba Esther Gordillo, the former Secretary-General of the official teachers' union, the SNTE, and one of the three founders of the Foro, is now one of the main leaders of the FNOC (Federacion Nacional de Organizaciones Ciudadanas—National Federation of Citizens Organizations)—which, along with the labor and peasant federations, is one of the three formal wings of the ruling party.

15. The flood of women entering the labor market has created great competition for scarce jobs. Currently there are, on average, 12 job seekers for every new job. The large enterprises have taken advantage of this large-scale entry of women into the labor force and further weakened collective bargaining agreements. The typical working woman today is married, with three children and with a secondary education, which is above the average education for male workers.

Globalization on Trial: Crisis and Class Struggle in East Asia

David McNally

Can someone find me an economist who knows what's going on?
—Ali Atlas, Indonesia's foreign minister

What a difference a year makes. As recently as last summer, economic pundits and global investors were singing the praises of the "Asian tigers." The World Bank basked in the glow of its 1993 report, *The Asian Miracle*. Throughout ruling circles, the "Asian model" was touted as proof that open markets and the free flow of capital would be the salvation of humankind.

Today, more than a year into the region's devastating economic crisis, the World Bank is preparing a new report. *Rethinking Asia's Miracle* it is to be called. Small wonder some rethinking is in order. Every day, 10,000 South Korean workers receive layoff notices—300,000 per month. The Indonesian economy is in a state of near-total collapse, with merely 22 of the 282 companies on the Jakarta stock exchange still viable. Japan is mired in its deepest recession in twenty-five years. Malaysia and Thailand remain in financial shock. Overall, more than $600 billion has been wiped off the balance sheets of the region's stock markets. With national budgets and public policy increasingly dictated by the International Monetary Fund (IMF), East Asia's increased integration into the world market now looks like the route to a new form of dependency.

The hype about "globalization" that has dominated economic analysis even on much of the left now stands severely shaken. True, capital's relentless drive to restructure—downsizing and "leaning" of production, outsourcing, casualization of much work, the creation of new capital markets, establishment of new trade and investment pacts—has reshaped the terrain of struggle and resistance. But rather than altering capital's essential dynamics and contradictions, the crisis in Asia reveals just how explosive those contradictions can be. In fact, the Asian crisis tells us much about two fundamental contradictions of capitalism in the age of "globalization." First, it reveals the severe problem of overaccumulation and overcapacity that plagues globalizing capital today. And, secondly, it illustrates how accelerated capital accumulation can give rise to powerful new working classes capable of fighting back against capital's dictates.

Globalization on Trial

If any region is a test case for establishment claims about globalization it is East Asia and its newly industrializing countries—South Korea, Thailand, Indonesia, Malaysia, and Taiwan in particular. In much of the world, claims for economic globalization seem laughable. After all, despite all the hype about globally-mobile capital, international capital continues to concentrate production and trade in the industrially developed nations. With a few exceptions, only parts of Asia have been more systematically incorporated into the global circuits of capital. Between 1980 and 1991, for instance, the share of world trade for which Asia (excluding Japan) accounted rose from 9 to 15 percent while the developed nations' share slipped from 72 to 63 percent. But the rest of the world economy—the "less developed countries" of Africa, Latin America, and the Caribbean in particular—experienced a catastrophic drop from 28 to 13 percent of international trade.[1] By 1994, East Asia was the destination of more than half of all investment flows to developing countries.

Take Asia away, therefore, and there was no globalization thesis; it was the sole success story. And East Asia's crisis now puts that at risk. More than that, events in Asia pose a serious threat to the world capitalist economy as a whole, "the biggest threat to global prosperity" since the 1970s, according to *Business Week*.[2]

Contrary to the facile descriptions of the business press, however, the collapse in East Asia is not fundamentally about corruption, crony capitalism, or overly regulated markets. Rather, it is about the classic problem of capitalist overaccumulation (and the profit squeeze that accompanies it). The enormous capital flows into Southeast Asia in recent years have contributed to a huge build-up in productive capacity, much of which cannot be profitably utilized. Capitalist development of the forces of production, in other words, is running up against its inherent limits. Yet, as market competition has intensified, corporations have responded by adding even more new capacity—new factories, mines, mills, and mega-farms, new infrastructure and service industries.

Adding new capacity at a time of general overcapacity may seem irrational—and for the system as a whole it is. But for the individual capitalist firm caught in the logic of market competition it is the only rational course. The objective, after all, is to insure that someone else fails in the scramble for market share. The survivors are likely to be those with the right combination of lean production, new technology, labor discipline, relatively low wages, and ready market access. So new capacity is added to achieve these, to construct the most efficient capitalist enterprises, despite the problem of overaccumulation as a whole.

In many cases, Asia has been the testing ground for much of the latest wave of capital accumulation. Auto, steel, electronics, computer chip, and fiber optics plants have been built pell-mell in the expectation that cheap labor, easy financing, and business-friendly governments with draconian labor regulations would guarantee good rates of return. Once the boom reached its limits, the results were predictable: enormous excess capacity and serious problems of profitability.

Take the case of the world automobile industry. Global excess capacity in autos today is around 21 to 22 million cars. That's roughly a 36 percent overcapacity relative to world markets, the equivalent of eighty efficient state-of-the-art plants. Yet, despite those realities—indeed, in capitalist logic, because of them—auto companies have been frantically building new capacity throughout Asia. Before the crisis broke, in fact, automobile firms planned investment projects that would see a doubling of Asian car manufacturing capacity outside of Korea and Japan, which are already staggering under excess capacity.

Similar problems of overaccumulation—of the creation of productive forces that cannot be utilized profitably—plague industries such as computer chips, semi-conductors, optical fibers, chemicals, and steel. The world market in dynamic random-access memory chips (DRAMs) is another case in point. Analysts estimate that the oversupply of DRAMs will be 18 percent this year, compared with zero as recently as 1995. The result has been a devastating collapse in prices (especially damaging for South Korea, which controls 40 percent of the global DRAM market). Prices of sixty-four-megabit DRAMs plummeted from sixty dollars in early 1997 to twenty dollars by the end of the year. This year, prices have fallen as low as eight dollars.[3] The root cause of the Asian economic crisis is this sort of downward pressure on prices and profits brought on by overproduction. That's why, sensing that an adequate return on further investment in these sectors was improbable, some investors got cold feet. They began to hedge their bets by reducing Asian holdings. Slowly but surely, plugs were pulled in precisely those areas, like East Asia, where hectic accumulation, exacerbated by huge inflows of speculative capital, had been the order of the day. "Market forces" responded, in other words, to real problems of overaccumulation of capital. *Rather than the result of inadequate marketization of society, then, the Asian crisis is all about the contradictions inherent in the capitalist market. It is, in short, a product of capitalist globalization, of the extension and intensification of capitalist contradictions on a world scale.*

All of this has been exacerbated further by flows of short-term financial capital. For while Latin American markets remained shaky, as Japan's stock and real estate markets were melting down, international banks and lending agencies saw great profits to be made in East Asia. They saw factories going up, new technologies being brought on stream, explosive growth of highways, airports, telecommunication systems, and luxury hotels—and they wanted in on the boom. As financial capital poured into the region, making it relatively cheap and easy to raise funds, manufacturing and construction firms kept bringing new projects on line. East Asia's economic upswing thus acquired all the classic characteristics of a speculative boom. As each new mega-project was announced to euphoric prediction, the bubble grew larger.

Inevitably, some investors bet against the euphoria. They recognized that too many factories, agribusinesses, mines, hotels, and highways were being built in a context of world overcapacity. Quietly at first, they withdrew from new investment projects in Asia. They pulled cash out of stock markets; they dumped Asian currencies. Once kick-started, the process snowballed. Whereas private capital flows into Indonesia, Malaysia, the Philippines, South Korea, and Thailand grew to nearly five times the original rate between 1990 and 1996, from $20 billion to $95 billion per year, those countries experienced in 1997 a net *outflow* of private capital to the tune of $20 billion. The crash was on, beginning with the run against the baht, Thailand's basic currency unit, last summer.

Suddenly, the business community discovered that East Asian debt—the very debt created by the offerings of global capital—was a festering problem. Only last summer, even after the collapse of the baht was underway, economists at the World Bank, the IMF, and a number of foreign banks all proclaimed the fundamental soundness of the Indonesian economy. No Thai-type problems were to be expected there. A few months later the capital flight began and the world market pronounced its verdict on the country's $80 billion foreign debt. So severe has the flight been that the devaluation imposed by global capital has now moved things to the edge of catastrophe, pushing the ratio of foreign bank debt to gross domestic product from 35 percent to 140 percent.[4]

All eyes turned next to South Korea. East Asia's major industrial power outside of Japan now appeared terribly vulnerable, especially in light of the long downward slide in the value of the Japanese yen brought on by Japan's crisis. Since South Korea competes directly with Japan in industries like autos, steel, and electronics, it has much to fear from the declining prices for Japanese exports that a lower yen creates. South Korea thus found itself in a conundrum: despite booming export growth, its export revenues stagnated as a result of downward pressure on prices. In 1996-1997, for instance, South Korean exports rose by 37 percent while export revenues crept up a mere 5 percent. But such meager increases were not adequate to finance the borrowing Korean businesses had done to build and retool factories. By the end of 1996, the top thirty chaebol—the industrial conglomerates that dominate the economy—had an average debt to equity ratio of 400 percent. As the crisis hit and exports and earnings slumped, prospects for financing those debts dimmed. More than one-quarter of the chaebol have now collapsed, including the automotive conglomerate Kia and the Halla Group, involved in shipbuilding, engineering and auto parts.

Meanwhile, the crisis in East Asia fed back into Japan where it had started. The Japanese slump began in the early 1990s with huge collapses in stock and real estate markets. After contracting about one percent in 1997, Japanese output slumped a staggering 5.3 percent in the first quarter of this year. Corporate profits and capital investment are down, business bankruptcies are soaring, and consumer spending is in a deep funk. Department store sales are falling at a rate of about 15 percent each month. Meanwhile, bad loans held by Japanese banks exceed $1 trillion and corporate debt averages four times equity, compared with 1.5 times in the United States.[5] All of this despite an injection of $1 trillion in government spending over the past six years to kick-start the economy. So pessimistic has much business opinion toward Japan turned that Paul Summerville, chief economist at RBC Dominion Securities, predicts (as he has since 1992) that Japan's slump will last fifteen years. Needless to say, that is more bad news for the "Asian tigers" for whom exports to Japan and local Japanese investments have been crucial. And it is one reason the crisis is unlikely to end any time soon.[6]

Across the region, a wave of stock market crashes, plant closings, mass layoffs, government cuts, and currency depreciations are wreaking havoc on the lives of millions. Massive capital investment and accumulation are colliding with the logic of production for profit. As a result, East Asia is now in the grips of "an epidemic that, in all earlier epochs, would have seemed an absurdity—the epidemic of overproduction."[7] That epidemic is now imposing untold hardship—and producing resistance and revolt.

Working People and the Natural Environment:
Some Dimensions of the Crisis

More than 5 million Indonesian workers have been laid off since July of 1997. The country's jobless number is likely to hit 20 million by the end of 1998, by which time nearly 3 million will be unemployed in Thailand, almost two million in South Korea, and a million in Malaysia alongside 1.5 million migrant laborers facing expulsion.

In concert with the layoffs goes the destruction of living standards. Between August and December of 1997, average incomes were halved in South Korea. That pales beside what's happened in Indonesia where the annual per capita income has plummeted from $1200 to $300. In Surabaya, the country's largest industrial city, the daily minimum wage has collapsed to less than thirty cents from two dollars a year ago. And this at a time when, as a result of the dictates of the IMF, food and fuel subsidies are being eliminated and prices are soaring. By year's end the number of people living below the poverty line will double to 58 million. And Indonesia is by no means alone. In Thailand, prices of rice and flour jumped 47 percent in February, spelling a calamity for the poor. More than simply shifts in trade and investment figures, the economic crisis in East Asia is fundamentally about soaring poverty, unemployment, malnutrition, and rates of disease. Relief workers in Indonesia report that many mothers, no longer able to afford milk which has tripled in price, are feeding their babies with tea. Rates of malnutrition and school dropouts are soaring. Young women have been hit particularly hard, as factories and stores close and girls are pulled out of schools. In Thailand, the crisis means that thousands more rural families will feel the pressure to sell their daughters into prostitution in Bangkok where, some experts suggest, as many as one million young women work in the sex trade, many of them susceptible to an AIDS crisis the government largely denies.

Devastation of the natural environment massively compounds the suffering. Frantic industrialization and grandiose mega-projects have already inflicted staggering environmental damage. The Asian Development Bank in Manila describes the continent as the "most polluted and environmentally degraded" in the world. Asia's rivers contain an average of twenty times more lead than do those in the West. The human toll is immense. According to the World Health Organization, more than 1.5 million lives are lost every year as a result of Asia's air pollution. Another 500,000 lives are claimed by untreated water and poor sanitation. The economic crisis will lead to further environmental degradation as companies, desperate to stay alive, reduce costs and cut corners on safety and pollution control. Recent events in Indonesia are a dire warning of what may be in store.

In sheer scale, commercial logging eclipses all other industrial undertakings in Indonesia which is home to 10 percent of the world's tropical rainforests. About 60 million people live and work in these forests, a third or more of them practicing slash-and-burn farming which has been sustainable for thousands of years. Yet millions of these people are being displaced by commercial logging, mining and the like. One third of the country's land mass—roughly 64 million hectares—is occupied by logging companies which routinely set forests ablaze as part of their logging and planting operations. The privatization and destruction of lands and forests has caused massive displacement of people. During the 1970s, for instance, more than 2.5 million indigenous peoples across Kalimantan were displaced. By the mid-1980s perhaps ten million people were "resettled" from Java to other islands. Last summer almost two million hectares were set afire in the lowland tropical rainforests of Sumatra and Kalimantan. The results have been devastating: global warming,

weather changes, adverse effects on coffee, cocoa farming, and the fishing
industry. Up to seventy million people in Indonesia, Singapore, southern
Thailand, Brunei, Malaysia and the southern Philippines have been affected
and thousands have sought treatment for respiratory problems, asthma, and
skin and eye irritations.[8]

Also devastating has been the impact of mega-mining projects, none more
so than the copper and gold mines run by New Orleans-based Freeport
McMoRan. The company, which has been charged with abduction, torture,
and murder of indigenous peoples, operates the richest mine in the world in
West Papua. The corporation extracts vast amounts of ore from Puncuk Jaya
Mountain and the tailings have poisoned the Ajkwa River, killing fish and
forests. The company now plans to double the output of the mine, something
we are likely to see more of as debt-strapped governments sell off natural
resources to raise cash for the IMF and global investors.[9]

Intensified destruction of the natural environment is a direct consequence
of the intensification of market imperatives throughout East Asia. Industrial
overaccumulation alongside the gyrations of financial capital have led to
classic capitalist assaults on working people and the environment, "simultaneously undermining the original sources of all wealth—the soil and the
worker," as Marx puts it.[10]

Resistance and Revolt: Asia's New Workers' Movements

Yet none of this is happening without resistance. The period of the last fifteen
to twenty years, the area of the celebrated "Asian miracle," has seen enormous
growth in the size of the employed working class and major progress in
working-class self-organization and struggle across the region. Throughout the
economic South, or the so-called "developing world," the number of industrial
workers alone increased from about 285 million in 1980 to over 400 million
by 1994, much of this growth concentrated in Asia. Moreover, women in East
Asia entered the paid workforce in huge numbers. Today, women constitute
42 percent of all wage-laborers in the region and often an overwhelming
majority in key industries like garments, electrical goods, and electronics. On
top of this, the late 1980s saw widespread growth in union organization. During
the years 1987 to 1989, for example, the number of organized workers
increased by 27 percent in Bangladesh, 38 percent in the Philippines, and fully
100 percent in South Korea. Over the years 1986 to 1989 the number increased
more than 50 percent in Taiwan.[11]

But it's not just numbers that matter here. The working class throughout
East Asia has also developed forms of militancy and self-organization that
often put western labor movements to shame. Frequently, young women have
been in the forefront of these struggles. And in many cases, these movements
have involved new, independent unions and labor federations which reject the

collaborationism of the older, state-tolerated, and state-regulated unions. In Taiwan, a new federation of independent unions emerged in 1988, while another was formed in South Korea in 1995. Meanwhile, unions like the National Garment Workers Union in Bangladesh and the Center for Indonesian Labor Struggle, an illegal workers' organization, have spearheaded major battles in those nations.

Indonesia is clearly a crucial case, given the growth of political dissent which brought on the student-led uprising that toppled dictator Suharto (who came to power in 1965 in a bloody coup during which at least half a million leftists were murdered). A crucial role in the street-level mobilizations that toppled Suharto was played by the banned People's Democratic Party (PRD) and its student allies in the Students in Solidarity for Democracy in Indonesia (SSDI). Significantly, the PRD, whose supporters are young radical democrats, champions the independence of East Timor, invaded by Suharto (with U.S. support) in 1975. And during the uprising against Suharto, the PRD distinguished itself by arguing against attacks on "our Chinese sisters and brothers" as tactics which "will only weaken our struggle and benefit Suharto." [12] Radically democratic perspectives such as these galvanized a movement whose courage was truly inspiring, as students waged months of daily protests, including hunger strikes, demonstrations, and occupations of government buildings in the face of club-wielding police and tear gas-firing soldiers who turned to bullets (and killed a number of students) during Suharto's last days.

But what most commentators on the Indonesian events missed was the emergence in recent years, alongside this youth- and campus-based opposition, of a small but militant workers' movement. In July of 1995, for instance, the banned Indonesian Center for Labor Struggle (PBBI), which has ties to the PRD, led a 13,000-strong strike of garment workers in Bogor. Last July, the union launched a strike and community protest movement of 20,000 in Surabaya. Then, last October, when the economic crisis led to rumors of IMF-dictated layoffs, the PBBI organized a strike of 16,000 workers at the state aircraft company in Bandung.

These may seem like small accomplishments. But in the context of police and military repression, the militant determination of Indonesian workers is nothing short of inspiring. And in the aftermath of the popular movement that toppled Suharto, workers' organizations are becoming more confident and self-assertive. During the struggle against Suharto, workers and the urban poor joined students on the streets on many occasions. On May 3, for example, 300 factory workers from Tangerang in East Jakarta responded to a student invitation to demonstrate against the regime. Moreover, the post-Suharto government's decision to free jailed union leader Muchtar Pakpahan has not quelled workers' protests. Workers at Garuda Airlines in Jakarta have taken strike action, as have 50,000 workers at Maspion Corporation in Surabaya. In fact, the strikers at Maspion organized the biggest protest since the fall of Suharto when, on June 8, more than 10,000 workers rallied and clashed with police in Surabaya. At the same time, transport workers in Jakarta struck the Public Transport Authority (PPD) and shut down seventy-three bus lines. At the height of their strike more than 9,000 workers demonstrated outside the PPD offices. Actions such as these raise hopes that the radical opposition among the young will take on an increasingly class character as workers' organizations come to the fore in the fight against poverty, layoffs, and the dictates of the IMF.

Nowhere is that prospect greater, perhaps, than in South Korea. Beginning in the late 1980s, a tremendous working-class upheaval swept South Korea. Between 1986 and 1990 union membership doubled from one to two million in the course of a huge strike wave. A classic weapon of militant working-class struggle—the sit-down strike—became increasingly common. In the industrial cities of Masan and Changwon, a virtual workers' revolt took place in 1987-88 when company assaults on a group of women strikers provoked an outpouring of solidarity strikes and the joining together of thirty new independent unions. So impressive was the solidarity and so widespread the militancy that radical workers described Masan-Chawong at the time as a "liberated zone." Then, after formation of the (illegal) Korean Confederation of Trade Unions (KCTU) in November 1995, with a membership of more than half a million, came the largest-ever mass strikes. The first round came in December 1996. That was followed, in January 1997, by a month of mass strikes involving 630,000 workers to protest new labor law restrictions and legislative changes that would make mass layoffs possible. In a mere decade, the South Korean working class had built one of the most combative union movements in the world. That movement is now being severely tested as a result of the current economic crisis.

The biggest challenge came when, as a condition of its $57 billion aid package, the IMF insisted that the South Korean government implement mass layoffs. Given that this question had prompted general strikes a year earlier, the state convened a tripartite commission of business, government, and labor leaders to negotiate an agreement. Representatives of the KCTU were invited, along with those of the more moderate Federation of Korean Trade Unions. On February 6 of this year, much to the dismay of many union activists, the leaders of the KCTU signed an accord which, in exchange for modest concessions, accepted mass layoffs and all the basic terms of the IMF bail-out. Within days, hundreds of angry KCTU delegates rebelled, voting down the agreement, removing the leaders who had signed the deal, and setting the date for a nationwide general strike. Only a few days later, however, the strike call was reversed as militants realized they did not have adequate support for the action.

Worker militants in South Korea now confront a dilemma. The scale of the economic crisis has shocked most Koreans. National pride has been deeply offended by the image of the IMF dictating national policy. Hundreds of thousands have responded to government calls for people to donate gold or U.S. dollars to state reserves. Incidents of people attacking foreign-made cars are frequent. In the midst of this patriotic upsurge, KCTU activists have found it difficult to mobilize against the South Korean state and ruling class. Yet that is precisely the task confronting the radical workers' movement: to develop a political program of action that targets international capital (and its agencies, like the IMF) *and* the Korean ruling class. To the traditional patriotism invoked by the Korean government, the radicals need to counterpose an anti-imperial- ism which is working-class in character, one which calls for socialization of the economy and workers' control of industry.

That will require the development of independent working-class politics alongside the new labor movement. There is no easy road to that goal. Prospects for mass resistance are made difficult as layoffs and economic collapse demoralize workers and grind down their confidence to fight back. Trying to raise the political horizons of struggle—to forge a class-based political opposition to the IMF and the local ruling class—is a daunting task under such circumstances. But a decade of struggle has created a militant and combative workers' movement with tens of thousands of dedicated union activists. And in the context of layoffs, economic crisis, and continued agita- tion for mass action by thousands of KCTU militants, there are real prospects for building working-class resistance. In fact, after stumbling in the early winter, unions are recovering their capacity to fight back. On May 27-28, about 120,000 workers in the KCTU participated in strike action against layoffs. Further mass strikes are now being planned. And on the heels of that mass strike, workers at Kia Motors forced concessions from management after waging a three-week series of strikes against wage cuts. Whatever the short- term outcome of the current struggles, a militant working-class leadership is being forged in the heat of struggle against economic crisis and IMF austerity.

An Asian Model of Resistance?

The working class and the poor throughout East Asia now find themselves locked in a ferocious battle with international capital. Economic and political struggles of immense importance—food riots, student demonstrations for democracy, workers' strikes against layoffs—are widespread. These struggles will not be easy ones. But in the crucible of the decaying "Asian miracle," forces of resistance are being constituted. The next few years will show if they are able to mount a major battle against the ravages of globalizing capital.

Already, however, the tremendous militancy and self-organization of East Asian workers ought to command respect. Strikes by young women in garment factories in Bogor and electronics plants in Kuala Lumpur, by aircraft workers in Bandung against IMF-directed layoffs, mass demonstrations by tens of thousands of workers in Surabaya, and weeks of strikes by workers at Kia in South Korea are all signs of working-class resistance to downsizing, austerity, privatization, unemployment, and poverty. East Asia has become the focal-point of the international class struggle. Out of these struggles a new "Asian model" may emerge—a model of working-class resistance to capitalist globalization. We have much to learn from these struggles. And we owe them our solidarity and support.

Notes

1. United Nations, *World Economic Survey* (New York: United Nations, 1993).
2. "What to do about Asia?" *Business Week,* 26 January 1998: 27.
3. Namju Cho, "Hyundai suspends chip output," *Wall Street Journal,* 4 June 1998.
4. "Survey: East Asian Economies," *The Economist,* 7 March 1998: 6.
5. Brian Bremner, "Japan's Real Crisis," *Business Week,* 18 May 1998: 139.
6. It is outside the bounds of this article to explore the unique dynamics of developments in China. Recent announcements of dramatic falls in China's growth rate and the layoff of millions more public employees, as tens of thousands of state enterprises close, suggest that major problems are in store, problems which will have reverberations throughout the region and the world economy as a whole.
7. Karl Marx and Friedrich Engels, *The Communist Manifesto* (New York: Monthly Review Press, 1998), 12.
8. Dianne Feeley, "Who Set the Fires?" *Against the Current* 72 (January-February, 1998), 17; and Curtis Runyan, "Indonesia's Discontent," *World Watch*, May-June 1998, 12-23.
9. Information on Freeport McMoRan comes from Runyan, "Indonesia's Discontent."
10. Karl Marx, *Capital*, v. 1, trans. Ben Fowkes (Harmondsworth: Penguin Books, 1976), 638.
11. Much of the data in this paragraph, and much of what follows on South Korean labor, is indebted to Kim Moody, *Workers in a Lean World* (London: Verso, 1997), 202. In addition to Moody's important book, useful sources are Jeremy Seabrook, *In the Cities of the South* (London: Verso, 1993) and Stephen Frenkel, ed., *Organized Workers in the Asia-Pacific Region* (Ithaca: ILR Press, 1993).
12. PRD Statement, 14 May 1998.

Communists and Workers in Ex-Communist Europe

Peter Gowan

The return to power of ex-Communist parties in a number of East Central and East European countries in the mid-1990s came as a shock to many in the West, largely because they had failed to notice the strength of the Communist electorate in the region during the so-called revolutions of 1989-1990. In all the countries of East Central Europe, the formerly ruling Communist parties emerged from the elections in 1989-1990 as the dominant parties of the left. In six of these first elections, they gained the largest vote of any party. And eight years after the beginning of the transition to capitalism, the ex-Communist parties remain the dominant parties of the left in all the countries of the region except two.

The official unions of the state socialist period have also emerged as the dominant trade union confederations during the transition to capitalism. They have done so despite concerted efforts on the part of governments of the right and of Western bodies such as the International Confederation of Free Trade Unions (ICFTU) and the AFL-CIO to weaken them. In Hungary, the main trade union center, MSzOSz, retained some 3 million of its 4.5 million 1988 membership in 1991. The Polish official unions, OPZZ, emerged with 4.5 million members in comparison with Solidarity's 2.3 million members. The same pattern emerged in Czechoslovakia where the official federation, CSKOS, predominated.

In Bulgaria, the official unions faced the most serious challenge with the emergence of an initially strong union center, Podkrepa. But this challenge later faded. After rising from about 350,000 at the end of 1990 to more than 600,000 at the end of 1991, Podkrepa's membership declined to about 225,000 by the beginning of 1993. The old official federation's membership also declined, from 3 million at the end of 1990 to 2.5 million at the end of 1991 and only 1.6 million at the end of 1992, but its dominance within the trade union field was maintained. In Romania, the official unions also remained the strongest, although they fragmented into competing centers in the early 1990s.

And the former official trade unions also remain dominant in the ex-Soviet republics.

There was thus a substantial trade union constituency remaining in these organizations to be won by parties of the left if they were prepared to orient towards it. But though still organizationally strong and electorally influential, the former Communist parties and the trade unions are facing extremely difficult problems. This is, of course, partly a result of ideological disarray following the collapse of state socialism. But the main reason is the catastrophic socioeconomic problems facing the mass of ordinary people in the region, the impoverishment and humiliation of tens of millions of people suffering the consequences of so-called "economic reform," and the lack of instruments available to the region's labor movements for tackling these problems.

The Continuing Strength of the Left

The widespread idea in the West that Communism had no significant popular support at the time of its collapse was simply the result of Western ideological preconceptions. The available evidence suggests that there remained a socialist electorate of at least 25-30 percent or more. Even in Poland and Hungary, where Communism had always been historically weak, support for the Communists remained significant in the late 1980s. Opinion surveys during the 1980s in Poland, Hungary, the Czech and Slovak republics, and the GDR showed that sizable minorities of the population supported the ruling parties. Such surveys also demonstrated that substantial numbers held socialist social values, particularly a commitment to egalitarianism and nationalized property.[1]

Thus, the strong showing of these parties during the first part of the 1990s is scarcely surprising. Indeed, the puzzle is why these parties did not do much better than they did in the first post-1989 elections—why their votes were lower in the GDR, Poland, Hungary, and the Czech and Slovak republics than polling evidence from the 1980s had suggested.

One explanation could be that erstwhile Communist supporters were temporarily swept up in the wave of enthusiasm for a transition to capitalism in 1989-1990 and switched their support to the parties of the free-market right. This does seem to have been an important factor in the GDR elections of March 1990. Polling in early 1990 showed more than 60 percent of the GDR electorate holding social democratic or socialist political and social opinions. Yet, Kohl's campaign promises swung a big majority for the right precisely in the traditional social democratic Saxon strongholds, leaving the Party of Democratic Socialism, successor to the GDR's ruling party, with only 16.3 percent, and the SPD with only 21.8 percent.

But this effect does not seem to have been very significant elsewhere. In the 1989 Polish elections, less than 50 percent of the electorate voted for Solidarity: the turnout in this first competitive election was low, with high levels of abstentions. Parties of the center and right in Hungary also failed to gain support from more than 50 percent of the electorate, and the party calling fairly explicitly for free-market capitalism, the Alliance of Free Democrats, gained only 21 percent of those who voted. In Czechoslovakia, the Civic Forum did not campaign on a free-market program in the 1990 elections.

A more likely explanation is that the post-Communist parties' earlier supporters, in large numbers, decided not to vote at all. This explanation is reinforced by the fact that the post-Communist parties that gained the smallest percentage of the vote were those of Poland and Hungary—the two countries where electoral participation was lowest. In Hungary, only 58 percent of the electorate turned out, and the figure was roughly the same in Poland—hardly, by the way, a sign of a popular revolution for "freedom" against "totalitarianism."

The high abstention rate in Poland and Hungary suggests another puzzle: in the only two countries where the ruling Communist Party leaderships made autonomous decisions (in February 1989) to move towards pluralist democratic political systems, those parties performed worst of all the Communist parties in the region. If the great issue of these elections was freedom from "totalitarianism," why did these two parties perform worse than the two parties that resisted democratic change—the East German and Czechoslovak parties?

This points to the possibility that the poor performance of the Polish and Hungarian parties had nothing to do with freedom versus totalitarianism, but was linked to another feature that distinguished these two parties from the Czechoslovak and East German parties: the fact that their party leaderships had for some years been vigorously promoting policies that tended to contradict the socially egalitarian ideologies of their parties, policies of increasing marketization and increasing social differentiation, with increasingly negative effects on those sections of the population in whose name they ruled. In contrast, such policies were not being promoted by the Czechoslovak and East German parties, whose economies were more successful under centralized planning.

Meanwhile, in Romania, Bulgaria, Serbia, and Montenegro, and later in Albania, the post-Communists tended to emerge from the first elections as the strongest parties. These parties retained strong support even if they were, in Bulgaria and Albania, subsequently to go into opposition.

The pattern of political change was different during the Soviet Union's collapse. The August 1991 coup and countercoup resulted in the banning of the CPSU and various republican Communist parties. They were therefore initially marginalized from political life. But when they were again able to operate openly in Russia, Ukraine, and Belarus, they quickly established themselves as the largest parties in their states.

The Attack on Labor

The single most important political fact throughout the region in the 1990s has been the disastrous conditions in which the great majority of working people have been forced to live. This has inevitably had major consequences for their self-confidence and for the possibilities of organization and resistance.

The breakup of Comecon, followed by the collapse of the USSR, caused a trade breakdown and consequent economic depression throughout the region. This situation made all the governments of the region dependent on the West for trade and finance. The G-7 governments, then, through the international financial institutions and the European Union, made access to Western products and financial markets dependent upon governments in the region taking two critical steps: first, proletarianizing labor by massively cutting its purchasing power and by making it dependent upon a capitalist labor market (unemployment and jobs being dependent upon criteria of private profit), and second, rapidly transforming their political economies in ways that made governments dependent upon future Western support, especially as a result of slump-induced fiscal crises, as well as trade deficits and debt servicing obligations.

The drive to proletarianize labor characteristically involved three steps. First, prices were liberalized and state subsidies for necessities were removed, while wages were frozen. This led to sudden cuts in living standards of 25-45 percent. Second, the deep market collapse undermined the revenues of state enterprises, while government policies were designed to make borrowing by enterprises virtually impossible. Third, therefore enterprises were under enormous economic pressure to lay off employees—a key objective in the move towards a capitalist labor market, as far as the international financial institutions were concerned.

The social attack on labor was most sudden and severe in those sectors most connected to intra-Comecon trade—often the most technologically advanced sectors in East Central Europe, but most seriously in Bulgaria, which had been deeply linked to the Soviet economy—and in those countries where anti-Communist governments were first appointed, particularly Poland, Czechoslovakia, Hungary, and Russia.

In these conditions, labor has had to find modes of resistance quite different from those familiar in advanced capitalist countries. Because of the historically unprecedented scale of the slump across the whole region in the early 1990s, involving, typically, a drop of industrial production of about 50 percent, resistance through Western-style strikes for economic demands had little rational meaning: big enterprises were facing bankruptcy because of collapsed markets.

Therefore, the first forms of resistance were concentrated upon trying to defend the state socialist forms of social relations within the state enterprise sector and forming labor-management alliances at enterprise, sectorial, and even national levels to defend the countries' industrial assets and the labor forces attached to them. Workers were prepared to absorb income losses, provided that they could block massive layoffs.

Under state socialism, links between workers and management had often been strong—through the nature of the planning system, which encouraged management to hoard labor and to avoid labor disputes; through Communist Party organizations; through pay and trade union structures: and through a strong, common culture of worker security. This meant that labor-management alliances were widely successful, at least in the initial phase of the slump. Where such corporatist strategies were impossible, as in the former GDR, employees turned to hunger strikes and protest marches in desperate efforts at resistance.

Almost nowhere did the pure concept of proletarianization work: enterprise managements did not shed large quantities of labor to make their enterprises immediately profitable. During the shock, few workers in state enterprises were laid off. Unemployment grew mainly through a complete end to new recruitment. At the same time, many went into retirement, especially those working past the permitted retirement age.

On the other hand, labor did experience a sudden, massive loss of purchasing power which came about easily through state action, because of the nature of consumption under state socialism. Since a very large part of consumption under the old regime was nonmonetized, the wage made up only a small part of workers' means of subsistence. Massively subsidized housing, fuel, transport, and food made up the bulk of employee living standards. Thus, ending these subsidies while freezing wages involved an enormous shift of wealth out of the hands of labor and made labor suddenly and overwhelmingly dependent upon the wage relation.

The failure of the initial proletarianization drive was most complete in the former Soviet republics. Here the creation of capitalist wage dependency was rarely achieved. Enterprise managements widely refused to implement the project. There were two main reasons for this. First, the social influence of labor was too strong because of the radical differences between the Soviet enterprise and capitalist institutions of the same name. Second, managements developed alternative strategies for capital accumulation outside the existing enterprise production systems.

The managerial class of the former Soviet Union looked for alternative ways of accumulating capital, bypassing the problem of reorganizing social relations at the level of the existing state enterprises. Creating networks among themselves, managers hoped to achieve accumulation essentially through pillage, trade, and capital flight, largely illegal and closely connected with political influence. These networks have not been centered on the enterprise structures so much as political networks, often with regional political bases or involving political clans that grew up within the CPSU.

In Belarus, the networks seem to have been centralized at a republican level and to involve functionally differentiated clubs (known as English Clubs). In Ukraine, the most powerful network is that based in Dnepropetrovsk (from where Kuchma comes), but another network has been centered on the old pre-independence leadership of Shcherbitsky. There are also increasingly powerful Russian-based networks in Ukraine.

The operations of these networks have very little to do with industrial capitalism. Thus, in the former Soviet Union, the social transformations are not mainly towards the rapid emergence of state-created industrial capitalism at all. Instead, the state socialist industrial structure is to a very large extent collapsing and being pillaged, with the result that very large parts of the population are reverting to subsistence agriculture and petty trade and production. In Ukraine, about 45 percent of food consumption is now outside all market exchange, and at least a third of large and medium-sized enterprises play no economic role whatsoever, despite continuing as legal entities. Other enterprises that do continue to function at some level do not do so on a capitalist basis.

Thus, very large numbers of workers attending these enterprises are not paid wages. In Ukraine in 1998, wages for workers at large and medium-sized enterprises were running, on average, six to nine months in arrears. On the other hand, workers attending the enterprise on a daily basis get their main meal there, and enterprises often have their own farms for their food supply.

Alongside the great energy and minerals enterprises of Russia, the main forms of capitalism in the former Soviet Union seem to be commercial capitalism, especially export and import operations. Exports take a mostly predatory form outside the energy and minerals sectors: acquiring and selling materials and assets left over from the Soviet period.

This situation, of course, is of questionable value to workers, but it does suggest that the implantation of capitalism, especially in the former Soviet Union, has been far from successful, and that the social power of labor has played an essential role in blocking it. The strength of labor's influence derived from the entire nexus of social relations in Soviet enterprises. These were typically not only economic organizations but also housing departments, health centers, food shops, childcare institutions, food producers and restaurants, and pubs and entertainment centers. To shed these roles in order to turn labor's relation to the enterprise into principally a wage relation was politically impossible for most enterprise managements. This explains why, for example, in the face of the Gaidar shock, very large numbers of enterprise managements formed alliances with their own employees in defense of the old system of social relations. This was also largely true in Bulgaria and in Romania.

By contrast, in Poland and especially in Hungary, market socialist reforms in the 1970s and 1980s had prepared the way for enterprises operating along capitalist lines. The tendency towards the quasi-autarkic enterprise of the Soviet type was generally far weaker in these countries, and in Hungary, in particular, workers' consumption was already far more monetized. The Czech case, on the other hand, is interesting in that the consumption shock was deeper than that in Hungary, but at the same time there was minimal unemployment. Unemployment levels in the Czech republic were only 2.6 percent in 1992 and 3.5 percent in 1993. These figures were more in line with former Soviet Union levels (of between 1 and 2 per cent) than with those of Poland, Hungary, or Bulgaria, where unemployment was at 12 per cent or more at a similar stage of transition. The Klaus government was prepared to allow the whole structure of industrial social links to remain largely intact, provided that there was a shift in income from employees to enterprise accounts.

The Politics of Labor Resistance: The Democratic Backlash

The attempts to resist through corporatist labor-management alliances at the industrial level were combined, of course, with a search for political levers for resisting, either through the incumbent government or through opposition political parties likely to support the demands of labor.

In both Romania and Bulgaria, the former Communists retained power in the first elections. The result in Bulgaria was that, throughout the period from 1990 to 1996, a strong link developed between labor-management alliances in the state industrial sector and the Bulgarian Socialist Party, which was in government most of the time. In Romania, there was at first a similar pattern, but the Iliescu government after 1993 turned increasingly to a kind of state capitalism involving strong government-management alliances and increasingly weak, fragmented, and uninfluential trade unions.

In Poland, uniquely, the first government was widely perceived to be both anti-Communist and pro-labor, and employees in the large enterprises initially expected that the government would hand ownership of the state enterprises over to the workers in those enterprises. But the government, pushed by the international financial institutions, had no intention of doing this and pursued a consistently antilabor drive. As a result, the worker base of Solidarity broke bitterly with its leadership, formed alliances with the formerly official Communist trade unions of the OPZZ, and switched their support to the former Communist Polish Social Democrats.

In Hungary, the first government (the Democratic Forum), though on the conservative right, was not a champion of neoliberal ideologies, and it gained electoral support from labor. But this declined dramatically by 1994, as labor

switched in large numbers to the former Communists in the Hungarian Socialist Party. And in Hungary as in Poland, labor-management alliances were much
weaker than in other countries of the region.

In Slovakia under Meciar, an effort somewhat similar to that in Bulgaria
was attempted: an alliance between management and labor in the big state
enterprises. But this alliance was cemented at a political level through nationalism, under nonsocialist leadership.

In the Czech Republic, the first government was ideologically as committed
to neoliberal ideas as was the Solidarity leadership in Poland. Yet the bargain
it offered to the Czech industrial workers was largely accepted: in return for
workers' acceptance of a large drop in purchasing power (greater than that in
Hungary), the government continued to offer the employees and managers in
the large enterprises a secure framework for the future. The entire nexus of
social, economic, and administrative links in the industrial sector was maintained and supported by the government, even while the government moved
to formally privatize the whole sector into the hands of (mainly publicly
owned) banks. In these conditions, the electoral support for the Czech Communist Party stagnated, a Western-oriented social democratic party became—
uniquely in the region—stronger than the former ruling party, and the Klaus
government won elections for a second term.

Only in the ex-GDR was labor too weak to establish significant labor-management alliances and to find a credible political lever for defending the
region's industrial assets and labor force. The West German trade unions came
into the region, marginalized the former Communist trade unions, and accepted
massive layoffs and closures. In such circumstances, the East German workers
had to resort to protest marches and hunger strikes in efforts to save their
livelihoods, while at the same time turning back towards the former Communist PDS as their electoral hope.

Lithuania was actually the first country where the former Communists came
back into power, and here there was both a strong labor-management alliance
in state enterprises and a link-up with the Socialists at an electoral level. In
Russia, the response was a kind of democratic backlash, in the form of a
popular, constitutionalist opposition to pro-market-reform forces that espoused
"democracy" while suppressing opposition. The Communist Party was banned
while the backlash developed strongly in 1993, and it was expressed first
within the Yelstin camp through the Khasbulatov-Rutskoi leadership of the
Russian parliament. At the same time, the labor-management alliance in the
industrial sector was stronger and "purer" in Russia than anywhere else, and
was expressed most articulately by Volski's Civic Union.

In Ukraine, the labor-management alliance expressed itself first in the rise
of the Ukrainian Socialist Party, formed after the banning of the Ukrainian
Communist Party in 1991, and later in the reformed Ukrainian Communist

Party, but it was also strongly expressed by the presidential challenger, Leonid Kuchma, who represented the politics of a management-led, manager-worker alliance based in the big enterprises.

Very generally, these industrial alliances formed by the post-Communists also had allies from the countryside: in Poland, in the form of the Communist-era Peasant Party, and in Bulgaria and the former Soviet Union, as various agrarian political groupings combining collective farm management with peasants under the leadership of the managers.

In most countries of the region, therefore, industrial workers were able to respond to the pro-capitalist onslaught through initial industrial alliances, democratic backlashes led by the former Communists, or a combination of the two. But that strategy was not possible in three countries: the former GDR, where the PDS was too weak in an all-German context, and Russia and Albania, where the state chose to confront and try to crush the democratic backlash rather than absorb it.

In Russia, President Yeltsin in the summer of 1993 broke with Russia's constitution (and Supreme Court) and ordered the disbanding of the Parliament. The leaders of Parliament then sought to gain Yeltsin's removal and were subjected to a military siege of the Parliament building and subsequent arrest. A new constitution was introduced, and elections were held, leading to the rapid rise of the Communist Party of the Russian Federation (CPRF) as by far the most powerful political party in Russia.

In Albania, the Berisha leadership chose electoral fraud and repression against the former Communist Albanian Socialist Party (imprisoning its leader) along with fraudulent pyramid credit scams. When the latter collapsed there was a full-scale national uprising, followed by Italian-led military intervention and the formation of a new government under the Socialists.

Some Conclusions

We can draw some general conclusions from these developments. It is possible to classify the current post-Communist parties into three main trends for the purposes of analysis, even though only one of these trends has a self-conscious, group identity. First, there is the West European social democratic trend, which has been heavily influenced by the path taken by the Italian Communist Party. The Polish and Hungarian Socialists are the most prominent examples of this trend. Their leaderships accept integration into the EU and NATO and the promotion of a full-fledged capitalist system. At the same time, they tend to support political liberalism, secularism, and constitutionalist values, unlike many currents in their countries on the supposed center-right of the political spectrum. In principle, they also support the preservation of a welfare state and of some continuing role for the public sector, even if, in practice, the Hungarian party leadership in particular has tended to cave in to the international financial institutions almost all the way down the line. But all these parties have sought to present themselves as champions of trade union rights and have sought to appeal for support to the trade union federations. And they contain left wings, including critical currents with some Marxist culture.

A second trend could be described as broad-church Socialist Parties, which combine Western-style social democrats with more Marxist trends supporting a large, continuing state sector and even central planning in their leading echelons. Examples of these parties are the Bulgarian, Albanian, and Ukrainian Socialist parties. The German PDS could also be included in this category.

Other parties can be loosely grouped together on the grounds that they have sought to defend at least some collectivist social structures through nationalist anti-West resistance. Elements of the Slovakia post-Communist left, the Serbian Socialist Party, the Iliescu Social Democratic Party in Romania, and, above all, the CPRF in Russia broadly fit into this category. They do, however, differ in many ways. For one thing, their respective nationalisms are not equally virulent and xenophobic. For another, the CPRF is more committed to legality and constitutionalism than the Romanian or Serbian parties. And the Iliescu party is formally seeking membership of the Socialist International, something that the other parties in this category do not contemplate.

The major question for the left internationally is, of course, the direction of the CPRF. It is not a homogeneously nationalist party, but the Zyuganov leadership dabbles in semi-mystical nationalist rhetoric and makes the distinction between patriotic and treasonous elements within Russia the governing division in the country—more central, for example, than the division between capitalism and socialism. He thus welcomes support for patriotic capital and presents the predatory power of the IMF as the main enemy facing Russia (although, in reality, the IMF has had far less leverage over Russia than over any other country in the region).

Finally, the Czech Communists, along with some other smaller Marxist parties in the region, have sought to continue a tradition of Marxist politics and to develop their links with West European Communist parties such as the French CP, Communist Refoundation in Italy, and the Spanish Communist Party. The Czech Communists have repudiated the idea of the one-party state but have had the will to attempt to set out on the long march to rebuild the European Marxist working-class movement.

Keeping in mind these differences among the various parties, we can draw some general conclusions from their common experience. A decade of capitalist expansion into the former Soviet bloc has revealed that throughout the region very large parts of the population have remained strongly attached to socialist values, and that large minorities have remained loyal to the political movements of the left that emerged from the former ruling Communist parties. The decade has also revealed that the attachment to the old single-party political system on the part of both the population and the former Communist parties was minimal. All these parties quickly repudiated the single-party system and supported pluralist democracy.

Indeed, forces for democracy in these regimes are more likely to be found in the former Communist parties than in the pro-West "democratic forces." These parties have, often alone, given voice to the value attachments of the majority of the electorates, and in the great bulk of the countries, they have championed democratic rights and freedoms.

In those countries where former Communist parties have espoused nationalist themes, their record is rather different, notably in Serbia vis-a-vis the Albanians and in Romania vis-a-vis the gypsies (the self-proclaimed Romani) and, to some extent, towards the Hungarian minority. But these have been exceptions to the general pattern of the region as a whole.

Another central lesson of the experience since 1989 has been the extraordinary difficulty for all labor movements in the region to produce an effective socialist policy. On the one hand, the entire regional division of labor has been shattered, and on the other hand, a substantial minority of the population—20-25 percent—is fully committed to and mobilized for a rapid transition to capitalism. The disruption of the regional trade and payments links made all these economies desperately dependent upon Western product and financial markets. And the pro-capitalist social groups, which included most of the intelligentsia, produced a powerful social linkage with the Western international financial institutions. This linkage was greatly strengthened by the very rapid transfer of media ownerships in many of these countries to Western proprietors at the very start of the transition.

In some countries, the socialist parties have played a crucial role in moderating the effects of the social shock. Without their mediating role in elections, there might have been social explosions, such as in Albania. In this and other ways, they have helped to carry forward the transition to capitalism. In other countries, the socialist parties did see a third path of continued social ownership along with democracy, but they were defeated, as in Bulgaria, by the country's external vulnerability.

In many cases, there is a danger that despairing sections of the population will turn towards authoritarian populist trends. The labor movements will face the task of rallying *truly* democratic forces against the continuing catastrophe of "economic reform" and against authoritarian currents that might appropriate popular resistance.

Notes

1. This section is based on Peter Gowan, "The Passages of the Russian and Eastern European Left," *Socialist Register 1998* (London: Merlin Press, 1998), 124-46. Details of the opinion surveys can be found on 129-30. The article also contains more detailed information about the development of the various Communist parties.

European Industrial Relations: Impasse or Model?

Gregory Albo and Chris Roberts

The long period of economic restructuring since the 1970s, combined with intensified international competition and instability, has set the North American labor movement back on its heels. There are hopeful signs of a labor movement resurgence—in the general strikes against neoliberalism in Ontario, in the militancy of the Canadian Auto Workers, and in the unexpectedly tenacious strike by the Teamsters against UPS. But these do not yet constitute a general trend that has altered the balance of class forces or congealed into a new socialist political formation. The dominant response in the North American labor movement and, indeed, most of the left, remains the defensive search for alternate approaches to competitiveness to set against neoliberalism.

The competitive pressures setting worker against worker are an immediate challenge. The popular image of globalization depicts nations and firms as competing national teams of capitalists and workers together. North American newspapers are filled with accounts measuring the performance of Team Canada or Team GM against the foreign competition. Global competitiveness rankings provide capitalists (and, increasingly, governments) with a helpful tool for wringing new work practices and wage concessions from fearful workforces. The message is that workers and unions must submit to the reality of global capitalism and do their part for national and firm competitiveness.

Workers, and even capitalists and managers, are continually exhorted to learn from the industrial relations practices that have produced successful national capitalisms abroad. Even the labor movement itself often points to alternative consensual European models of competitiveness. Typically, the Swedish or German examples are invoked in the struggle to resist intensification of coercive North American-style management practices and labor-market flexibility, and more recently the even more unlikely example of New Labour's Britain is being cited by some social democratic unionists. The North American labor movement often looks favorably on European national training systems, labor market regulation, forms of worker representation, patterns of collective bargaining, social welfare supports, and legal frameworks safeguarding workers' rights. Liberals sympathetic to the labor movement—notably Robert Reich and Richard Freeman—are fond of recommending these alternate forms of mediating the labor market as a way of avoiding cutthroat competitive practices.

There is much to be said against this habit of invoking foreign models. For one thing, although it is true that capitalism imposes universal imperatives of competition, which oblige enterprises and national economies to keep up with competitors often by imitating them, these universal pressures always work in historically specific and variable conditions. Each national economy has its own specific history, its own specific location in the world capitalist economy, its own specific balance of class forces, and its own specific class struggles, which have produced specific social and institutional arrangements that cannot simply be transplanted.

But our object here is not simply to expose the limits of imitation. Instead, we want to look at some of the models often invoked by the left, to see if they really do justify the claims made for them. Beginning with a general survey of industrial relations in Europe after the Second World War, we will then explore three specific cases—Germany, Sweden, and the United Kingdom—to see how they have responded to capitalist restructuring in recent years.

We take it for granted that there are many national differences among advanced capitalist countries, but also that workers in all of them are facing common problems in this period of economic restructuring. The question here is whether European models really represent progressive alternatives to North American ways of confronting these common problems, or whether we are now seeing European variants of intensified exploitation—the same intensified exploitation as in North America but mediated by historically specific European institutions.

Industrial Relations in Postwar Europe

The postwar reconstruction of Europe was a moment of intense class conflict and institutional creativity in the forging of national identities, political systems, and forms of industrial relations. Although earlier patterns of class formation persisted, national union movements were strengthened by the rise of socialist parties, their role in wartime governments, the discredit of capitalist classes for their fascist sympathies, and the economic dominance of manufacturing industries where unions were strong.[1]

European industrial relations systems are commonly classified according to their degree of trade union organization and the extent of national coordination of economic and wage policies. The Nordic and German-speaking countries, together with the Netherlands, form a corporatist group with extensive coordination and strong unions; the Mediterranean countries form a group of fragmented and isolated labor movements (and thus have held the least appeal as models); and Britain is characterized by pluralist bargaining, combining strong sectorial unions and weak central coordination largely confined to state involvement in pay restraint.

The British industrial relations system most clearly resembles the North American in the separation of politics from industrial relations in the sense that the union movement has been marginal to economic policy-making. There is also a parallel in the decentralization of postwar collective bargaining institutions, although in Britain this system was regulated by voluntary norms and in North America by industrial law.

The rising level of industrial conflict in the 1960s in Britain, however, sparked a large number of industrial commissions seeking to limit working-class unrest and impress upon unions the need to reverse the decline in Britain's competitive capacity, supposedly resulting from restrictive work practices and rank-and-file militancy. But free collective bargaining also became more constrained as wage advances interacted with deteriorating competitiveness to erupt in balance of payments crises through the 1960s and 1970s. This politicized industrial relations even more as Labour governments increasingly resorted to incomes policies to deliver pay restraint.

In the Federal Republic of Germany, the new Trade Union Federation (DGB) emerged out of the ashes of fascism as a unitary structure with unions demarcated by industrial sector. The new industrial relations system was built on the dual structure of interest representation: unions and employers associations bargaining collectively over wages and hours at the sectorial level (dealing with quantitative issues related to income distribution and productivity); and at the company level, managers and workers meeting in works councils (discussing qualitative issues, such as skills and competitiveness).

In a highly legalistic union environment, class conflicts in Germany are mediated through social partnership processes of national coordination and "codetermination" *(Mitbestimmung)* between workers and employers. These processes are kept separate from formal state institutions and national economic policy, which the Christian Democratic Union has dominated. High unemployment in the immediate postwar period allowed the emergence of the German social market model, in which coordination held labor costs in line with external competitiveness, and the federal state combined a strict monetary policy with a moderately redistributive social policy.

As labor market conditions tightened in the 1960s, the policy of the Social Democratic Party (SPD), entering government for the first time, further encouraged wage restraint through national coordination while modestly extending the role of the works councils. The legal constitutionalism of the German union movement proved profoundly contradictory: it restricted working class gains when German economic performance was rising but also restricted management's range of manoeuvre in periods of economic decline.

In contrast, in Sweden the social democratic party SAP dominated government from the 1930s, and their policies, as much as the union confederation LO, shaped the Swedish model and its industrial relations system. Swedish social democracy eschewed public ownership for a policy of high employment through Keynesian demand management (and later currency devaluation) and expansion of the public sector. The industrial relations system tightly controlled wage bargaining by means of central negotiations between LO and the employers group SAF without extensive regulation by the state.

Wage negotiations in the postwar period were intended to match productivity growth with real wage growth to sustain external competitiveness, while preventing inflation and wage drift through implementation of pay norms at a sub-national level. Setting central wage norms for the whole economy also meant that firms with low productivity, hence low wages, would be squeezed out.

In the 1950s, the system of labor market boards expanded to focus even more on achieving high employment and productivity by means of active labor market policies such as training and employment subsidies. With high union density and low unemployment into the 1970s, the Swedish unions concentrated on wage solidarity to lessen wage differentials, relations between the growing white-collar unions and LO, and, through plant-level activism, the slow evolution of a formal shop-steward system. The long, steady consolidation of the Swedish model, however, was just as quickly subjected to the imperatives of capitalist competition as was the rest of Europe in the 1970s.

The popular uprisings at the close of the 1960s signaled not the end of class conflict in Western Europe, but rather the beginning of a prolonged period of mounting challenges to national industrial relations in the region. Since the 1973 oil shock, economic instability across the advanced capitalist countries has resulted in weak employment conditions and an increasingly unequal distribution of labor-market incomes. There has been a consistent pattern of *labor-market failure* that no state has overcome.

Adjustment to slower output growth has, however, taken different routes. In the United States, labor markets have become the most flexible in compressing wages and disguising unemployment in the form of low-productivity, low-wage, and frequently precarious employment.[2] In Europe, capitalist pressures toward social polarization have been somewhat relieved, more than reinforced, by labor market institutions (although this is less true of the Mediterranean countries). Many countries of the European Union (EU) have cushioned high rates of joblessness with unemployment and welfare benefits that reduce income inequality, as in Germany and many of the Nordic countries; or relatively egalitarian income distribution (in terms of capitalism) has been combined with disguised unemployment in other forms, principally low labor-force participation rates and underemployment, as in the Netherlands. But where wages and employment have been spread more evenly across the working class as a whole, the consequence has been stagnant—and even falling—living standards for workers, fiscal pressures, and capital flight.[3]

While the adjustment experience has varied, it can be said that in both North America and the EU, trade union movements confront labor markets failing to deliver equitable living conditions for increasing numbers of workers. This is an outcome that labor movements have found increasingly difficult to arrest in conditions of high unemployment and growing part-time and casual employment. It has also affected wage setting. The wage share of GDP (the grossest measure of union capacity) fell sharply throughout the EU during the 1980s, in some countries hitting postwar lows, and remains flat in the 1990s. Similarly, strike actions almost everywhere in Europe have dropped to record lows and, although there is considerable variation in union density levels and patterns, union membership has slipped throughout the EU, with the exception of Denmark.[4] The consequences of the growing failure of the labor market and the retreat of labor across Europe are fears of social exclusion, right-wing extremism, and deepening poverty.[5]

There are, then, deep-rooted forces for instability across Europe's industrial relations systems. Intensified competition in slow-growing markets within Europe has brought growing demands for union sacrifices in the interest of competitiveness. This has further aggravated existing class tensions within consensual corporatist arrangements such as those in Sweden and Germany. As Leo Panitch argued long ago, even under the buoyant economic conditions of the postwar period, corporatist arrangements were vulnerable to destabilization from below because of the contradictory position of unions: as class organizations for the expression of workers' demands, and, at the same time, as institutions administering wage restraint through incomes policies to meet the accumulation requirements of capital.[6] The economic crisis following 1973 intensified this contradiction for the labor movements in Sweden, Germany, and Britain.

The European union movements thus faced a critical challenge: to try sustaining the postwar pattern, as did Sweden and Britain, by Keynes-plus measures that matched incomes policies with labor market and industrial policies to raise output; to resist by defensive measures the growing offensive by capital (the North American pattern); or to launch a broader political project to begin actively socializing capital, as both the Swedish Meidner Plan for wage-earner funds and the French Common Programme proposed.

The last option barely got off the ground, especially as even industrial policies were bitterly opposed by European capitalists in the 1970s. What emerged was an expansion of labor market policies at the national level and union attempts to resist neoliberalism at the sectorial and local levels through the 1980s. Moreover, European industrial relations systems, especially in the national models with strong unions and corporatist bargaining, now functioned quite differently. The postwar bargaining norm of *nominal* wage restraint in collective bargaining to control inflation, in return for higher and more stable output through low inflation, was transformed into a norm of *real* wage restraint to spread employment and prevent layoffs.

Industrial relations systems in the leading economies of post-war Europe had sought to maintain working-class shares of a growing output. That objective was limited enough, but now, in the face of slower growth, their goal was even more restricted, since they were distributing a declining share of wages. In Sweden, this was negotiated centrally through the LO and the governing social democrats in the SAP. In Germany, it worked itself out at the sectorial level through the constituent components of the DGB. In Britain, the experience of Thatcherism finished off an already marginal corporatism. Unions in the Trades Union Congress (TUC) were pushed into concessions negotiations at the sectorial or company levels in a manner similar to North American unions.

Where union movements did not suffer outright defeat, then, they sought to impose a kind of shared austerity on the working class. But this could last only as long as workers agreed to lower incomes and higher taxes in exchange for a strong social sector that spread work, and capitalists were compelled to maintain domestic investment and allow a large and expanding public sector.[7] Increasing European integration soon began to place heavy strains on such corporatist bargains.

Contrary to some conventional assumptions, European integration has meant not only increasing cooperation among European states but intensified competition among their economies. Throughout the 1980s, as competition became more intense, corporatist bargains were subjected to the pressures of maintaining profitability. Slowing private sector investment and minimal but continuous productivity gains meant weak employment conditions and thus greater wage compression and taxation of workers to ensure external competitiveness, sufficiently high rates of return on investment, and stable budgets.[8]

In other words, national union movements were being transformed into the guarantors of capitalist economic stability. Capitalists were induced to invest by means of wage restraint, and employment was spread by means of higher taxes, at the expense of workers' immediate material interests. These practices, then, hardly represent models of economic and political advance, as their North American advocates maintain. Instead, these institutional arrangements have become the particular form in which the rate of exploitation has been intensified for European workers.

The intense pressures placed on working-class solidarity and egalitarianism, in the context of widening inequalities between the social classes and capitalist offensives, have begun to erode the redistributional component of Swedish and German industrial relations. In Sweden, austerity within one class has broken down as employers have balked at low profits, high taxes, and a large public sector and begun to export capital rather than invest in Sweden.

Workers have strained under the burden they have been asked to bear alone. In Germany, the continued offensive by German capitalists, the bureaucratic inertia of the DGB, and the added burden of unification signaled the long-term crisis of the social partnership model. In countries such as Britain, where unions have been defeated and remain under attack, the result has been increasing social inequality, with political rebuilding not yet on the horizon.

Germany: The Social Market Model in Crisis

The fiscal shock of German reunification, the sharp economic recession of the early 1990s, and the persistence of mass unemployment have created profound uncertainties about the future of the German social market model.[9] The German industrial relations structure has historically had some success in establishing a uniform labor market by extending collective bargaining coverage to all workers and partly insulating wage costs from direct competition (although the situation of "guest workers" is quite a different story). But high and rising unemployment since the 1980s has led to a segmentation of labor markets and the marginalization of a growing stratum of workers, a low employment rate, and consequent fiscal pressures.[10] The DGB faces the challenge of dealing with chronically high unemployment in declining sectors; employment growth in areas that have proven more resistant to organizing, such as the service sector; and a German industrial relations system under severe internal and external strain.

Statutory rights to workplace representation for employees in the form of firm-level codetermination require that changes to employment relations be negotiated. But broader political and economic forces have generated severe pressure for deregulation, so far mainly in the form of loosening regulations on labor markets rather than their wholesale removal.[11] German firms in high-quality, medium-technology industries, once thought to be immune to competitive pressures for cost-reduction and often envied as a model of flexible adjustment on the basis of labor-management cooperation, are also experiencing pressures from Japanese and American rivals.[12]

With codetermination in the works councils unable to control capital allocation, these firms have increasingly expanded foreign direct investment abroad and moved elements of the production chain eastward to circumvent regulation and high costs. This movement has been given added incentive by the anticipated entry of Central and East European countries into the European Union, with the likelihood that the low-cost, highly-skilled labor in the high-unemployment zones of the East will add to existing pressures for cost reduction in the German system.[13] Indeed, there is evidence that capitalists have begun to defect from the employers associations crucial to sectorial bargaining. This is happening even as pressure is being exerted through works councils and on the unions to deliver concessions in the form of hardship clauses and moderate wage demands to encourage employment growth.[14]

The external environment also poses challenges to the export-driven German model, which has typically relied on strong growth in international markets and export surpluses to maintain low unemployment and rising incomes. The continued stagnation, intensified competition, and instability of the world economy have added to domestic industrial restructuring to produce chronically high unemployment (even with sharply falling participation rates among older male workers).[15] Ironically, this problem is compounded by the fact that Germany's principal trading partners in the rest of western Europe are deflating to meet the requirements of the European Monetary Union set out under the Maastricht Accord, and under the competitive pressures transmitted by the Bundesbank's own disinflationary policy.

The pressures on fiscal resources from a large, dependent population of unemployed, inactive, and older pensioned-off workers, combined with austerity measures to meet the convergence criteria of Maastricht and transfers to eastern Germany on the order of $100 billion yearly, are stretching the limits of the social bargain.[16] Just at the moment when the German stakeholding model is so much in vogue among social democrats for its flexible adjustment, cooperative labor relations, and the patient capital it supposedly provides to domestic industry, in Germany itself the model is in crisis.

Some observers have hoped that the German model could be universalized across Europe through the EU. But this hope is contradicted by the fact, acknowledged even by the German model's strongest advocates, that codetermination cannot be extended even to other EU countries without fundamentally changing existing legal systems and imposing a German-type industrial relations system. And within Germany itself, capitalists are attempting to redefine and, in many areas, eliminate that system. Indeed, even the transfer of the system to eastern Germany is proving difficult to consolidate.[17]

The labor movement itself is suffering a crisis of strategic direction. The German model of industrial relations has had significant effects on the movement's capacity for struggle.[18] The system of sectorial collective bargaining has become an established ritual to which the individual union member has no direct relationship, since the benefits of the agreement are reaped regardless of membership. More generally, the effect of the social partnership model has been a political demobilization of the labor movement. While unions are wrestling with that legacy, German capitalists have seized the opportunity to break many of the restrictions imposed on them by the partnership model.[19]

The political opening offered by unification and the disintegration of the state-led East German trade union system illustrates the impasse of the labor movement. The impulse of the DGB was to transfer existing structures to the East, adding East German workers to its own rolls. It failed to use the moment for organizational reform, determined instead to meet the challenge of expansion by avoiding the uncertainties of organizational restructuring.[20] In West

Germany, the DGB has confronted the problem of a declining membership with a similar strategy, merging its member unions and making only minimal efforts to strengthen union organization and rank-and-file identification with the union.[21]

There have, however, been a few dramatic and successful strikes, especially the massive 1993 strike in the metalworking sector led by IG Metall, as well as its successful campaigns to reduce labor supply by means of reducing (and redistributing) work time. Such developments have the added advantage of forging better political links with the German ecology movement, which has been estranged from the workers' movement. Similarly, in 1997 the coal miners successfully struck against job cuts. Finally, the DGB has opened some political space apart from the Social Democratic Party (SPD), and vice versa, although a political realignment of the left still seems distant.[22]

These developments may be promising signs of revival, but for the moment they are exceptions in the general picture of a union movement strategically disoriented and lacking sustained capacity for mobilization. And only dissident sections of IG Metall, primarily in the auto sector, have broken with German capital's competitiveness agenda.

Sweden: After the Model

If the German labor movement has been struggling with German employers over competitiveness and the institutions of industrial relations, Swedish unions have confronted an aggressive and mobilized capitalist class. Since the 1980s, Swedish transnational firms have expanded operations abroad and aggressively pushed for flexibility and decentralized wage bargaining at home, effectively undermining the Swedish model.[23]

The employers organization SAF began to mobilize politically in the early 1980s against the labor movement's wage earner funds proposal, called the "Meidner Plan," By the end of the decade SAF had successfully replaced centralized wage negotiations with industry- and firm-level bargaining. In 1991, it unilaterally abandoned peak-level negotiations. It also advocated deregulation and the sell-off of public assets, and led public campaigns protesting social democratic fiscal policy and public expenditure.[24] With the rise of mass unemployment in Sweden and the acceptance of neoliberal austerity by the new SAP government, peak-level corporatist bargaining may in the future simply be unnecessary to deliver wage restraint, permitting decentralized bargaining without risk of bidding up wages.

While mass unemployment is of more recent origin, the malaise of the Swedish model is of longer standing. One early symptom was the resort to employment-spreading as the principal, and often unintended, social outcome of political bargaining between LO, SAF, and the SAP in government. There were other symptoms, too. After narrowing over the 1960s and 1970s (and while still low by international standards), wage differentials began to widen in the second half of the 1980s.[25] Periodic currency devaluations as a response to problems of competitiveness, combined with stagnant productivity growth and wage spreading, also took their toll on working-class incomes. For example, the average after-tax wage fell roughly 20 percent between 1973 and 1985, and by 1990 was still well below 1973 levels.[26] The result was a stagnation of working-class living standards, which, despite far more developed provision of public goods, resembled the stagnant wages confronting North American unions.

The LO was unable to correct this situation, in which one class alone, the working class, carried the burden of austerity. That inability reflected a more significant rupture in the Swedish model that followed capital's opposition to the Meidner Plan. The export of capital by Swedish employers in the 1980s signaled a shift in private investment strategies, dissolution of the postwar system of capital controls, and more fundamentally, the undermining of the material basis for the domestic class collaboration that had formed the high-employment, high-productivity Swedish model.

Outward foreign direct investment jumped from 10 percent of all business investment in 1985 to 28 percent in 1989, reaching 6 percent of GDP the following year, the highest among the advanced capitalist economies.[27] In 1988, more than 60 percent of profits earned internationally by Swedish multinationals were reinvested abroad, and the share of total employment in Swedish firms located in foreign subsidiaries tripled between 1960 and 1987.[28]

The deregulation of financial markets during the 1980s boom, intended partly as a response to growing internationalization, prepared the way for the mass unemployment and stagnation of the 1990s. Moreover, the SAP, back in power after a brief period of conservative government, followed the neoliberal policies of fiscal and monetary constriction and openly campaigned for an even more complete break with the solidarity policies of the past.

The LO has, therefore, had to respond by charting new directions. It has, among other things, distanced itself to some extent from the rightward-leaning SAP. For example, a Union Opposition has been formed, largely out of the Metal Workers Union, to oppose the continual retreats in collective bargaining and the failure to adequately challenge the SAP government. But the LO has as yet no coherent strategy, except for a return to revamped solidarity wage bargaining, and there is even some rather blithe invocation of German social partnership models.

There has, however, been some regrouping of unions and bargaining at the sectoral level. The strength of white-collar unions has been especially important in realigning the union movement. The main innovation has been the strategic rethinking of solidaristic work, especially in relation to women workers. Although the participation of women in the labor force is quite high compared, for instance, to Germany, much of women's employment is part-time and vulnerable to casualisation, and income differentials are more common because of highly gender-segmented labor markets. Attempts are now being made to address the occupational segmentation and unequal integration of women into the labor force that have generated tensions between private- and public-sector unions.

The political mobilization of women has thus been on the rise in the LO and its member unions, as part of the defence of the public sector.[29] Although its child care and parental policies were won in order to support the equitable integration of women into the labor market, the LO has also begun to inject gender equity directly into a range of issues in its efforts to revitalize the union movement. In the 1990s, it has supported the emergence of a separate women's caucus and the independent political organization of women employees and non-employees. Kommunal, the largest union organizing employees in the health and social services sector, more than 80 percent of whom are female and among the worst paid, has also been active in defending public services against market rationalization.

British Unions Under Blair: More of the Same?

If large employers led the offensive against established industrial relations practices in Sweden, it was the state that assumed the responsibility of removing union restrictions on competitiveness in Britain. In the 1980s, Margaret Thatcher led a direct frontal assault on the already weak British system of employment rights, rolling back workers' gains and earning the admiration of neoliberals everywhere.

As a consequence of market-led adjustment, Britain combined the most flexible labor markets in western Europe with one of the highest unemployment rates. Unemployment climbed to an average of over 9 percent from 1980 to 1995, owing in part to the continued de-industrialization of the British economy.[30] This rise in the official rate of unemployment was accompanied by an exodus from the labor market of 1.3 million non-student, working-age Britons, mainly with low skills, between 1979 and 1992.[31] The official unemployment rate of about 6 percent in 1997 is thus a result of cyclical economic recovery and the expansion of low-wage jobs, together with long-term trends of labor withdrawal. This form of growth in labor reserves, although it does not appear in official unemployment figures, still puts downward pressure on the labor market, keeping British unions on the defensive (in much the same way that a similar trend has done in the United States).

Partly as a direct consequence of Thatcher's anti-trade-union legislation, which aided union derecognition battles by employers, and partly as a consequence of continuing deindustrialization, British union density has fallen from 55 percent over the years 1976 to 1980 to about 40 percent in the 1990s.[32] Declining membership has combined with the replacement of centralized industry-level collective bargaining in several major sectors by firm-level negotiations. This has effectively reduced workers covered directly and indirectly by union contracts from more than 70 percent in 1984 to 54 percent in 1990 (a figure that continues to fall), one of the worst declines among the OECD economies.[33]

These trends are the result of a whole series of flexible labor policies introduced by Tory governments: Britain's already minimal employee protection and labor standards legislation was diluted, benefit replacement rates for the unemployed fell dramatically, and so on. The consequences of the government and employer assaults on British workers have been ghastly: since the end of the 1970s, pay inequality has increased faster than anywhere else in the advanced industrialized world, apart from the U.S., and is now at its widest in Britain for perhaps over a century.[34]

Part of the growth of wage inequality has been a polarization in the distribution of working time—with the increase of lower-paid, part-time, insecure jobs during the 1990s recovery.[35] The toll on the British industrial relations system has been enormous: by the 1990s, Britain had become a low-wage zone for European production by Japanese transplants in greenfield sites. Many of the major unions, and the TUC itself, have at least passively accepted lean production.

The election of Tony Blair's Labour Party in 1997 has meant little: a Low Wage Commission to install a standard minimum wage for the first time and modest and, to a degree, coercive and neoliberal work-to-welfare and youth employment schemes. There has been no reversal of the anti-union reforms of the Thatcher and Major governments. Owing to the desperation of union members to be rid of the Tories, New Labour has maintained favor with much of the labor movement and the TUC, despite the Party's efforts to diminish union influence—though recent developments like the government's hard line on conditions for union recognition and its reluctance to accept even some of the milder EU provisions concerning, for example, workplace consultation may push the tolerance of unions to its limits.

Some British unions, especially the Amalgamated Engineers and trades unions like the Electricians, have adopted their own brand of neoliberalism and have sought to forge a productivity alliance with manufacturing capital in the interests of competitiveness and employment stability, but this effort has found little support. It has not gone beyond an enterprise unionism that discards old work practices and allows greater company flexibility, as many unions have been doing since the mid-1980s, especially in the wake of the miners' strike.

The stakeholder capitalism envisioned by Blair and company faces the enormous obstacles created by the long assault on the British union movement, not to mention the employers' offensives against the German and Swedish models that have broken these kinds of productivity alliances in their own countries. Hopes for a strong "social" Europe, with social protections throughout the EU, are also dimming. Such hopes are likely to be dashed by the combined impact of the deflationary bias of the EMU and competition throughout the EU (including Germany and Sweden) to attract capital investment by means of competitive austerity.

The European Monetary Union (EMU) is tying the hands of national economic policy, leaving few options for coping with restructuring, apart from state policies to promote supply-side labor market flexibility. So some sections of the European left have begun to look favorably on Blairism. This is especially the case for social democratic parties (and their allied unions) in high unemployment zones, as with the Olive alliance in Italy, part of the Jospin government in France, and the PSOE in Spain.[36] The same search for "flexibility with a human face" explains why the Dutch model is also often evoked. Similarly, Blairism appeals to business unionists in the U.S. simply because it offers relief from hard right governments and speaks the language of cooperation in coping with globalization. But the real experience of British workers should make it clear that the cool Britannia model of New Labour should hold little appeal for labor movements outside Britain, on the continent or in North America.

Labor Movements and Models Forward

There have been many paths of transformation in European industrial relations systems. But there have been common challenges from the intensification of capitalist imperatives over the past two decades, as the contrasting cases of Germany, Sweden, and Britain, with their distinct industrial relations systems, vividly illustrate. None of the national models are producing the social benefits for workers they once did. They have offered little protection against the ravages of capitalist restructuring. The cornerstones of postwar collective bargaining are crumbling, and in some cases, the old arrangements have themselves become mechanisms for imposing austerity and intensifying exploitation.

This has entailed a search for new strategic directions by national union movements in Europe, but the process has been slow and hesitant. As national systems of industrial relations have proved inadequate, the EU project has raised hopes for multinational cooperation among the European labor movements. But apart from more formalized meetings in the European Trade Union Confederation, some negotiating pressure for EU provisions, and a few cases of transnational bargaining coordination, there has been no clear strategic direction for unions at this level either.

While the labor movement looks for new directions, European capital is transforming itself rather more quickly. The drive for European economic and monetary union, accompanying the corporate integration of production and circulation on a continental scale, is generating further competition over investment and employment throughout Europe. The creation of a Single European Market and the EMU convergence criteria set out at Maastricht, accompanied by weak provisions for a Social Europe and a system of European

Works Councils, have intensified political and legal efforts to harmonize standards and regulations across EU countries. So European labor movements are facing a new challenge: the need for strategic transformation and political mobilization, not only at the national level but also at the transnational level of the European Union.

In Europe as well as in North America, despite the growing instability of world capitalism, the ideology of TINA ("There Is No Alternative") is widely accepted. This has led to a search for alternatives within capitalism that might be capable of delivering some measure of social welfare while submitting to the requirements of capitalist accumulation. But it is simply an illusion to think that there are crisis-free models of capitalism—effectively, capitalisms that are not capitalist—available for universal adaptation.

Not only is a notion of crisis-free capitalism chimerical, the urge to find more cooperative and competitive models of capitalism rests on questionable assumptions about the nature of capitalism, modernization, and progress. The supposition is that model states or systems of industrial relations are advanced, while other societies are backward and need modernizing.[37] Economies held up as models are effectively abstracted from history, as if they were not themselves the products of specific class struggles, and as if they were themselves immune to the pressures and crises of capitalist change.

The objectives, strategies, and terrain of socialist struggle in any given time and place will always be affected by their specific historical context. At the same time, those specific conditions cannot be considered apart from their capitalist character. To the extent that all capitalist societies are subject to the same capitalist "laws of motion," their labor movements can learn from each other.

But the lessons to be learned should not be about how different national—and now, within the EU, multinational—models of capitalism can be imitated. That approach asks the workers' movement to accept the capitalist logic of competitiveness and treats capitalist imperatives as permanent, not historically specific and transitory. The effect is to undermine the principles of the labor movement—egalitarianism, solidarity, cooperative economies and not competitive ones, and production for use and not for exchange. The workers' movement should reject such an approach, not out of some purist and unrealistic utopianism but because it threatens the historical gains of workers' struggles, the very existence of independent working-class organizations, and the possibility of democratic institutions for economic coordination and provision outside of market imperatives.

Labor movements need to go on the offensive instead of submitting themselves completely to the imperatives of capitalist accumulation and competition. This means seeking ways of constraining and reducing the scope of the market with the aim of increasing the time and space *disengaged* from the market. In this respect, labor movements in various countries *can* learn from each other and find ways of confronting common problems in diverse political settings, while offering support and solidarity across national boundaries. North American labor movements might, for example, support efforts by the Swedish labor movement to reestablish capital controls and the wage-earner funds. Or the German labor movement might lead European-wide campaigns supportive of American strike actions for reduced work-time.

This implies a strategy for transforming European and North American labor movements that is very different from what is commonly on offer from the left. It means no longer relying on the social partnership models so often invoked in a futile effort to *tame* capitalist competition instead of replacing it.

Notes

1. See especially the essays by Richard Hyman in *Industrial Relations in the New Europe*, ed. Anthony Ferner and Richard Hyman (Oxford: Blackwell, 1992); and Hyman and Ferner, eds., *New Frontiers in European Industrial Relations* (Oxford: Blackwell, 1994).
2. Michael D. Yates, *Longer Hours, Fewer Jobs: Employment and Unemployment in the United States* (New York: Monthly Review Press, 1994).
3. International Labour Office, *World Employment 1995* (Geneva: ILO, 1995), 137.
4. Stephen J. Silvia, "The Social Charter of the European Community: A Defeat for European Labor," *Industrial and Labor Relations Review* 44, no. 4 (1991): 630.
5. John Vinocur, "Poverty Becoming Ugly Routine in Europe," *International Herald Tribune*, 17 October 1997.
6. Leo Panitch, *Working Class Politics in Crisis* (London: Verso, 1986).
7. Gregory Albo, "A World Market of Opportunities? Capitalist Obstacles and Left Economic Policy," in *The Socialist Register 1997: Ruthless Criticism of All That Exists,* ed. Leo Panitch (London: Merlin, 1997).
8. Andrew Glyn, "Social Democracy and Full Employment," *New Left Review* no. 211 (1995): 54.
9. Wendy Carlin and David Soskice, "Shocks to the System: The German Political Economy Under Stress," *National Institute Economic Review* 159, no. 1 (1997).
10. Stephen J. Silvia, "Political Adaptation to Growing Labor Market Segmentation," in *Negotiating the New Germany,* ed. Lowell Turner (Ithaca: Cornell University Press, 1997).
11. Richard Hyman, "Industrial Relations in Western Europe: An Era of Ambiguity?" *Industrial Relations* 33, no. 1 (1994).
12. Birgit Mahnkopf, "Between the Devil and the Deep Blue Sea: The German Model Under the Pressure of Globalisation," in *The Socialist Register 1999*, ed. Colin Leys and Leo Panitch (London: Merlin Press, 1999).
13. Hans-Georg Betz, "The German Model Reconsidered," *German Studies Review* 19, no. 2 (1996): 316-17. This latter point is cautiously raised by Michael Fichter, "Unions in the New Länder: Evidence for the Urgency of Reform," in *Negotiating the New Germany,* ed. Turner (Ithaca: Cornell University Press, 1997), 105.

14. Stephen J. Silvia, "German Unification and Emerging Divisions within German Employers' Associations: Cause or Catalyst?" *Comparative Politics*, 29, no. 2 (1997).
15. Carlin and Soskice, "Shocks to the System": 69.
16. Ibid.: 64.
17. Wolfgang Streeck, "German Capitalism: Does it Exist? Can it Survive?" *New Political Economy* 2, no. 2 (1997).
18. Silvia, "German Unification."
19. Michael Fichter, "Trade Union Members: A Vanishing Species in Post-Unification Germany?" *German Studies Review* 20, no. 1 (1997): 100.
20. Ibid.: 85.
21. Ibid.: 99.
22. Stephen J. Silvia, "The Forward Retreat: Labor and Social Democracy in Germany, 1982-1992," *International Journal of Political Economy* 22, no. 4 (1992-93).
23. Jonas Pontusson and Peter Swenson, "Labour Markets, Production Strategies, and Wage Bargaining Institutions: The Swedish Employer Offensive in Comparative Perspective," *Comparative Political Studies* 29, no. 2 (1996).
24. Stuart Wilks, "Class Compromise and the International Economy: The Rise and Fall of Swedish Social Democracy," *Capital and Class* 58 (1996): 107.
25. Per-Andrers Edin and Bertil Holmlund, "The Swedish Wage Structure: The Rise and Fall of Solidarity Wage Policy?" in *Differences and Changes in Wage Structures,* ed. Richard Freeman and Lawrence F. Katz (Chicago: University of Chicago Press, 1995).
26. Glyn, "Social Democracy and Full Employment": 51.
27. Wilks, "Class Compromise and the International Economy": 103.
28. Jonas Pontusson, "Sweden: After the Golden Age," in *Mapping the West European Left,* ed. Perry Anderson and Patrick Camiller (London: Verso, 1994), 42.
29. Rianne Mahon, "From Solidaristic Wages to Solidaristic Work: A Post-Fordist Historic Compromise for Sweden?" *Economic and Industrial Democracy* 15, no. 3 (1994).
30. William Brown, Simon Deakin, and Paul Ryan, "The Effects of British Industrial Relations Legislation 1979-97," *National Institute Economic Review* 161, no. 3 (1997).
31. John Schmitt and Jonathan Wadsworth, "Unemployment, Inequality and Inefficiency: The Rise in Economic Inactivity," in *Paying For Inequality,* ed. Andrew Glyn and David Miliband (London: IPPR/Rivers Oram Press, 1994), 114.
32. Brown, Deakin, and Ryan, "The Effects": 73.
33. Ibid.: 74-5.
34. Glyn and Miliband, "Introduction," in *Paying For Inequality*.
35. Andrew Glyn, "The Assessment: Unemployment and Inequality," *Oxford Review of Economic Policy* 11, no. 1 (1995).
36. Andy Robinson, "Why 'Employability' Won't Make EMU Work," in *The Single European Currency in National Perspective: A Community in Crisis*, ed. Bernard Moss and Jonathan Michie (London: Macmillan, 1998).
37. Ellen Meiksins Wood, *The Pristine Culture of Capitalism* (London: Verso, 1991).

The ICFTU and the Politics of Compromise

Gerard Greenfield

In whatever form of engagement we undertake, negotiations must never become a substitute for mass struggle, and we must never allow ourselves to become jointly responsible for the management of a system which seeks to destroy the very constituency we claim to represent.

—Roger Ronnie, General Secretary,
South African Municipal Workers Union (SAMWU)[1]

"Think Globally, Act Locally" has become a familiar catch-phrase among trade unionists and labor activists around the world. In one sense, it simply acknowledges the importance of international solidarity in our struggles—which, of course, is not new. In another sense, it reflects a greater awareness of the common crisis faced by working-class people under globalization, and asserts the necessity of combining a critical consciousness of the global capitalist system with collective action in the local terrain of class struggle to challenge the logic of this system. But it is rarely used in this sense.

Instead, globalization is used by the majority of national union leaders to justify the abandonment of collective action locally, and even nationally, as ineffective or irrelevant. Based on what they see as the inevitability of capitalist globalization and the weakness of organized labor, they are instead seeking a new set of compromises with global capital. Or to put it more accurately, they are seeking a continuation of the old compromises with national capital at a global level. This involves engagement with international capitalist organizations such as the World Trade Organization (WTO) and the Asia-Pacific Economic Cooperation (APEC) so that, at best, labor can be represented in the global arena. It seems, then, that we are faced with quite a different slogan: "Talk Globally, Give Up Locally."

But clearly, workers are not giving up locally, and neither are they just talking globally. There are organized, militant struggles taking place all over the world which are gaining support from workers' movements in other countries. Much of the movement in the international labor movement is in fact found in those international exchanges, networks, and cross-border solidarity campaigns which take place outside the official union hierarchy—in what Kim Moody calls rank-and-file internationalism.[2] However, there are also a series of new and important solidarity campaigns involving international union federations that have chosen to support local struggles through concerted international action that challenges global capital. This includes the campaign by Public Services International (PSI) to support the struggle of the South African Municipal Workers Union (SAMWU) against the British transnational, Biwater; the International Federation of Chemical, Energy, Mine, and General Workers Unions (ICEM) campaign against Rio Tinto, the biggest minerals company in the world; and the International Union of Food, Agricultural, Hotel, Restaurant, Catering, Tobacco, and Allied Workers Associations (IUF) campaign against the attack on workers' and trade union rights in the Philippines by the world's largest fresh-fruit company, Dole Food Company.[3] The IUF has also played a central role in confronting transnational corporations (TNCs) by building links between workers in different countries employed by the same TNC, and exercising transnational collective bargaining power rooted in local organizing and struggle.

However, the question remains as to whether the strategies of confrontation adopted by a minority of the international union federations will lead to a shift in the politics of official international unionism overall. In contrast, the leadership of the largest representative of organized workers internationally, the International Confederation of Free Trade Unions (ICFTU), continues to promote a strategy of compromise that displaces rather than supports militant workers' struggles. This is particularly evident in Asia, where the affiliates of the ICFTU are predominantly pro-government, pro-business unions seeking partnership with capital at regional and international levels to legitimate their own claim to represent workers locally. Ultimately, another layer of representation from above is imposed on workers, and the possibility—let alone the threat—of organized struggle is further diminished.

The ICFTU and the Economic Crisis in Asia

On February 10-11, 1998, the Asia Pacific Regional Organization (APRO) of the ICFTU called an emergency meeting in Singapore to discuss the economic crisis and develop a plan of action. The nature and outcome of this conference, "Meeting the Challenges of Economic Turmoil," gives us an insight into the ICFTU's politics of compromise. From the start, there was little promise of setting an agenda to fight for workers' rights and interests. On the contrary, it was announced that workers and unions would need to make sacrifices. In the opening speech given by the general secretary of the National Trades Union

Congress of Singapore (who is also a government minister), it was stated that cooperation with governments and business was necessary to solve the problems in the financial markets before we can push for upholding workers' rights and the abolition of child labor. A conservative argument about the basics was advanced: survival first, rights later. This ignores the fact that millions of workers throughout the region are facing a threat to their survival precisely because their collective rights, including the right to organize and bargain collectively, the right to job and income security, and the right to work, have been repressed or systematically dismantled.

This theme has been used by authoritarian political regimes in the Asian tiger economies over the past three decades to impose social and political sacrifice on subordinate classes while consolidating the rise of capital. In the dominant ideology of pro-government trade unions in Asia, workers' rights and interests have been narrowly defined in terms of rice-and-fish (bread-and-butter) issues. Top-down intervention by these unions has often transformed workers' self-organized protests, in which they demand the right to work and respect for their dignity, into quiet acceptance of their dismissal and redundancy payouts. Should workers continue their protest, they are deemed a threat to the interests of the nation. When 3,000 workers from the Thai Summit auto parts factory in Thailand took to the streets in January 1998 to oppose wage cuts, the loss of bonuses, and the threat of losing their jobs, the Thai Labor Congress joined the ruling class in condemning the action as an act of violent unrest and called for greater sacrifice by workers for the sake of national economic recovery.

This concern for national economic interests tends to view capitalists as fellow travelers rather than perpetrators of the crisis faced by workers, and it places the nation rather than the working class at the center of trade union responses to globalization. At the same time that the Thai Summit auto workers took to the streets in Bangkok, global union leaders were participating in the World Economic Forum in Davos, Switzerland. Here the ICFTU leadership reiterated the claim that nation-states, and not the working class, are victims of global markets.[4] Not surprisingly, defending individual nations requires a partnership between the state, labor, and capital based on social contracts and compromise. Ironically, the World Economic Forum itself is one of the clearest expressions of the collusion between TNCs and national governments, with 1,000 of the world's largest TNCs joining 250 political leaders to set the priorities for the twenty-first century.

Given the devastating impact of the Asian economic crisis on workers in Indonesia and South Korea, it is significant that only union officials from the government-controlled FSPSI and the pro-government Federation of Korean

Trade Unions (FKTU) were present at the Singapore conference. No representatives from the independent union in Indonesia, SBSI, were present, despite the fact that the release of its leader, Muchtar Pakpahan, has been a major international campaign for the ICFTU and a number of national and local unions. The absence of the KCTU was related to the rank-and-file revolt against the union leadership only a day before the ICFTU meeting in Singapore. In an extraordinary convention of 270 delegates and 500 observers held on February 9 in Seoul, a three-to-one vote rejected the tripartite accord signed by the KCTU leadership with the government and business leaders, along with the FKTU. The accord included an agreement on the law on layoffs that brought an end to lifetime employment and dismantled job protection. It was argued that accepting the terms of the existing agreement would destroy workers' livelihood and lead to a greater deterioration in workplace conditions. Delegates demanded that the agreement be renegotiated, asserting that if the new terms were not accepted, general strike action must be called. In a sharp criticism of the KCTU leadership, some delegates likened the signing of the accord to business union leaders who absolutely ignore opinions of their rank-and-file union members.[5]

In sharp contrast, union officials from the pro-government FKTU, who were supposedly representing Korean workers at the meeting in Singapore, reiterated their commitment to the tripartite accord, stating that the FKTU will play a role to find solutions of labor issues through conversation and compromise.[6] Ironically, it was this compromise that forced the leadership and staff of KCTU to resign in the face of the rank-and-file protest in Seoul less than twenty-four hours earlier. Despite the overwhelming rejection of the accord, and the immediate resignation of the KCTU staff and leadership as a result of its failure to follow through with rank-and-file demands, a few days later KCTU again joined FKTU in supporting the tripartite agreement.

This rank-and-file rejection of the compromises embodied in the tripartite agreement had little effect on the proposed solutions and plan of action drawn up at the Singapore conference. The statement adopted at the conference calls for the setting up or strengthening of high-level national tripartite councils and offers no challenge to mass layoffs or givebacks. Thousands of workers have been laid off in Hong Kong and Malaysia, tens of thousands in South Korea and Thailand, and close to 4 million in Indonesia. By the end of 1998, there will be 2.8 million unemployed workers in Thailand, 12 million in Indonesia, 1.5 million in South Korea, and 1 million unemployed in Malaysia with up to 1.2 million migrant workers facing expulsion. Rather than facing this challenge, the ICFTU's plan of action consists of such measures as petitioning the World Bank, the IMF, and the leaders of the G-8 countries, and setting up a hotline for laid-off workers.

Real Problems, False Solutions: Representing Labor Without Organizing

The most revealing thing about this statement and action plan is the demand for increased funding for the IMF and the World Bank.[7] This stems from a belief in the need to bail out corporations and help them regain their financial health in order to save jobs and promote economic growth. It is already clear that the IMF's multibillion-dollar loans to Asian governments will ensure the recovery of most of the losses suffered by finance capitalists, although transnational banks and international securities firms are demanding more intervention, calling for the radical restructuring of Asia's debt— nationalizing and securing it. Having failed to oppose privatization over the past two decades, unions are now failing to oppose the nationalization of private-sector debt. So the mass of the working-class population will be left to pay off these debts for generations to come.

Mass unemployment, the threat of unemployment, rapidly falling real wages, and food shortages are combined with the accumulation of massive national debt (on top of existing debt) to save capitalists and political elites from their own crisis. While recognizing the anger and frustration of workers in these countries, the statement adopted by the Singapore conference offers no real solutions. Nor does the plan of action involve any real action. The task of trade unions in Asia is merely to voice the fears and needs of working men and women who are victims of forces beyond their control, whose only salvation is corporate kindness and responsibility. Hence, in his speech to the Singapore conference, Bill Jordan, the general secretary of the ICFTU, concludes, "What we need is globalization with a human face!"

Another significant feature of this plan of action is the ICFTU-APRO's resolution that it will urge employers to set up a regional association as a vehicle for discussions on matters of mutual interest with APRO. The fact that a regional organization of unions is demanding that employers establish a parallel body reflects the underlying logic of partnership and social contracts, in which the institutional representation of workers' narrowly defined economic interests and basic rights is contingent upon a forum created by capital. Ultimately, APRO cannot set an agenda for workers; it can only set an agenda with capital, and in the absence of a regional structure representing employers, it is unable to define its role. Rather than seeking its legitimation in the 32 million workers it claims to represent, the APRO union leadership can only seek legitimation from its inclusion in top-down structures established by business and governments, a framework that strengthens its own internal hierarchy.

A similar motivation underlies their demand for institutional representation in the Asia-Pacific Economic Cooperation (APEC). It is argued that since employers are represented in the APEC Business Advisory Council (ABAC), labor should be included, too. However, instead of using this forum to oppose coercive trade and investment liberalization, privatization, and labor market deregulation planned under APEC, APRO has instead sought the participation of its Asia-Pacific Labor Network—which includes the AFL-CIO and CLC— in the working group on Human Resource Development (HRD). It is already evident that the HRD policies being proposed under APEC combine labor flexibility (destruction of job and income security) policies with a shift in public resources to training and (re)skilling the workforce to serve the specific, medium-term needs of transnational capital. Like Human Resource Management (HRM) in the workplace, national and regional HRD strategies seek to co-opt unions and gain their acquiescence to these policies. This politics of inclusion is particularly important for those national union centers that have turned (re)training and (re)skilling into a business in itself.

Ironically, the majority of the ICFTU's affiliates in Asia are so close to their governments that they form part of the official delegations to APEC anyway. While hundreds of thousands of workers, farmers, fisher-folk, and indigenous peoples protested against APEC in Manila in November 1996, the Trade Union Congress of the Philippines (TUCP) joined the government delegation inside the official meeting. Even the violent eviction of tens of thousands of squatters, followed by the demolition of their houses as part of the cleansing of Manila prior to APEC, was conveniently forgotten. What was important for the TUCP and its allies in the NGO community was recognition by government and business of their role as the legitimate representative of labor. This legitimacy was contingent upon accepting the authoritarian structures and coercive neo-liberal agenda of APEC, while ignoring the absolute rejection of APEC by the mass of the people. In doing so, TUCP leaders were acting not only in accordance with their own political agenda, but also with the ICFTU's global strategy of engagement rather than opposition.

The ICFTU's most recent engagement is with the World Trade Organization (WTO), again despite the long history of massive grassroots resistance to GATT. As its central response to globalization, the ICFTU has demanded the inclusion of a social clause on basic labor standards in the multilateral agreements under the WTO. According to this proposal, the International Labor Organization (ILO) would work with the WTO in monitoring the respect of core International Labor Conventions in member countries. Missing altogether is a critical reflection on the failure of the ILO and its tripartitism to enforce these conventions in the first place, and the fact that the WTO will assess violations of labor standards only on the basis of whether such violations constitute unfair trading practices (that is, unfair to other capitalists). More important, the entire agenda of the WTO is about speeding up economic liberalization and increasing the power of TNCs. Liberalization includes the deregulation of labor markets and the consolidation of labor flexibility, privatization, cuts in government subsidies, reductions in public spending, and severe restrictions on the ability of states to regulate capital. These are precisely the policies that will exacerbate the crisis faced by workers and their communities and undermine their capacity to defend their rights and interests. For example, more than a million textile workers have been sacked in China as a result of the cut in textile production capacity demanded by the WTO. At the same time, the privatization program devised by the World Bank and the Chinese government (which borrows US$3 billion from the Bank every year) has seen more than 15 million workers dismissed from the state sector, with another 15 million to be sacked by the year 2000. On what basis, then, can a clause on labor standards really protect workers' rights under conditions of mass unemployment and free-labor markets?

In fact, the ICFTU failed to get agreement on the social clause at a meeting of the WTO in Singapore in December 1996. Renamed "core labor standards" to emphasize the limited definition of workers' rights, it was agreed only that the proposal would be open to future discussion. What did happen at the Singapore meeting was the move to establish a working group, similar to the MAI, on an investment agreement within the WTO. This group, the MIA, will extend the protection of TNCs and foreign investment beyond the OECD countries and create a level playing field for foreign direct investment globally. So while transnational capital made significant gains in securing greater cooperation from national governments and diminishing their regulatory capacity, the ICFTU leadership held on to the promise of talking about labor standards another time.

In an attempt to present this as a victory for global labor unionism, the ICFTU leadership now behaves as if the social clause were actually adopted. For example, the ICFTU recently issued a report on the violation of trade union rights and discrimination in Japan, revealing the unfair dismissal of public sector workers, including teachers and workers in public enterprises, for attempting to strike and bargain collectively and documenting extensive gender discrimination. The report also notes that for several years the Japanese government has ignored the recommendations of the ILO Committee of Experts on the Application of Conventions. This is where the ICFTU draws a bizarre conclusion:

> At the Singapore meeting, the WTO said that it would work with the ILO to ensure WTO members observed ILO standards. The ICFTU is calling on the WTO to remind the Japanese government of the commitments it made and to work with the ILO to ensure that these standards are implemented.[8]

Simply passing these issues on to the WTO is highly problematic since, under its neoliberal agenda, the WTO seeks more flexible labor markets, which exploit the gender division of labor and remove rigidities such as equal pay for equal work. And given the belief in a smaller, more efficient or competitive public sector, it is possible that the WTO will use these findings to argue that labor standards would improve after the privatization of public sector enterprises and the contracting-out of public services to private corporations.

In the not-so-distant past, most of the major national centers affiliated with the ICFTU supported privatisation as a means of attacking left unionists and breaking the power of militant public sector unions. Support for privatization was one of the ways in which the Japan Private Sector Trade Union Confederation (JPTUC-Rengo) finally forced the dissolution of the General Council of Trade Unions (Sohyo) in 1989, incorporating public sector unions into its own structures and forming a new national center, JTUC-Rengo. This consolidated the power of pro-business unionism and took the movement out of organized labor in the public sector. That explains the weak position of public sector workers, the continued repression of their rights, and the inaction of the ICFTU's major Asian affiliate, JTUC-Rengo.

Ultimately, global union strategies like the social clause do nothing to enhance workers' capacity to challenge the power of capital locally and it further marginalizes nonorganized workers, including the vast majority of women workers, who do not have access to these mechanisms. Even among the majority of organized workers, including most of the 125 million workers the ICFTU claims to represent, there is little or no knowledge of social clause proposals, let alone how, why, and at what cost they have been arrived at. Even where the social clause/WTO proposal is supported, as in the case of Hong Kong, this support is not based on a movement from below, but merely on a directive from above.[9]

The problem lies in creating more structures within international capitalist organizations through which labor issues are raised and in which labor is represented, but without any organic link to a real movement which challenges capital and seeks to shift the balance of forces in favor of the working class. So while labor is included, the form of representation chosen and its disarticulation from local struggles leave it with no bargaining power at all. At best, trade unionists can only point out that workers will be adversely affected by certain policies and that such policies ought to be revised. If they are not, nothing will happen.

Increasingly, local unions have turned to other local and national social movements and their regional and international networks to maintain the struggle against APEC and the WTO/GATT. According to Robert Reid, secretary of the New Zealand Footwear and Clothing Workers Union:

> [A] section of the international trade union movement has a policy of rejecting the whole free trade ideology and system. Its strategy is to build up the international solidarity of workers and trade unions. While it acknowledges that the power of GATT and APEC is far beyond what workers and trade unions have, it seeks to confront that power. It believes that this is done not by getting into bed with the transnational corporations and their agents but by building up

our own networks, our own solidarity, so that over time we can build a counter-power to that of the big trade organizations and the big TNCs.[10]

Conclusion

For many on the left, the ICFTU seems largely irrelevant, a benign presence in the post-Cold War world that poses neither possibilities nor constraints for workers' struggles. The reality is that the ICFTU continues to play an active role in international politics and is often the only representative of labor in the global arena. The World Federation of Trade Unions (WFTU) has all but collapsed with the demise of the Soviet Union (a testimony to its Stalinist orientation), while other international networks, such as the International Trade Union Conference (ITUC), are still in the process of building the institutional capacity necessary to follow through with an international agenda of pro-worker unionism and opposition to privatization. In fact, a number of the unions involved in the ITUC initiative are members of the WFTU or the ICFTU, or are in the process of joining the ICFTU.[11] The ICFTU can legitimately claim to represent 125 million workers in 206 national trade union centers in 141 countries, including radical union locals and rank-and-file union members actively engaged in militant struggle.

At the same time, we should recall that throughout the struggle of the independent union movement in South Korea and its repression by the authoritarian military regime, the ICFTU supported the pro-government Federation of Korean Trade Unions (FKTU). It is also worth remembering that in South Africa, COSATU joined the ICFTU only after the militant years of anti-apartheid struggle were over, and only after adopting a pragmatic strategy "promoting competitiveness and co-responsibility."[12]

On the one hand, this reinforces the notion that links between unions committed to working-class struggle and the ICFTU are forged out of compromise, and a convergence with the mainstream politics of social contracts and partnership. On the other hand, there are unionists within the ICFTU, including its international departments, who are genuinely committed to working class struggle and believe that there is a possibility for a fundamental shift in the unions' agenda to effectively promote workers' collective rights and interests. This shift would require the active participation of militant unionists in making demands on their own leadership and on the international departments of their national union centers, thereby bringing about change at the top. These unionists recognize that many rank-and-file members and union locals actively engaged in struggle constitute a part of the ICFTU's constituency and, as such, should use it.

Whether or not this is a viable strategy, the point is that local unionists and members need to take this claim to represent them seriously. It is all the more important because the politics of compromise being advanced by the ICFTU leadership and national union leaders is about comprehensively displacing alternative forms of action, including attempts to build class-struggle unionism or social movement unionism. Yet, as the other essays in this volume show, we are faced with the absolute necessity of organizing such a challenge to the global capitalist system. So the call to "Think Globally, Act Locally" must involve concerted rank-and-file action to shift international unions, including the ICFTU, towards active support for local struggles and away from global compromise.

Notes

1. Roger Ronnie, "For defensive unionism and socialism," *South African Labor Bulletin* 20, no. 2 (April 1996): 25.
2. Kim Moody, *Workers in a Lean World: Unions in the International Economy* (London and New York: Verso, 1997), 249-68.
3. Details of these campaigns are available on the Internet sites of these unions: *http://www.world-psi.org/; http://www.icem.org/campaigns/riotinto/; http://www.iuf.org/iuf/.*
4. *ICFTU Online,* 28 January 1998.
5. This was reported by Eric Lee. See "KCTU delegates reject the Tripartite Agreement," *http://www.labornet.org.uk/1998/Feb/kctu1.html.*
6. Kim Yoo-kon, vice-president, Federation of Korean Trade Unions, "The economic crisis in Korea and its impacts on labor and FKTU strategies," talk given at Trade Union Forum for East and Southeast Asia, Singapore, 10-11 February, 1998.
7. Statement by the Forum on the Asian Economic Turmoil held by the ICFTU-APRO, Singapore, 10-11 February 1998.
8. *ICFTU Online,* 29 January 1998.
9. *Asian Labour Update,* no. 20 (November 1995-March 1996): 15.
10. Quoted in Aziz Choudry, "APLN seeks APEC Labor Forum: Others not so sure," *The Big Picture,* November 1997: 7.
11. General Confederation of Trade Unions (GEFONT) and Asia Monitor Resource Center (AMRC), *Strengthening Pro-worker Trade Unionism* (Nepal: GEFONT; Hong Kong: AMRC, 1996), 61.
12. Roger Ronnie, "For defensive unionism."

Notes on Labor
at the End of the Century:
Starting Over?

Sam Gindin

In the fifties, socialism wasn't on because things were so good.
Now, socialism isn't on because things are so bad. . . .
—Chrysler Canada retiree

With the publication of *The Communist Manifesto* 150 years ago, came modern socialism. To the many critiques of capitalism that already existed at the time, one of Marx's most important contributions was to add the dimension of agency: the emerging working class was placed at the center of a conscious movement to go beyond capitalism. As workers struggled within capitalism, they would, Marxists argued, transform themselves and develop the potential to transform society.

Socialism depended on the working class, but that dependency ran both ways. The socialist dream inspired, among workers and especially among their formal and informal leaders, both a working class politics and the movement to form their unions. Socialism was the vision that sustained them. It was the perspective that provided the daily counter-common sense so crucial to expose, engage, and build confidence. It was the reference point that guided tactical discussions. This wasn't the case just in Europe, but even in North America, where collective memory recalls the socialist idea as being comparatively weak and marginal.

Yet by the middle of this century, socialism was already stumbling as a player in the domestic politics of most of the developed capitalist countries—long before the collapse of the Soviet Union, long before social democracy stopped pretending it had anything to do with socialism, long before globalization found its way into the opening paragraph of every speech about the new reality. And by the last quarter of this century, even the moderate gains previously made by workers were being rolled back. The ideological hegemony of capitalism was such that, for labor, being radical was reduced to arguing for the recovery of the welfare state. What the left once scoffed at as liberal reformism had for many become the outer limit of the possible.

As the century comes to a close, socialism remains dependent on the development of the working class. But the potential of the socialist idea to inspire a more militant working class, never mind the kind of movement that might in turn restore socialism as a serious option, seems lost. At best, the socialist project has been postponed, replaced with a more modest and immediate challenge: can we at least build and sustain an oppositional base to challenge the capitalism that is marching over us? Can we develop a culture of resistance and struggle—a movement—rich enough to keep alive the possibility of an alternative to capitalism?

The Polarization of Options

> ... *this new breed [of labor leaders] has recognized that the global economy has changed forever the role of Europe's unions. If unions are to survive ... workers will have to accept cuts in their safety net, while unions find new ways to boost productivity. The union agenda should be competitiveness, and making things smarter and more efficiently, says John Monks (head of the TUC, Britain's central labor body).*
>
> —*Business Week*, December 16, 1996

Globalization is indeed forcing a rethinking of the role of unions. But it is also polarizing the options: accommodate to capitalism or take it on, give up or fight back. The coffin being nailed down by globalization is not, as it turns out, socialism and working class militancy but social democracy and the illusion of class-blind, nonradical reform.

Consider the modest goal of restoring the welfare state. The welfare state emerged at a particular time in capitalist history. It was preceded by the specific circumstances of the Great Depression and a set of unique conditions that followed the Second World War. It emerged at a time when the international order was semifragmented and international finance was semiregulated. The subsequent attack by capital on the welfare state wasn't gratuitous; it happened because, in the new world order of intensified competition, previous concessions made to the working class now seriously threatened profitability (and in the minds of some, even the viability of the system).

What does it mean, then, to restore the good old days? Given the shift in power since those relatively more hopeful days, a return to the welfare state is now a radical idea—it implies a radical attack on current trends in corporate power and globalization (e.g., at a minimum, a return to a greater degree of regulation in domestic and global finance). And even if we did go back, the very same conflicts that subsequently led to the attack on the welfare state would also be restored, with their same insistence on the same necessary changes. The past provides no escape from the present.

Similarly, what does it really mean to tell workers that the union agenda should be competitiveness? The acceleration of capital's internationalization (i.e., globalization) and the resulting increased pressures to meet the test of competitiveness do of course confront us with constraints that we must address. But if we are seduced into accepting those constraints as *goals*—no matter how progressive-sounding the spin is, no matter the qualifications about doing it smarter—we are, as an independent movement, finished. Those constraints end up dominating all economic and social decisions. What is good for competitiveness (like strengthening corporate power) is good; what is bad for competitiveness (like higher wages and more security for workers) is bad.

Fundamental to the very existence of unions—and inscribed on workers' early banners and in their minds—was the replacement of competition among individual workers with worker solidarity. Having limited that competition within a workplace, how can we then accept the re-creation of that competition across workplaces? What is the moral basis of a unionism that defines success in terms of getting investment and jobs at the expense of other workers? What can class solidarity possibly mean if the core strategy is an alliance with the employer or with national capital on terms favorable to the companies? What can be left of working class autonomy if the ultimate test of any policy is, as the logic of competitiveness rigorously demands, the impact on corporate bottom lines?

Even at the most practical level, a competitiveness-derived strategy represents the most questionable trade-off: we are weakened and lose our independence yet get no guarantee, short- or long-term, that this will provide a steady improvement in our lives. The real world has, in fact, already and very clearly revealed that competitiveness can't be generalized as a solution for all workers.

Competitiveness is inevitably uneven and exclusionary. Winners imply losers, and even if some high-tech, high-skilled workers temporarily win, what about the much larger numbers of workers in the rest of the economy? Even workers seemingly outside the traded sectors and apparently outside competitive pressures, such as service workers in both the public and private sectors, are dragged into the downward spiral. They represent a cost to the sectors directly facing competitive pressures. And the very process of trying to become competitive undermines standards and working-class power, thereby setting logical limits to sustained economic growth. If everyone follows this downward spiral, who will buy the goods? Deeper recessions, fragile recoveries, permanent insecurity, and growing inequality are built into the very core of this strategy.

It's also worth keeping in mind that, although competitiveness is supposed to be synonymous with "productivity" and "efficiency," capitalist competitiveness can accommodate only certain kinds of "efficiency" and "productivity," those that increase profit and capital accumulation. It rules out other forms of "efficiency," for instance, the efficient production of high-quality goods or the efficient provision of services under conditions controlled by workers, not to maximize the profits of capital but to fulfill social needs. But even if we consider just the conditions of survival in a competitive capitalist market, we need to remember that capital's criteria of viability are very different from those of workers: a plant may be competitive enough to stay in the market, or an uncompetitive plant may be capable of conversion to some other activity that would allow it to stay open, but if it isn't profitable "enough," or if the employer can't be bothered to undertake the conversion, by capital's standards it simply isn't "competitive."

As part of its restructuring dynamic, competitiveness also performs a powerful ideological function. It declares as a matter of unquestionable fact that there is only one basic way forward; any variations are minor and secondary. That path to social development necessitates a greater dependence on corporate priorities and hence corporate power. And this implies the rejection of any alternative vision and the postponement of contrary goals to an always-deferred future. The competitive agenda won't deliver the goods. But along the way it will destroy the capacity of working-class organizations to defend their members. Nothing is more naive, more disorienting, or more debilitating to the construction of an independent labor movement than the acceptance of the competitive framework.

Unity vs. Solidarity

> *You don't need a union to go backwards.*
> —Bob White, former Canadian Auto Workers president

If we want to take on capital and build a broad movement, it follows that unity within labor itself should be crucial. Yet a superficial unity only signals that the crucial debates and struggles over direction are being blocked. Since the defeat of the left within labor in the early postwar (and Cold War) years, the labor movement has certainly been much more unified. But along with this came the inertia responsible for much of labor's subsequent weakness. Building the kind of solidarity we need can't happen without controversy, as recent experience within the Canadian labor movement has certainly made clear. We can't have unity without a struggle over the question: unity for what?

This controversy should not be all that surprising. It reflects both the times and the long-standing problem of bureaucratization within sections of the labor movement. The general crisis within socialism has left us, in the words of

Dennis Potter's Singing Detective, with clues but no answers. Fundamental debates about direction are now not only necessary and unavoidable but inherently difficult. The options have become more polarized, and this is in turn polarizing the debate.

Within labor, one side in the debate has a world-view that supports the kind of unionism that is uncomfortable with membership mobilization. That side argues for realism (modifying expectations) and responsibility (accommodating to the constraints of capitalism). It ends up increasingly distancing itself from labor militancy, the politics of the street, and any rhetoric that challenges capitalism. It channels workplace bargaining demands towards membership-excluding longer agreements or towards new partnerships with employers, and it limits politics to social democratic electoralism. Mobilization is consequently not just secondary, but because of the possible loss of centralized control, a threat. It might undermine potential deals with business or government or, at critical moments, embarrass labor's political arm (where there is one). The call for unity, in this context, becomes a conservative blanket smothering debate and precluding the building of real solidarity.

In contrast, the perspective that calls for an oppositional movement emphasizes that trade unionism has nowhere to go unless it addresses the challenge of mobilization. Once such a perspective extends beyond an isolated minority within unions and establishes itself as the official direction of key unions, and so has a solid organizational base, serious divisiveness in the labor movement will emerge. Divisions are, of course, painful and dangerous, but experience confirms that they do not paralyze the labor movement. On the contrary, they can, as the two examples that follow indicate, even lead to the discovery of new energies.

In the early 1980s, the Canadian Auto Workers union (CAW) rejected the response of its parent, the UAW, to the new corporate agressiveness. We would have liked to stay and fight the corporations alongside our American brothers and sisters, but the direction of the U.S. leadership—selling concessions to the membership—pre-empted any fight, made solidarity irrelevant, and limited our own ability to fight. (Recently, hints of change within the UAW have led to an improved relationship.)

Our divisive departure did not weaken but strengthened and energized us. We subsequently committed a higher share of our resources to organizing, education, and international contacts; established a Department of Work Organization to help cope with workplace change; and played a leading role within Canada both in bargaining and in building coalitions to take on the corporate agenda. As other like-minded unions merged with us, our union not only increased in numbers but also came to represent a broader group of workers linked not by sector but by a particular ideological commitment.

At another level, in Ontario, Canada's largest and most industrialized province, the past three years have been the most divisive for the labor movement since the Cold War, while the level of mobilization and degree of politicization has been at a postwar peak. There has been no consensus on this mobilization, so it has risked aggravating the divisions. Yet a more substantial solidarity has emerged: public sector workers have remained a strong part of the movement instead of retreating into isolation after the lack of support from some unions; teachers, formerly outside the Ontario labor movement, have participated in very large numbers and have begun their integration into the labor movement; and the emergence of new activists and local coalitions holds out a promise of a broader-based movement.

The Ontario Days of Action

Corporations have raised the stakes and moved the issues to a whole new level. If we don't also move to a new level, then even just hanging on to what we have—never mind achieving real change—will become harder and harder. . . .
—1993 CAW Collective Bargaining and Political Action Program

The 1990s began with some promise in Ontario, where the population approximates that of Sweden. In apparent rebellion against the corporate agenda, the people of Ontario, for the first time in history, elected a social democratic party—the New Democratic Party (NDP)—to government.

By the summer of 1995, however, the NDP had traveled down a road familiar to postwar social democracy. Some very important pieces of legislation were introduced, but they were lost in the sudden repudiation of other central promises (like public auto insurance) and by direct attacks on both its trade union base (through imposed collective agreements) and the poor (with welfare cuts and Big Brother policing).

Meanwhile, the government's rhetoric and focus shifted toward establishing its credibility among corporate executives, bankers, and the business press. The NDP left in its wake a movement demoralized by disappointment after finally winning office, demobilized by confusion over how to protest the betrayals of a friendly government, and divided by conflict between long-standing principle and loyalty to the party leadership. This set the stage for the NDP's replacement by a right-wing populist government.

Given the harsh and destructive attacks the new government immediately introduced, with the next election too far down the road and with elections in any case now being viewed with particular skepticism, the labor movement turned the need to do something into an innovative politics of the street. The movement had neither the unity nor the ability to act on a provincewide shutdown, so it looked to a series of community shutdowns. This allowed the labor movement both to choose the locations on a strategic basis and to concentrate its limited resources on these one-at-a-time local protests.

Within a surprisingly short time, labor and the coalitions were able to act. On December 11, 1995, the labor movement (now including teachers) and its coalition partners organized a two-day protest in London, Ontario, a mid-size and traditionally conservative city, but one with a strong labor base. The first incredible day saw workers taking direct action to shut down workplaces and services for social and political—not collective bargaining—reasons. The second day mobilized what turned out, in each of the community protests that followed, to be the largest demonstrations anyone had ever seen in that community. The Toronto demo had an estimated quarter of a million people.

The emphasis on workplace shutdowns and not just protests at the legislature, highlighted successfully the employer base behind the government's attacks on working people. The public sector shutdowns of transit, schools, and post offices were directed toward reminding people of the importance of the social services they had taken for granted: if their loss for one day was so valuable and disruptive, what would the permanent loss of such services mean? The call on workers to lose a day's pay and risk employer retaliation forced, in the weeks leading up to the action, local leaders and activists to engage their members in debates over the issues. That discussion spread into the community, directly through labor and coalition activists, and inadvertently aided by business, political, and press hysteria that exploited nervousness over the lawlessness to come as the shutdowns and mass demonstrations hit each community.

These events did not push the government off its course. Nor can it be assumed that such actions can be accelerated or even sustained. The excitement didn't force any significant rebellions among workers within unions who remained on the sidelines. The movement that emerged didn't resolve the dilemma of needing friends in high places yet being turned off by electoral politics. And any serious rethinking of the purpose, structure, and role of a political party remains distant. Yet those of us involved in those incredible Days of Action knew they were a success and knew that something had changed. That something started with the way we began to define success.

The Days of Action were about building an opposition and changing the mood, and therefore the range of options, in Ontario. They revived the flagging hope of some, deepened the commitment of others, and brought new people into politics. They led to new links across union-coalition lines, developed new organizational skills, and exposed weaknesses we would later have to address. They increased economic and political literacy and developed a conscious need to continually educate ourselves about capitalism. They made serious inroads into the hegemony of right-wing ideas. They created that intangible space and collective self-confidence that set the stage for future struggles, big and small, over jobs, collective bargaining, municipal democracy, and rights of citizenship.

The mobilization of workers in the Ontario Days of Action did not come about by avoiding divisive issues and maintaining an artificial unity within the labor movement. But at some point, of course, existing divisions must be overcome—that is, they must become constructive debates over how, not whether, to fight. This is unlikely to happen through leadership compromises at the top. Change will come only when internal pressures develop within those unions that have been on the sidelines—when their members demand to join the growing solidarity. We can't change the world if we can't change our unions.

Movement Unionism

> *The issue isn't about being pure. . . . It's because we understand how difficult the problems really are, that we view the central problem as one of building: building our union, building a movement, building the party—so the limits on what we can do today can, over time, be overcome.*
> —Discussion Paper, 1994 CAW Convention

The real issue of alternatives isn't about alternative policies or alternative governments but about an alternative politics. Neither well-meaning policies nor sympathetic governments can fundamentally alter our lives unless they are part of a fundamental challenge to capital. That is, making alternatives possible requires a movement that is changing political culture (the assumptions we bring to how society should work), bringing more people into everyday struggles (collective engagement in shaping our lives), and deepening the understanding and organizational skills of activists along with their commitment to radical change (developing socialists).

It's not that policies are unimportant but that their importance should be judged first and foremost by their ability to mobilize people and, therefore, to help create the conditions that will make those policies truly possible. Nor is it that electoral participation is of no consequence but that it, too, should be judged, both during and after an election, on its contribution to building the movement and developing people's consciousness of their rights and potentials.

A unionism that not only identifies with, but also plays a leading role in, developing such a movement might be called movement unionism—a unionism that is workplace-based, community-rooted, democratic, ideological, and committed to building the kind of movement that is a precondition for any sustained resistance and fundamental change.

Movement unionism doesn't start by looking out, but by looking in. The workplace remains fundamental. It's here that workers are most likely to first experience the relevance—or irrelevance—of collective action. It's from their workplace base that workers continue to have meaningful power.

Globalization doesn't end this reality. Alongside national and international economic restructuring comes a higher degree of integration of components and services, specialization, and lean inventories. So in spite of globalization, or in a sense precisely because of it, corporations are at one level more vulnerable to disciplined local and regional actions, such as the 1996 strikes at GM in Dayton, Ohio, and in Canada, and the 1998 GM strike in Flint, Michigan. This is acknowledged and reflected in the corporate emphasis on counter-strategies to incorporate workers into a company perspective and thereby neutralize the independent capacities of unions.

Since unions are voluntary organizations whose members are dependent on corporations for work, the precondition for mobilizing workers to fight capital is that they view the union as their own. This means that the union must first be organizationally and ideologically independent of capital. And union democracy must be more than formal. It must maximize the forums for discussion and debate about the direction the union will take; it must structure educational programs to develop the capacity and therefore the confidence to actively participate; and it must include engagement in struggles that demonstrate the union as an effective vehicle for change (effective democracy).

By expanding its structures to expand the issues addressed, movement unionism moves to place the union at the center of workers' lives, thereby reinforcing the emphasis on the democratic character of the union as an institution belonging to workers. Consider, for example, the creation of new local union committees that are open to workers' spouses and teenage sons and daughters and directed to addressing what is happening to working-class kids in the school system. Such an initiative necessarily engages the union with the community, but in a way that doesn't set up an artificial distinction between the union and others in the community. Rather, it moves towards the kind of coalition work that organizes workers around other aspects of their lives: the air in our community, the safety of the neighborhood, the schools our kids attend.

The leadership role that movement unionism can play in such coalitions comes not from throwing around its organizational weight and access to resources, but from using its potential to lead concrete struggles with wider implications, such as the fight to open up new jobs through reduced work time, and the recent mass mobilizations in Ontario.

As such a movement unfolds and forces all kinds of questions on the left, one crucial issue is finding the theme(s) that could bring the separate and localized struggles together so they are more than the sum of their parts. Since unions exist to set limits on corporate and management power in the workplace, and since unions can be effective in making significant change only if they themselves are democratic, it seems natural—and turns out to be strategic—to develop and use democratization as that unifying theme: the goal of politics is to democratize the economy; politicization is the democratic process of developing the capacity to challenge those with power.

Thinking About Alternatives: Job Development Boards

If we have schoolboards to guarantee the right to an education,
why not job boards to guarantee the right to a job?
—Leo Panitch, York University

Let me give an example of the kind of immediate objective that a movement unionism could embrace and that could move workers' struggles beyond the workplace. The most important thing for an individual worker is his or her job. Yet the ability to influence jobs and job security is one of the weakest links in unionism. How can unions play a role in addressing jobs and making the creation of decent jobs a national priority? And can we structure this engagement over jobs in a way that creates new political possibilities down the road?

Suppose we called for the formation, at the municipal level, of elected Job Development Boards. The mandate of these boards would be to guarantee everyone an opportunity (as opposed to the enforced labor of workfare) to participate in either a paid job or in training or education. The board would supervise a number of supportive institutions involved in conducting research, disseminating information, carrying out training, holding public information meetings, etc.

Once established, such boards would have to start quite modestly; we clearly know very little about how to make decent jobs happen. A board might begin by obtaining from the municipality its list—they all have one—of all the things that must be done in the community to maintain or improve the neglected infrastructure (housing, roads, parks, schools, and hospitals). The board could invite proposals on services the community needs but is not providing (e.g., childcare, adult education, delivering medicine, food, or entertainment to the aged, and environmental clean-up and protection). It could initiate steps to prevent losing jobs that already exist or to facilitate expansion of existing jobs (e.g., before a plant can close, investigate the reason; if marketing or technological help or temporary financing is the key, provide it).

Let's elaborate a little on the last example. We're not going to get far in creating new jobs if we can't even hang on to the jobs we already have. At first, we might be limited to developing some understanding of why plants close. Then we might reach the point where we can intervene in a constructive way. At some point, we might be able to go further and lead a move to convert workplaces that would otherwise close into workplaces that are making new products. We could, for instance, start with a few accountants who would check the books of a company threatening bankruptcy, but over time we might have a research center linked to a university that includes some marketing and technological skills, or a conversion center that looks at new possibilities related to import substitution or new directions linked to environmental imperatives. We might also want to have an educational component so workers and unions could learn how to figure out whether their company is failing to invest or to keep up, and could intervene before it's too late.

The long-term advantage to the community of this approach isn't just that it preserves and develops its capacities, but that those capacities aren't only in private hands (which can move). Some are community-owned or linked to public institutions (which won't move away). This strategy works on two tracks: the community and the sector. Economic activity occurs within communities, but it also cuts across communities, and it often makes sense to approach issues sectorially. In each sector, there would be a committee (e.g., Aerospace Committee, Airline Committee) with representatives of the sector's companies and unions. The point would be to develop a plan for each sector that would go to the government for approval. Governments would make the final decisions, so if business refused to cooperate, the movement would mobilize to get the government to act. Note that the distinction between communities and sectors, while useful, is not always clear. For example, in Ontario, to address the issue of tool-and-die technology and stampings in the auto parts industry, we might set up a tool-and-die technology center in the community of Windsor, and in Kitchener, a research center looking into future stamping needs.

The above structures could not work without access to funding, and they would need something more than minor adjustments in government budgets. There is already little room in current budgets for existing social programs, and the amounts needed for the strategy proposed here are simply too large to get from normal budgets. Something more radical would be needed to get direct access to the funds sloshing around in the private financial markets. Again, the problem isn't the overall shortage of funds but who controls them. There is so much money around that business is furiously lobbying to remove some of the restrictions that limit its outflow.

Suppose, for example, that every financial institution in the country had to place a percentage of its assets (maybe 5 percent rising to 10 percent over time) in a National Investment Fund. The money invested would pay less than the market rate, though still a fair and safe return (e.g., inflation plus 1-2 percent). Individuals wanting to invest in this fund out of solidarity could buy Canadian Investment Bonds and, since this would be optional, the return might be higher (perhaps inflation plus 2-3 percent—enough for a future decent pension income). The fund would have a board of directors appointed by the government with the responsibility of allocating the funds according to regional and sectorial priorities.

This strategy isn't a quick-fix, risk-free answer to complex problems. Such a central fund could certainly be bureaucratized and diverted from its true intent. Local elites might dominate the community boards. Corporations, with their privileged access to information and possibilities, might get unions to buy into their agenda at the sectorial level. Lack of adequate financial support and resources might mean that whatever we succeed in establishing would end up as an irrelevant talkshop.

Despite these potential pitfalls, this strategy could build and politicize the movement if it can effectively accomplish its broader goals. It would address concrete demands, particularly the fundamental right to a job. The strategy broadens the definition of needs that jobs address. It would build our capacities—individual, collective, and institutional—in the community and in our unions. Through it, labor can act locally while learning the limits of local action and the need to address national issues like the power of capitalism's financial institutions; engage in democratizing the economy by gaining some control over its finances; and refocus on democratizing the state, as we try to create new and accessible institutions like the Job Development Boards. This alternative supports an ideolgical and practical perspective that shows some independence from the dominant view that links jobs with competitiveness—a view that strengthens, at our ultimate expense, corporations and corporate rights.

Internationalizing the Struggle

Though not in substance, yet in form, the struggle of the proletariat with the bourgeoisie is first a national struggle.
—Karl Marx, *The Communist Manifesto*

The kind of local and national strategy I've been suggesting here immediately raises a question: if capital is international, doesn't labor have to follow suit? Don't we have to turn our attention to changing existing (reactionary) international institutions and developing new (progressive) ones?

Any focus on lobbying international institutions like the International Monetary Fund or the World Bank, or creating comparable alternatives, will get us absolutely nowhere. These international institutions do not exist in a vacuum; they are not castles in the air. What they do necessarily reflects the national constellation of powers at their base. Until we have built countervailing power in each of our own countries, and have been able to put financial capital on the defensive in a significant number of major countries, it is the silliest kind of utopianism to talk about influencing the economy through these distant and secondary international bodies.

International labor bodies, in apparent contrast, make constructive contributions to our struggles. They are useful vehicles for exchanging information and analysis and mobilizing modest acts of solidarity and support. But here, too, we should be clear about their limits. Strategic international coordination is dependent on the strength of national movements. For example, what kind of internationalism can we expect among the United States, Mexico, and Canada if the American labor movement can't yet organize its own South; if the Mexican labor movement doesn't yet have a common union across workplaces within a single company like GM; if the Canadian labor movement hasn't yet been able to acheive major organizing breakthroughs in its own key private service sectors?

The key to international solidarity isn't international institutions but internationalizing the struggle, carrying on the fight (for example, over work time) in each country and thereby reinforcing and creating the space for working-class struggles in other countries. For example, the pressure on German Metal workers to surrender the work-time gains they had made since the 1980s wasn't rooted in the lack of cross-country institutional coordination, but in the failure of other labor movements to aggressively follow the lead of the German workers. Similarly, if we want to eventually see global finance regulated, the most effective starting point would be to launch a series of national campaigns to regulate finance in each industrially developed country. Progressive internationalism can only be built on a strong and progressive national base.

If capitalism has demonstrated anything over the past two decades, when the right has so controlled the agenda and so ambitiously applied the solutions that reflected capitalist necessity, it is that under modern capitalism there is no humane alternative. Can we translate the failed promises of capitalism into an anticapitalist movement? Can we combine the impatience essential for a culture of resistance and the patience fundamental to building labor into a movement that doesn't ask whether change is possible but how to make it possible? A new century, a new movement?

CONTRIBUTORS

Gregory Albo teaches political science at York University and works with a number of Canadian unions.

Johanna Brenner is coordinator of women's studies at Portland State University in Portland, Oregon.

Bill Fletcher, Jr. is director of education for the AFL-CIO.

Fernando Gapasin is a longtime union activist and labor educator currently teaching at the Center for Labor Research and Education at UCLA.

Sam Gindin is assistant to the president of the Canadian Auto Workers and author of *Canadian Auto Workers: The Birth and Transformation of a Union* (1995).

Michael Goldfield teaches at Wayne State University and is the author of *The Color of Politics* (1997).

Peter Gowan is a principal lecturer in European politics at the University of North London.

Gerard Greenfield is a labor research activist working in East and Southeast Asia.

Doug Henwood is editor of *Left Business Observer* and author of *Wall Street* (1997).

Eric Mann is director of the Labor/Community Strategy Center in Los Angeles and a former assembly line autoworker and UAW activist.

David McNally teaches political science at York University and is the author of *Against the Market* (1993).

Peter Meiksins teaches sociology at Cleveland State University and is co-author with Chris Smith of *Engineering Labor: Technical Workers in Comparative Perspective* (1996).

Kim Moody is director of *Labor Notes* and author of *Labor in a Lean World* (1997).

Chris Roberts is completing his doctoral research in political science at York University.

Richard Roman teaches sociology at the University of Toronto.

Edur Velasco Arregui teaches economics at the Universidad Autonoma Metropolitana in Mexico City, is one of the founders of the Intersindical, and is the former secretary-general of the Sindicato Independiente de Trabajadores de la Universidad Autonoma Metropolitana (SITUAM).

Ellen Meiksins Wood, co-editor of *Monthly Review*, wrote the afterword to *The Communist Manifesto* by Karl Marx and Friedrich Engels (Monthly Review Press, 1998) and is author of *The Origins of Capitalism* (forthcoming from Monthly Review Press).

Michael Yates, a labor educator, teaches at the University of Pittsburgh at Johnstown and is the author of *Why Unions Matter* (Monthly Review Press, 1998).

Index